FISCAL FEDERALISM IN NIGERIA

Facing the Challenges of the Future

Published by
Adonis & Abbey Publishers Ltd
P.O. Box 43418
London
SE114XZ
http://www.adonis-abbey.com
Email: editor@adonis-abbey.com

British Library Cataloguing-in-Publication Data
A catalogue record for this book is available from the British Library

ISBN: 9781906704032(HB)

Printed and bound in Great Britain

FISCAL FEDERALISM IN NIGERIA

Facing the Challenges of the Future

Edited By

J. Isawa Elaigwu

Adonis & Abbey
Publishers Ltd

PREFACE

Debates on Nigeria's fiscal federalism preceded the gradual evolution of Nigeria into a colonial federal state in 1954. Issues of distribution of scarce but allocatable resources had often beclouded the desires of Nigerians to generate these resources that were expected to be shared. Throughout its history, it has been evident that Nigerians have always been sensitive to the fiscal dimensions of its federation.

Nigeria's media have been replete with the debate over the nature of resource generation, distribution, and challenges of equalization in the federation. At the National Political Reform Conference in 2005, delegates from some states of the federation staged a walk-out because of the nature of resource distribution.

It was in recognition of fiscal federalism as cardinal to the stability and progress of the federation, that the Institute of Governance and Social Research (IGSR) developed a project schema. This schema is planned to be implemented in four phases:

a) **Phase One:** "Fiscal federalism in Nigeria: Facing the Challenges of the Future". This first phase deals with the clarification of global and national issues of debate in the area. It was executed in March 2007. This workshop was sponsored by Canadian International Agency for Development (CIDA), British Department for International Development (DFID) and IGSR.

b) **Phase Two:** *"Transparency and Accountability In Nigeria's Fiscal Federalism".* In this phase, the emphasis is on confidence–building among the various stakeholders – federal, state and local governments – given the current level of collection, custody and distribution. It involves the identification of the desirable reforms which would re-establish confidence in the country's process of fiscal federalism. Consensus – building is important here.

c) **Phase Three:** *"Intergovernmental Relations and the Delivery of Services: Towards Cooperation for Development".* This phase deals with an analyses of the expenditure patterns of government sectorally, and finding out more efficient and less wasteful means of alleviating poverty through intergovernmental relations. It involves looking at sectors such as Health, Environment, Housing, Education and Water. The emphasis here is to encourage practitioners to cooperate across tiers and even within the same tier of government to deliver services in a more efficient and cost-effective manner, cutting out, as much as possible, duplications and wastes.

d) **Phase Four**: *"Monitoring Fiscal Federalism"*. In this final phase, we shall focus on collective monitoring of the fiscal process in order to sustain material confidence; continue and expand the modes of inter-governmental relations in service delivery, and ensure accountability and transparency in fiscal federalism. All stakeholders, in addition, to constitutionally stipulated monitors (such as the Revenue Mobilization, Allocation and Fiscal Commission – RMAFC) shall come to regard themselves as monitors. Each stakeholder can signal alarm when it feels that the consensus has been broken or side-tracked.

The essence of all these activities, for IGSR as a neutral, non-governmental agency, is to help mediate among stakeholders and encourage them to carry out desirable reforms in the Nigerian federation, especially the fiscal health of the federation.

It is our hope to continue collaboration with all stakeholders and friends of Nigeria as the federation makes necessary adjustments in response to the exigencies of the 21st Century.

J. Isawa Elaigwu
President, IGSR

Table of Contents

PART I

AN OVERVIEW OF NIGERIAN FEDERALISM

INTRODUCTION

Nigeria is a federation with thirty-six states and 774 local government councils. Since 1954, the politics of federalism in Nigeria had highlighted the importance of fiscal federalism. Infact, under unitary colonial administration, the issue of distribution of resources had become an important moot-point. Under the 1946 Constitution, Sydney Phillipson was appointed to review the fiscal system in Nigeria. Further pressures for the review of revenue allocation system led to the Hicks-Phillipson Commission Report of 1950. Again, in 1953, the Louis Chick Commission was tasked with the review of tax powers and their effects on public expenditure.

Thus, even before her independence, in 1960, and before the federalization of Nigeria under colonial rule in 1954, the concern of Nigerian leaders and colonial officers over fiscal issues had become clear; it has taken additionally heightened dimension since independence.

Among attempts to deal with the issues of equitable generation and distribution of resources are the following fiscal commissions and Laws: the Chick Commission (1953); Raisman Commission (1958); Binns Commission (1964); Decree No. 15, 1967; Dina Commission (1968). Decree No. 13, 1970; Aboyade Commission (1977); Okigbo Commission (1979); National Revenue Mobilization, Allocation and Fiscal Commission (1989), and Revenue Mobilization Allocation and Fiscal Commission (2004).

The fiscal dimension of federalism lubricates the wheels of the federation. It deals with the generation and distribution of scarce but allocatable resources, as federations attempt to create *equality* among its citizens and component units. Yet, equality "is the most widely proclaimed ideal of the modern age; but is one of the most imperfectly achieved". Like other aspects of federalism, fiscal federalism is infinite in its adjustments over time.

In 1973, Mr. Allison Ayida, (a former Federal Permanent Secretary, and later Secretary to the Government of the Federation) predicted that:

> The next threat to the continued existence of Nigeria will not come from the East. The next crisis is most likely to have its origins in basic economic issues and social conflict – the equitable allocation and proper management of increased disposable resources of the federation and the familiar conflict between the haves and have-nots[1].

Mr. Ayida hardly anticipated the enormity of the crises of distribution of scarce but allocatable resources we have today. He probably never projected that the Adaka Boro[2] resistance in the Niger-Delta would escalate to the Niger-Delta crises of today.

Since 1973, there have been serious debates and conflicts of interests over resource distribution, even under military regimes[3]. Often Nigerian elites, at all tiers of government, quarrel over resource distribution and pay little attention to resource generation by governments.

At the National Political Reform Conference of 2005, representatives of the South-South zone walked out because their demand for 25% revenue on the basis of derivation was rejected. Currently, there is intense and much mutual suspicion among tiers of government over the machinery of distribution. Obasanjo's eight years of command approach to federalism had alienated state governors, whom he treated as prefects. Similarly, Local Government chairmen opposed the high-handedness of many governors who allegedly recklessly violated the constitutionally guaranteed autonomy of local government councils.

By May 29, 2007 when Obasanjo left the political scene, the process of fiscal federalism had become corroded by mutual suspicions and lack of confidence in the existing institutions and processes of fiscal federalism. In 2007, the Revenue Mobilization Allocation and Fiscal Commission took the Obasanjo federal government to court for illegally withdrawing ₦2.071 trillion from the Federation Account. It had earlier accused the Nigeria National Petroleum Company (NNPC) for not accounting for over ₦300 billion naira. The Commission also frowned on the practice of the federal government keeping a dedicated account at the Central Bank for NNPC. All revenue collected, according to the 1999 Constitution, must be deposited in the Federation Account.

In similar vein, state governors have demanded for an "impartial revenue sharing organ" as well as the details of the Federation Account. The lack of transparency and accountability in the fiscal process has compounded existing crises of confidence in the process.

For our purposes, it has become a political imperative to critically assess the process of fiscal federalism in Nigeria in order to make its governments respond to emerging exigencies of the times.

Thus, a few questions come to mind. What is the nature of fiscal federalism in Nigeria? Is there a balance between the tax powers by each tier of government and the constitutionally allocated powers and responsibilities? Why is revenue sharing such a sensitive issue in Nigeria's federation? What kinds of fiscal equalization do we have—vertically and horizontally? Can modalities be established for intergovernmental relations among units of government to effectively deliver services? What impact have these on poverty alleviation?

These are the main issues tackled by the National Workshop on "Fiscal Federalism in Nigeria: Facing the Challenges of the Future", in March 18-21, 2007 at Abuja. The content of this book are the revised versions of presentations and the summary and conclusions at that workshop. Part I gives an overview of the Nigerian federation. In this part are two papers—"The Challenges of Federalism in Nigeria: An overview" by J. Isawa Elaigwu; and "Distribution of Powers and Responsibilities" by Habu Galadima.

Part II which discusses fiscal federalism and the Political Economy of Distribution, has three papers. Philip Usman writes on "Resource or Revenue Sharing" in Chapter 3; Akpan Ekpo's "Fiscal Federalism in Nigeria: The Challenges of the Next Decade" is Chapter 4; while Chapter 5 contains Eghosa Osagie's "Revenue Sharing (Vertical and Horizontal).

Part III discusses Intergovernmental Fiscal Relations: Financing National Development". In this section, Mike Obadan and I. B. Bello-Imam write in Chapter 6, on "Intergovernmental Relations in Nigeria: Financing National Development". In Chapter 7, Lev Frienkman looks at "Intergovernmental Relations in Nigeria: Improving Service Delivery in Core Sectors".

Part IV deals with Fiscal Federalism: Towards Coping and Resolving Future Challenges. Attahiru Jega in Chapter 8 and Milton Iyoha in Chapter 9, look at "Fiscal Federalism: Towards Coping with and Resolving Future Challenges". Chapter 10 by Eghosa Osaghae is on "Reforms and Fiscal Federalism". The conclusion is really a report of the proceedings of the Workshop.

NOTES

1. Allison Ayida, *The Nigerian Revolution, 1966-1976* (Ibadan: Ibadan University Press, 1973), p.7.

2. Isaac Adaka Boro was a police officer from Niger-Delta area of the former Eastern region. He and his group demanded for the Sagbama Republic in the 1960s.

3. See J. Isawa Elaigwu, *The Politics of Federalism in Nigeria,* (Jos: Aha Publishing House, 2005), Chapter 9.

CHAPTER 1
THE CHALLENGES OF FEDERALISM IN NIGERIA: AN OVERVIEW

J. Isawa Elaigwu

Introduction

After thirty years of military rule, Nigeria embarked on democratic rule on May 29, 1999. Of Nigeria's forty-seven years of independence, she has had only about 17 years of elected civilian government. About thirty years of that period witnessed military rule of all shades. As the country embarked on a new democratic journey eight years ago, what are the challenges faced by the Nigerian federation? What problems have arisen in the federal process? How are these being resolved or tackled? What are the prospects of federalism in the new century -- especially in the first decade of this century?

In order to answer these questions, it is suggested that:

i) the Nigerian federation, at the dawn of the 21st century, is characterized by strong unitarist streaks as a response to almost three decades of military rule;
iii) there are, therefore, intense pressures for a review of the legislative list to devolve many of the powers concentrated at the centre to subnational units;
iv)the issues of resource distribution and/or management have become important issues of debate as Nigerian groups reassess the federation;
v) in the context of the new democratic polity, new issues have emerged as part of the politics of federalism in response to the explosion of subnational identities;
vi) there is a friction between the federal grid and the democratic process; and
vii) the quality of leadership is important in effecting necessary compromises in Nigeria's reconciliation system.

The Federal Principle

Federalism is essentially a compromise solution in a multinational state between two types of self-determination—the determination provided by a national government which guarantees security for all in the nation-state on one hand, and the self-determination of component groups to retain their individual identities on the other. Federalism emanates from the desire of people to form a federal union without necessarily losing their identity.[1] Thus, federalism is an attempt to reflect the diverse political, social, cultural and economic interests within the broader framework of unity. It therefore attempts to satisfy "the need for cooperation in some things coupled with the right to separate action in others. Only federalism fulfills the desire for unity where it coexists with a determination not to smother local identity and local power".[2]

Federalism emphasizes non-centralization of powers. Each component unit of federal system has its powers and functions delineated and guaranteed in a constitutional document. As the doyen of federalism, K.C. Wheare wrote, federalism is "the method of dividing powers so that the general and regional governments are each, within a sphere coordinate and independent".[3]

There is greater interdependence among component federal units and less autonomy for subnational units than Wheare had anticipated; but he was correct to emphasize that the division of powers should be such that "whoever has the residue, neither general nor regional government is subordinate to the other".[4]

In essence, this is what distinguishes a federal system from a unitary system of government. In the latter, "the state governments are legally subordinate to the central government". It also differs from confederacy in which the "central government is legally subordinate to the state government".[5] Thus, in a federal system of government, the very structures and their concomitant functions and authority should reflect dual legal *sovereignty* in areas of jurisdiction of the federal and subnational political units.

In practice, no country has been able to embody all these federal principles in its traditional definition. In fact, it is generally agreed that federal systems vary in content from one country to another. The particular political colouring that a country's federal government takes, is often reflective of its historical experiences, its political, cultural, social, and economic environment and the disposition of its people at a particular point in time. There is no ideal model of federalism. Federalism responds to local problems. The old Whearist model of federal association in terms of relations among component units does not exist anywhere in the world now. As Justice Ranjit Sarkaria of India correctly observed:

> The classical concept of federation which envisaged two parallel governments of coordinate jurisdiction, operating in isolation from each other in watertight compartments, is no where a functional reality now. With the emergence of the Social Welfare State, the traditional theory of federalism completely lost its ground. After the First World War, it became very much a myth even in the old federations... By the middle of the Twentieth Century, federalism had come to be understood as a dynamic process of cooperation and shared action between two or more levels of government, with increasing interdependence and Centrist trends.[6]

The complexity of modern governance, the need for homogeneity within the state, as well as the nature of foreign trade (among other reasons) have contributed to the increase in the power of central government in most federal states, except perhaps in countries such as Belgium.

The United States of America is regarded as one of the best examples of federal government in practice. The United States example, which is buttressed by various discourses documented by its founding fathers,[7] has experienced adjustments over time in response to new problems and political exigencies. Thus, U.S. federalism in the 1890s or even in the 1930s is different from federalism in the U.S. of 1990 or 2000. This process of adjustment is normal. As integrative processes in a nation-state positively advance, so also will adjustments become necessary in intergovernmental relations. In addition, the complexity of modern government (thanks to technological revolution) makes the traditional concept of federalism inappropriate, especially after the Second World War. Thus, as mentioned earlier, a greater degree of interdependence of component units in a federal state has become inevitable. In the same vein, the traditional concept of 'independence' or 'autonomy' of component units has also changed. The very process of interdependence implies some erosion of that traditional concept of independence of component units.

Given the U.S. experience, which in itself is very interesting and complex, many Western scholars gave the impression that unless the practice of federal government of other countries approximate the U.S. experience, they are not yet operating 'federal government'. This has led to the use of the term *quasi-federalism*. While the U.S. experience has reflected the cardinal principles of federalism, the fact that the adoption of the federal compromise is a response to the peculiar problems of a particular nation-state operating within a particular environment, makes differences in federal experiences inevitable. The important point is that the cardinal principles of federalism are constitutionally guaranteed and practised. Perhaps Ivor Duchacek hit the nail on the head when he observed that:

> Using the American measuring rods, we are, however, far from suggesting that the United States federalism should be considered the only 'true' or 'pure' one. Neither do we suggest that its birth and evolution are relevant to other countries that in the twentieth century may contemplate the adoption of a federal system. Some of the characteristics and aspects of the United States federalism are so anchored in the American soil that its experiences and lessons can hardly be transplanted elsewhere. Furthermore, its record of preserving unity with diversity is much less impressive than some textbooks on American Government would have one believe.[8]

The experiences which led to the adoption of federalism in the U.S. differ from those of Germany (after 1945), Australia, Nigeria, Switzerland and Canada. The practice of federalism in each of these countries would reflect the local settings and the peculiar nature of these countries. We shall return to this issue later. But let us look at conditions that led to establishing of Nigerian federalism.

Federalism in Nigeria

The Foundations of Nigerian Federalism

The current Nigerian State came into being as a colonial quasi-state in 1914, after the amalgamation of the colony of Lagos, and the Northern and Southern Protectorates of Nigeria. The British colonial authority did nothing to integrate these political units until after the Richards Constitution of 1946. This constitution recognized three regions — the Northern, Western and Eastern regions and the colony of Lagos. The dissatisfaction of Nigerian nationalists with the level of Nigerian participation in government led to a number of constitutional reforms between 1951 and 1957. These reforms saw the gradual federalization of

Nigeria's unitarist colonial state. As the prospects of independence became clearer, Nigerian politicians withdrew into their ethnic cocoons to mobilize for competitive politics. Mutual fears and suspicions of domination among ethnic and geo-ethnic groups generated intense pressures on the colonial administration for a federal Nigeria.

In 1956, Eastern and Western Regions secured self-governing status, while the Northern Region's self-government had to wait till 1959. By 1957, a *political dyarchy* had been established which saw Alhaji Abubakar Tafawa Balewa as the Prime Minister. Nigeria attained her independence on October 1, 1960, after the 1959 federal elections. The first Nigerian constitution provided for a federation operating in the context of a parliamentary democracy. By December 1965, the temperature in the polity had risen so high that politics had become dangerous for both players and spectators, as violence accompanied political disagreements.

It was therefore not surprising that in January 1966, the military staged a coup, which was followed by another military coup in July 1966. Nigeria became drowned in the vortex of crises, which climaxed in a thirty-month civil war. The military ruled Nigeria from January 15, 1966 to October 1, 1979; from December 31, 1983 to August 27, 1993; and from November 17, 1993 to May 29, 1999.

By May 1999, there were many complaints that the Nigerian federation had become excessively centralized. If there had been clamours in the 1960s for a federal system with a strong centre, there are now demands for a federal system with a weaker centre by some Nigerian groups. Why did Nigeria's central government become so centralized?

It is our suggestion that the high unitary streaks in the Nigerian federation were the result of a number of factors. These were - i) military rule, ii) the civil war, iii) the creation of states, iv) the increase in petro-naira; v) demands for federally desirable harmonization, and vi) international trade and globalization.

The military rule by decrees, and this meant that the central or federal government could assume functions reserved for the erstwhile regions through decrees, without opposition from politicians. Popular institutions of representation were, in any case, banned under military regimes in Nigeria. Politicians were shoved into the backwaters. Thus, many matters in the concurrent list such as university education, television stations were moved, at a point, to the exclusive list of the federal government. Under this provision, the federal military government took over the *New Nigerian Newspapers* and *Television Stations* in some states and some tertiary institutions. In addition, the emergency powers acquired by the federal government during the civil war were hardly reversed. Thus the federal government acquired powers which, because they were not reversed after the civil war, made it more powerful vis-à-vis the states.

Furthermore, the creation of additional states from the four regions which existed by 1966, meant weaker states, with narrower resource bases. General Gowon created twelve States in 1967. These were increased to nineteen States by Murtala Mohammed in 1976; General Babangida created two additional States in 1987, thus making twenty one States. He increased the number of States to thirty in 1991, while General Sani Abacha increased the number of States to thirty-six in 1996.

Paradoxically, as additional states were created to meet the demands of subnational groups for greater autonomy, the greater the number of States, the stronger the federal centre, and the more imperative its role as a centre for taking necessary homogenizing or harmonizing actions in matters transcending each state.

The advent of revenues from petroleum resources and the gradual dependence of the economy on this source, made a huge difference to fiscal federalism in Nigeria. The federal government derived greater resources than subnational units, especially from profit tax. Similarly, as from 1966, the federal military government adjusted the revenue formula in favour of the centre. The nature of military rule meant that there were little debates, if any, before such formula was adopted by the military's highest ruling body. Finally, the federal government's role in international trade and foreign relations in a world caught up in globalization fever, give advantages to the federal centre at the expense of states.

What we had in Nigeria, by May 29, 1999, therefore was a highly centralized federation in which the federal centre had enormous political and economic powers, with an apparently suffocating hold on the subnational States. It was therefore not surprising that various Nigerian groups had called for *Sovereign National Conference (SNC); National Conference*; a *Conference of Ethnic Nationalities; Devolution of Powers; Restructuring of the Federation*; and others. While some Nigerian groups called for a federation with a weak centre as at January 15, 1966, others called for a conference to enable ethnic nationalities negotiate the nature of their association in the federal polity.

When the military handed over power to the civilian politicians in 1999, the federation was characterized by a very strong central government; popular agitation for a more decentralized structure; dissatisfaction with the distribution of available resources; communal conflicts, and demands by some subnational groups for greater self-determination. What has been the nature of Nigeria's federation since May 1999? What new challenges has the new democratic federation faced, and how has it coped with them?

The Politics of Federalism in Nigeria's New Democratic Polity

In the terminal days of Nigeria's transition to civil rule, a number of issues had become evident in the political horizon. Given many years of the military rule, the Nigerian polity was like a bottle of wine, properly corked and airtight. With the dawn of democracy and the opening of the bottle, the wine explosively popped up. It took a while for the bubbles to settle down.

The Nigerian federation is faced with a number of challenges. Among these were: i) issues of centralization and decentralization in the relations among the three tiers of government; ii) resource distribution and/or management; and iii) the politics of federalism and aggressive subnationalism. There are many issues of interest in the current dynamics of Nigerian federalism, but let us concentrate on these three major points to illustrate the trend in the operation of the Nigerian federation.

Federal – State Relations

The military had left behind a highly centralized federation. Some Nigerian observers have argued that if the centre gets decentralized in its functions and accompanying powers, there would be less to fight among politicians for the centre, and there would be greater political stability in the system. This is not really as simple as it seems. It does seem that the federal government will continue to attract politicians who feel that their political stature and ambitions transcend the state level.

In the relations among Federal-State- and Local governments, there are signs of *residual militarism* in the actions of political executives. The ghost of the military's politics of control has had difficulty leaving the scene. Under the Obasanjo regime, federal officials treated state and local government officials with overbearing arrogance. In similar ways, state governors patronizingly related to local government chairmen.

In federal-state interactions, the relations between President Olusegun Obasanjo and state governors oscillated between 'hot' and 'cold'. The State Governors were not pleased with the President's way of operating as if he was still a military President.[9] They accused him of taking actions in flagrant disregard of federally desirable and constitutionally guaranteed autonomy of state governments—especially as provided in the legislative lists. Let us illustrate these concerns with some cases.

The first source of conflict between both tiers of government was the *National Minimum Wage* (NMW). On Labour Day (May 1, 2000) President Obasanjo announced a national minimum wage of ₦5,500 for state governments and ₦7,500 for the federal government.[10] Apparently under pressure from the Nigeria Labour Congress, the President did not consult the state governors or the National Assembly. The governors were livid with anger and reminded the President that the era of centralization under military rule was over.[11] They insisted that only the states could negotiate wages with their employees. While recognizing the powers of the federal government to set the minimum wage, they held that the President could not announce such a wage without due consultations with state governments (as employers of labour) and without sending a bill to the National Assembly.

For almost a year the country was gripped by wage crises[12] and strikes because many state governments could not afford to pay the new wages and arrears as demanded by their labour force. Some analysts believe that the President hastily announced the NMW in order to court the support of the labour force against the National Assembly with which he was having problems. General Obasanjo's military background and unilateral actions goaded him into a number of political hot waters with the state governments.

In a similar manner, the federal government introduced the *Universal Basic Education* (UBE) programme. This programme is aimed at providing free universal basic education from Primary School to the first three years of Secondary School. The federal government announced this programme and went ahead to launch it in Sokoto, before a bill was sent to the National Assembly. State governors complained of lack of consultation. They claimed that the matter was under the concurrent legislative list, and that since the federal government was going to depend on states for the implementation of the programme, states should have been adequately consulted.

In addition, some state governments were controlled by political parties different from the one at the federal level. Each political party had its own programme on education. They therefore frowned on the *military* fashion in which federal programmes were announced in areas of concurrent legislation, without regard to the priorities of states, especially where states were to be the implementing agency. The state governors and the Vice-President later met to harmonize areas of disagreement over this programme, but many grey areas remained. Adequate political consultations could have reduced tensions in federal-state relations. While, the federal government accused state governments of sabotaging the UBE programme, state governments felt that they could not abandon their programmes in order to execute federal programmes. The federal government had similar problems in getting the cooperation of state governments in the implementation of its *Poverty Alleviation Programme* (PAP), now replaced by the *National Poverty Eradication Programme* (NAPEP). Again the states reminded the federal government that each government had its own poverty eradication programme. If the federal government desired the cooperation of states in the implementation of its programmes, it should carry state governments along. Unlike the German Basic law, the Nigerian Constitution of 1999 does not provide for states as implementors of federal laws.

There is also the issue of the *Nigeria Police Force* and the maintenance of Law and Order. Given the ineptitude and inefficiency of the Nigeria Police in the maintenance of law and order, governors of states with large urban centres and high rates of crimes, found themselves helpless in dealing with crimes. Police is a federal matter, even though the Governor of a state is the Chief Law Officer of the State. As it happened in the Second Republic, many governors complained that State Commissioners of Police ignored orders from them but took orders only from their boss, the Inspector-General of Police.[13] In frustration, some state governors demanded for a review of the Constitution to enable the states to establish their own police forces. However, some state governors were opposed to the idea of establishing state police forces. They expressed their reluctance to spend their meagre resources on maintaining state police. These governors opted for a greater level of decentralization of the Nigeria Police to enable it respond to problems on the ground more effectively and promptly. In some states, the government officially resorted to using *vigilante* groups to maintain law and order.[14]

The issues of Revenue Allocation and local governments have also been areas of conflict between the Federal and State governments. Only recently, (December 10, 2004) the Supreme Court gave judgment in favour of the Lagos State government making it clear that the federal government had no power to withhold the funds of state governments, which had created additional local councils.

Nor has the relations between the National and State Assemblies been smooth. In view of the confusion over the actual tenure of Chairmen of Local Governments, State Houses of Assembly had made laws limiting the term of office of these chairmen to two years in some states, and three years in others.

In an attempt to sort out the problem, the Senate set up a committee to make recommendations to the National Assembly. The State Houses of Assembly felt that this was an usurpation of the powers given to them under Section 7 of the Constitution that the "Government of every state shall... ensure their existence under a Law which provides for the establishment, structure, composition, finance and functions of such councils."

Similarly, some state governments created or tried to create additional local governments in their states. Bayelsa State, for example, created new Local Government Councils, and deployed the chairmen of the old local governments to new local governments. The Senate of the Federal Republic declared this action a nullity because it violated Section 8(3) of the Constitution which provided elaborate processes for the creation of new local governments including a referendum.[15] In addition, the Senate argued that unless the list of local governments as contained in the first schedule, Section 3, Part 1, was duly amended, no new local government was legal. The action of the Senate was declared a nullity by the Supreme Court. In the case of Lagos State vs. Federal Government, the Supreme Court declared that while states had the power to create local governments, they should send these to National Assembly for constitutional amendments.

In state-local government relations, there had also been a cold war. Local Governments complained about undue interference from State Government. As an illustration, the Sokoto State government was taken to court by 15 Local Government Councils in the State and the court restrained the state government from deducting 3% of their statutory allocation for funding the Sokoto Emirate Council as passed by the State House of Assembly.[16]

In addition, local government Chairmen argued that state governors, (especially where the Chairman came from a party different from the Governor's) plotted to remove such chairmen by using the Audit powers of the state. State Governors were also accused of plotting with the State Houses of Assembly to shorten the tenure of three years of elected local government officials in order to put their supporters in office. In some states there were protests by elected local government officials against attempts by State Houses of Assembly to reduce their term to two years. Thus, in Imo State, the police arrested 11 Local Government Councillors along with 300 others who had gone to the State House of Assembly to protest the reduction of their tenure from three to two years.[17] In the case of Bayelsa State where new local governments were created, some Councillors took the Governor and Chairmen of the Local Government Councils to court because they believed that it was 'illegal' to share funds from the Federation Account with new and "illegal" local governments. Similarly, these chairmen also went to court to protest their deployment to new local governments as a form of illegality and disenfranchisement of the people, being perpetrated by some state governments.[18]

However, many Governors claimed that a majority of Chairmen and Councillors of Local Governments, only sit down to share money drawn from the Federation Account and hardly embark on development projects. President Obasanjo publicly chided the Chairmen over this issue. The Governors were at pains to point out that the Chairmen of Local Governments did not have the powers they had under the 1989 Constitution, and that they should be enlightened on this matter. In addition, the Governors were angry that the Federal Government related directly with Local Government Councils, which operated under them. They argued that the 1999 Constitution, Section 162(6) provided for the *State Joint Local Government Account* into which statutory allocation from Federal and State Government accruing to the Local Governments should be deposited.

The states were therefore opposed to what they perceived as attempts by the Federal Government to relate directly to local governments under them. They cited the case of the Federal Government aiding the local government chairmen to buy security vehicles and gadgets for the maintenance of law and order at local level without the knowledge and involvement of state governors, as evidence of federal government's interference in matters under state governments. The state governors are the Chief Security Officers of the state and should be involved in this kind of arrangement.

Let us turn briefly to the issue of centralization and decentralization of power in the federation. Federalism presupposes non-centralization of powers among the component units of the federation.[19] No one component, federal, state or (as in the 1999 Constitution) local government, is superior to the other. They all act directly on the people. If there is no superior government, which tier devolves powers to the other? Herein lies the difficulty of devolution of powers in the Nigerian federation, like some others in the world. A review of legislative list is one effective way of dealing with the devolution of powers. It is hoped that the process of constitutional review/amendments will take care of some of these issues.

Given the post-military rule situation and the emergence of a very strong central government, some Nigerians have called for *true federalism.* By *true federalism,* the protagonists of a weak central government refer to a confederation or what they claim to be the classical model of federalism delineated by K.C. Wheare. This is evident in the 1995 *Report of the Constitutional Conference Containing the Resolutions and Recommendations,* Volume 11, which recommended 'innovation' to Nigerian federalism thus

> It should be true federalism with clear demarcation of powers and functions among the levels of government. In the exercise of those powers and functions assigned by the Constitution, each level of government should be autonomous.[20]

In reality, the old sense of autonomy of component units in their areas of jurisdiction, have given way to cooperation, interdependence and interaction. That there is still a call for a return to a nostalgic classical model of federalism, however, is a reflection of the extent to which centrifugal forces are at work in the current Nigerian federation, as groups seek greater autonomy or self-rule at sub-national level in order to control their destiny. Paradoxically, the greater the number of states, the less autonomous the content of this self-rule, and the stronger the federal centre.

However, the prospects of a review of the legislative list in favour of subnational units are high. The future is most likely to witness a relatively less strong centre than Nigeria has now. But it is unlikely that Nigerians would revert to the loose federation they had between 1960 and 1965, or even adopt a confederal constitution.[21]

It can be argued that the Federal Legislative List (or the Exclusive List) is overloaded. It does seem more appropriate that the federal government should make policies for agriculture, health, education and others, for purposes of uniformity in policy direction. Thus, there should be no need for a Federal Ministry of Agriculture. A unit should be responsible for agricultural policies. It can also provide for federal forms of intervention in research, capacity and funding. On the other hand, given the peculiar development of Nigeria's formal Western education, the recommendation by the 1995 Constitutional Conference on Education may be unworkable. The Report left Primary Education to local governments; and transferred education at secondary and tertiary levels to states' legislative list. The intention of such action is understood, but Nigeria's experiences show that the problem with the educational sector is not just funding. There are human problems of capacity and attitude. The gross anti-intellectual posture in the country is part of these. May be, Universities should continue to be in the concurrent list. But they should be rationalized. There is no reason why seven good Medical Schools, six Faculties of Law; six or seven Faculties of Engineering; seven Faculties of Information and Computer Science, as well as Architecture and others – spread out across the country, properly staffed and appropriately funded – should not serve as centres of excellence for the country. No single state can handle these problems. It lies squarely at the door of the federal government. Paradoxically some state governments are requesting the federal government to take over their universities, while new universities are springing up in other states of the country.

In essence, the democratic pressures in the Nigerian federation, is likely to respond to the current centrifugal swing in the federal pendulum. It seems unlikely that Nigeria will eventually have a federation with a weak centre in the next decade, unless something dramatic happens. In addition, as political leaders imbibe greater democratic values; as democratic institutions get grafted and embellished by the federal grid; and as new cultures of tolerance and cooperation in intergovernmental relations are imbibed, Nigeria may witness a gradual adjustment in its vertical federal structure in favour of more appropriate power-sharing formulae among the levels of government. For now, centrifugal forces are likely to continue to push for a drastic reduction in the strength of the central government, beginning with the revenue sharing formula in the federation.

Another important challenge to Nigerian federation is the issue of resource distribution and management.

Resource Distribution and Management

Resource distribution includes both statuses and material resources. In fact, it includes the distribution of all scarce but allocatable resources. The location of government projects as well as the pattern of recruitment into political offices and the public services is also a yardstick for measuring the fairness of leaders in the distribution process in Nigeria.

In order to ensure relative fairness in the appointment of people from various groups into the Federal Public Service, government established the *Federal Character Commission* to monitor the pattern of appointment into all the public services of Federal, State and Local Governments, in order to give Nigerians, a sense of belonging to the nation. Cries of discrimination and marginalization by groups have not been abated since the establishment of this commission. But, at least, there is an office to which complaints can now be addressed for redress.

The 1999 Constitution provides in Section 162 (2) that the *Revenue Mobilization, Allocation and Fiscal Commission* (RMAFC) has the function of tabling before the National Assembly a draft revenue allocation formula. The National Assembly shall then deliberate on this document, taking into account the principles of "population, equality of states, internal revenue generation effort, landmass, terrain as well as population density". The National Assembly shall note that the principle of derivation applied on all proceeds from all natural resources will not be less than 13%. Since the advent of the new democratic polity, State Governors have argued that a new allocation formula should be put in place giving the states, at least 40%. As a matter of fact, a delegation representing state governors made the same point to the members of the RMAFC. This point was reinforced by the resolution of the Governors' Forum meeting in Abuja in August, 2000.

Generally, given the centralization of political power under the military, the centre became a financial titan, as military rulers altered the revenue formula[22] as they deemed fit. They did not need to debate the formula at any legislative forum, except at the Armed Forces Ruling Council or the Provisional Ruling Council. There have been calls for the revision of the legislative list and accompanying tax powers in favour of local and state governments. The argument is that the federal centre has too much funds at its disposal, thus encouraging it to engage in policy adventures into areas it should not, and into activities reserved for other tiers of government.

On the horizontal level, there have been cries of 'marginalization' by all groups. The oil producing states of Niger-Delta are angry that the dividends of oil produced in their area go to other parts of the country, without adequate concern for their own interests. Basically while oil accounts for over 80% of the country's annual revenue, it has not changed the lives of the Niger-Delta people. While the Constitution provides for 13% revenue (on the principle of derivation) to the oil producing area, the governors of these states argue that the federal government only agreed to pay these funds to the oil-producing states from January 2000, and has failed to do so between May 29 and December 1999. In response, the governors of the South-South Zone decided to demand for 100% control of its resources. As Governor Ibori of Delta State put it:

> ...the Federal Government has not, and we believe does not intend to resolve that very provision of the constitution, so we are not asking for 13 per cent any more, what we are taking now is everything, the 100% per cent control.[23]

The point is that, as in Canada and Australia, the Revenue Commission should be tasked to carry out two functions, in addition, to its current functions. It should carry out fiscal equalization on a vertical dimension, to ensure that funds are available to all three tiers of government to carry out their functions. Furthermore, its fiscal equalization measures on a horizontal level should carry out relative equalization among states in order to ensure some political stability.

In response to the complaints of neglect in the Niger-Delta, a new body *the Niger-Delta Development Commission* (NDDC) has been established, to replace the old *Oil Minerals Producing and Development Com-*

mission (OMPADEC). The NDDC is designed to alleviate poverty in the Delta area and embark on development projects aimed at improving the quality of lives of the average Niger-Delta person.

Similarly, states with solid minerals also complain that inspite of environmental degradation as a result of mining activities in their areas, they have not been adequately compensated. They are therefore calling for the establishment of the *Solid Minerals Producing Area Development Commission* (SOMPADEC). Interestingly, all the states from which hydro-electric power is generated have also called for the establishment of *Hydro Power Producing Areas Development Commission* (HYPPADEC) to compensate them for the consequences of any environmental damages caused by the activities associated with the generation of hydro-related energy.

Since the current quarrels are over the nature of distribution and not over the recognition of claims by contending parties, compromises will continue to be found. While the federal government went to court to seek the definition of the on-shore and off-shore minerals (or oil) in the context of resource distribution, there were pressures for a political, rather than a legal solution of the matter. This was done when a law was passed merging off-shore and on-shore. Since then, however, some Northern states have gone to court to challenge this law. In addition, the politicians are likely to strike compromises over the percentage of resources in the federation account which should be allocated on the basis of derivation. Currently, all mineral resources belong to the federation, and the 13% of the proceeds return to the state of origin of such minerals (including petroleum). Given the centrifugal pulls in the federation, the percentage of the derivation principle may go up gradually in the decade.[24]

One disturbing trait in the politics of leadership and resource distribution is the extent to which actions of leaders (military and/or civilian) can be easily ethnicized. It is very easy for a leader's mandate to be ethnicized or geoethnicized by his people, by the way they lay claim to him. It is also easy for a leader to ethnicize his mandate by his policies and actions. Usually, a leader's mandate being ethnicized by his people becomes more dangerous if the leader also ethnicizes his mandate through his official actions in government. The qualities of fairness and justice in a leader cannot be over-emphasized in the process of nation-building in a federal context. Let us now turn to the challenges of aggressive subnationalism.

Aggressive Subnationalism, Democracy and the Politics of Federalism

At the terminal period of transition from military to civil rule in 1998-99, there were signs of resurgence of aggressive subnationalism which had been suppressed under the regime of General Abacha. After May 29, 1999 when the military handed over power to civilians, latent aggressive subnationalism exploded into violence.

One effect of the over-centralization of power by various military regimes was the emergence of strong centrifugal forces which felt disadvantaged in the system. Many subnational groups felt that if the Nigerian federation were not as centralized as it was, they would have had a fairer deal in the federation.

Under this *democratic* polity, the suppressed *angst* of various groups with the Nigerian federation found expressions in many ways. The emergence of a fiscally and politically titanic centre had questioned the basic sense of security of groups. Let us illustrate this with some cases.

As a result of the Constitutional Conference of 1994/95, Nigeria was informally divided into six geopolitical zones.[25] These zones were regarded as development zones and zones for sharing resources among Nigerian groups. The Southwest zone, from the Abacha days had pressed for a Sovereign National Conference to discuss the restructuring of Nigeria. In essence, it was asking for a return to the old regions with their accompanying autonomy. This demand was partly predicated on the assumption that the federation was too centralized and that those who controlled political power at the centre also controlled resources, including their extraction and distribution. They therefore opted for the old regional autonomy (between 1960 and 1965) in order to control their resources and pace of development.

After May 1999, the *O'dua People's Congress* (OPC) declared its stand for the freedom of Yorubas to go it alone as an independent unit. It declared its desire to protect and defend Yoruba interests anywhere in Nigeria. The first eruption of crises was in Shagamu between OPC-backed group and Hausa settlers. Many people were killed and goods were destroyed. The corpses of Hausa men which were carried back to Kano generated a retaliatory wave of violence in that city against Yorubas. In response, Northern youths formed the *Arewa People's Congress (APC)* to challenge OPC violence.

OPC violence at Ketu and other places in Lagos angered the Ibos, who also set up the *Igbo People's Congress* (IPC) to deal with what they considered OPC's unwarranted meddlesomeness and violence. The OPC violence in Lagos got to a point at which the President threatened the Governor of Lagos State with a declaration of a State of Emergency in the State, unless he could restore law and order. Lagos had become extremely unsafe. Many people saw OPC's espousal of Yoruba nationalism as the reason for OPC leaders who had been declared wanted being shielded from the police. There were also allegations that the freedom attained by the two leaders of OPC – Dr. Fasheun and Ganiyu Adams— is not unrelated, to the fact that they are Yorubas from Obasanjo's ethnic group. They compare these cases with those of Major Al-Mustapha, General Bamaiyi and others who were, like Adams charged with murder. These men (Bamaiyi and Al-Mustapha et-al) had spent eight years in prison without the conclusion of their cases.

If OPC activities were not properly curbed by former President Obasanjo, because of the logic of federal autonomy of Yorubas espoused by that group, why should President Obasanjo deal with political manifestations of autonomy in other states? Some Northern states then chose to use *Shari'a* law to declare their federally desirable autonomy. Since May 1999, it was clear that the old North had lost political power, even though it had voted massively for General Obasanjo. The announcement of the introduction of *Supreme Shari'a* in Zamfara State, introduced a new factor in the politics of federalism. Up till then, state governments had operated *Shari'a* law as provided in the Constitutions of 1979, 1989 and 1999 – it was applicable only to civil proceedings involving Islamic personal law (such as inheritance, divorce and others). The *Supreme Shari'a* expanded the parameters of *Shari'a* Law to include criminal matters. As a result of this *Shari'a* Law, two thieves were amputated in Zamfara State. A seventeen year old girl was also flogged eighty times for fornication in the same state. In Kano and Katsina States a number of people were convicted for consuming alcoholic drinks and were sentenced to varying number of strokes of the cane.

Since its introduction in Zamfara State, *Shari'a* Law has been adopted in ten other northern States.[26] News of its introduction in Kaduna State (which is multi-ethnic and multi-religious in nature) led to gross communal violence and death of many Nigerians. The killing of Ibos and others in Kaduna extracted reciprocal killings of Hausa-Fulani Muslims in Abia and Imo States. In fact, the State governors of Abia,

Imo, Enugu, Anambra and Ebonyi States (of the Southeastern zone) called for a Confederal Nigeria.[27] The governors were quickly backed by the Yoruba *Afenifere* leader, Chief Abraham Adesanya, who argued that there was hardly any difference between "true federalism as demanded by Yorubas" and "confederacy which the *Igbos* are now demanding." In his usually blunt style, President Obasanjo described the call for a confederation as "highly mischievous and extremely unpatriotic.[28] Mischievous or not, the demand for confederation by the Southeast zone sent shivers down the political spine of the North, which then sent emissaries to the Southeast on reconciliation mission.

Following closely to these developments was the announced intention to declare a *Republic of Biafra* by the Movement for the Actualization of the Sovereign State of *Biafra* (MASSOB), on May 27, 2000. Disowned by Ojukwu and the pan-Ibo *Ohaneze* group, MASSOB hoisted a *Biafran* flag, while the leader escaped on motorcycle during the so-called ceremony. Was the call for confederation, like the *Shari'a,* a political card? If it was, other zones were soon to put their cards on the political table.

As discussed above, the governors of the South-South had complained about the non-release of 13% derivation fund to their states from May 29 to December 31, 1999. From the days of the military rule, the Niger-Delta had always been an area of conflicts. Devastated by oil exploration, inadequately touched by the benefits of oil, and overwhelmed by an army of unemployed youth, the area has seen violence aimed at extracting positive responses from the federal government and oil companies.

In fact, oil pipelines had been sabotaged at various times, while communities involved in illegal oil bunkering had suffered tragic consequences resulting from unexpected explosions and inferno. In a demonstration of anger, Bayelsa youths in Odi had captured policemen, ambushed and killed four soldiers. In reaction, government ordered military action which razed Odi village. It was a wanton military operation, illustrating clearly the need for Nigeria to establish a paramilitary unit appropriately trained for dealing with civil disobedience.

With this background of restiveness among the youth and their pressures on state governments, what was seen as the refusal of the federal government to release the 13% derivation fund, due to the states from May 29, 1999 to December 1999, soon took another dimension. The Governors of the states in the South-South Zone met and issued a communiqué that they had set the machinery "in motion to assume full control of its resources within the framework of true federalism."[29] Was this constitutional? Could states control mineral resources, when mining is under the exclusive legislative list of the federation? Again, the reaction by State governors of the South-South zone reflects the level of dissatisfaction among Nigerians with the operation of the federation.

Similarly, the Middle-Belt (or the North Central Zone) reacted to a number of issues in the federation. The trigger for the Middle Belt reaction was the complaint by the core North or Hausa-Fulani that the Service Chiefs of the Armed Forces came from the Middle Belt and not the North. There were spontaneous reactions to what was regarded as Northern hypocrisy – using the Middle Belt when it was convenient, to fight its war, and turn around to dump them. The Middle Belt Forum made it clear that it was no longer interested in being part of the old Northern geopolity, or share Northern identity with the Hausa-Fulanis.[30] The Middle Belt declared its support for a federation with a strong centre, with equity of opportunities for all. It called for equity in the distribution of resources and the need to encourage solid minerals, agricultural, and industrial development in the zone. Like the South-east, Southwest and South-South zones, the Middle-belt or the North-Central zone called for a national conference to discuss all outstanding issues in the Nigerian federation.

In essence, the violent protests in the Niger-Delta over perceived injustice in resource distribution; the Itsekiri–Ijaw violence in the Niger-Delta; the resumption of the Ife-Modakeke communal violence; the Odi violence and the sacking of the community by Obasanjo administration; the menace of *O'dua People's Congress* (OPC) and the accompanying violence in Lagos and Shagamu areas; the formation of the *Arewa People's Congress* (APC) and the *Igbo People's Congress* (IPC); the MASSOB feeble attempt to resuscitate *Biafra;* the *Shari'a* crises and the demands for a confederation; the South-South demand for the control of its resources, are all part of the bubbles of the Nigerian federation.

That these political bubbles worried President Obasanjo, is reflected in his address to the members of the Obasanjo Leadership Forum when they paid a courtesy call on him. Obasanjo claimed that the *Shari'a,* OPC and Niger-Delta crises were all programmed to destabilize Nigeria. According to the President, "... some people want to secede.

Some people want to break away from Nigeria while others want a stronger federation".[31]

Let us now turn to the challenges of federalism in the Fourth Republic.

The Challenges of Democratic Federalism in the Fourth Republic

The Challenge of Democracy

a) Politicians

We have made a transition from military to civil rule. So far, many of our politicians are still learning democratic values. They exhibit 'residual military' psyche in their actions. We do not seem to be ready for democratic practices. Our politicians see democracy in instrumental terms. They are more concerned with the perquisites that politics provides under a democracy.

This is why we have three groups of politicians—*politicians, political contractors* and *political touts*— in the political terrain. The *politician* is one who is dedicated to politics and seeks to acquire and use power in the interest of his electorate— for the maintenance of law and order, provision of welfare, and the pursuit of the interest of the State in relations with other states in the international system. There are very few of these available in Nigeria today; even these have become endangered specie.

The *political contractor* is a businessman in the political terrain. For him, democracy is tolerable nuisance, which provides greater access to resources. The ends of democracy and values are unimportant, even though he may be shouting them at public fora. The *political tout* is the hireling of the contractor and does his bidding, even if it involves maximum dispensation of violence. For the tout, democracy means 'democratization of violence' and democratic access to the instruments of violence and at times these undercut the state's ability to maintain law and order. This point is illustrated by the violence in most states of the federation, especially during the elections and after. Anambra and Oyo States illustrate the dangerous dimensions of the activities of political contractors. The Ngige-Chris Ubah and the Ladoja-Adedibu crises are current examples. It is our hope that in the next twenty years, political contractors and touts would have fizzled out of the system in favour of politicians.

b) Political Leadership and Statesmanship

Since 1999, the political class had not learnt that leadership entails listening to your followers, persuading them when necessary, and providing guidance and foresight. At the federal level, General Obasanjo, as President, still exhibited *messianic arrogance* and *residual militarism*. Many chief executives in the states shared the trait of residual militarism with him. These leaders, at all levels, did not learn that once elected, they must transform themselves into statesmen. Our experience has shown that many of our leaders are still politicians – there is no principle they cannot mortgage, there is no value they can not adulterate, and there is no law or rule they can not bastardize. From the election of the Senate President in 1999 through attempts to remove the former Speaker of the House of Representatives (Alhaji Ghali Na'abba) and those of states, the abortive 'coup' in Anambra, to the fraudulent actions by leaders in the process of passing electoral act, and the election of Senator Wabara as Senator and President of the Senate, the politics of self-interest, not statesmanship dominated the polity. The political class must wake-up, demonstrate better understanding of the kind of leadership required in a multinational Nigeria, otherwise they would be committing class suicide. The Presidency excessively engaged itself in a war, especially between President Obasanjo and Vice President Atiku Abubakar, which detracted from the dignity of that exalted office.

c) Political Tolerance

Political Tolerance of the opinion of others and the extension of the democratic space is another challenge. In Nigeria, the present actors seem not to understand democracy or have not learnt from the politicians of the past Republics. There is so much political intolerance among politicians. It is amazing and yet disgusting intra-party squabbles have led to deaths. How, for example, does one explain the show of force demonstrated by the Nigeria Police in Kano at the ANPP rally on 23rd of September 2003? What good excuse did the police have for denying ANPP the permit to hold the rally— beyond the usual 'security reasons'? There were excessive abuse of human right and freedom of association, using the Public Order Act to arrest and intimidate political opponents. The decision of the court voiding the Act is a victory for democracy, because that act was unconstitutional. How does one explain government's use of force during the Nigeria Labour Congress

(NLC) demonstration against its hike in fuel prize? How can one explain the abuse of court process by the federal government— after having its case against the NLC thrown out in Abuja, taking it to a court of coordinate jurisdiction in Lagos? The Lagos court granted the injunction, which has become popularly known as *black market* or *bolekaja* injunction. Political leaders must not only be responsive to the yearnings of the people, they must demonstrate a high sense of constitutionalism in their actions. They must tolerate the opposition because this country belongs to all of us. We must nurture the democratic plant of freedom with demonstrable understanding and mutual respect for one another. The excessive dependence of Obasanjo regime on coercion was anti-democratic, and was even dangerous for the political class.

d) Security to Life and Property

Since 1999, an atmosphere of insecurity has enveloped the polity. Initially, one thought that the removal of the tight lid under military rule had led to a new sense of freedom in which freedom had been transformed into license. Over the last eight years, there have been at least 140 cases of violence – communal and others. Armed robbery has become part of our normal life. Political and other homicides have become rampant in the system— not different from the situation under the military. The assassinations of the late Minister of Justice, Chief Bola Ige, Marshall Harry, the PDP Chairman in Kogi State and Chairman Anambra Bar Association and his wife, gubernatorial aspirants in Lagos and Ekiti, (Eng. Funsho Williams and Chief Daramola respectively) among others, illustrate how life has become really unsafe. The entourage of the Governors of Niger, Lagos and Benue were also attacked by those believed to be robbers. Democracy presupposes responsibility. It presupposes that politicians will be responsible enough to be crisis dampers rather crisis escalators. It also means that government should effectively maintain law and order to encourage the 'rule of law' and prevent the aggrieved from taking laws into his/her hands. Unfortunately, the Nigeria Police Force seems to be overwhelmed, while the constant use of the military for police duties is dangerous for everyone. Government must also stop the intimidatory technique of using the Nigeria Police to enable it get away with illegalities. Government must demonstrate civility, decency and caution in the use of its security services, which are paid from our tax funds. They are paid to maintain the system for all of us and not for a few incumbents in government.

e)The Electoral Process

While winners would call the 2003 elections free and fair, some losers would call it fraudulent. On balance, as a political observer, the 2003 elections in many parts of Nigeria were very fraudulent. Politicians, because of their insecurity, put their rigging machines on overdrive and ended with overkill. It was a disastrous exercise—detracting from our democratic learning process and potentially challenging our process of national integration. Given the cynicism in the polity, let me suggest, as I have consistently done since 2003 that:

i) all members of the current Independent National Electoral Commission (INEC) be relieved of their duties, while consultations be undertaken for a new and more neutral INEC comprising members of all political parties, NGOs and CSOs. Currently, INEC does not have any credibility as it does not command the respect of most of the political parties.
ii) there is a need to revisit the voters register by such after new INEC,
iii) laws governing contributions to party and individual campaign funds be established, and there should be a **one-term of five years for all Chief Executives at** all levels of government. As if the electoral tragedy of 2003 was not enough, General Obasanjo umpired also the election in 2007, which was at best, a shameful sham. Both domestic and international observers confirmed this.

We need to sanitize our electoral process to help restore electoral legitimacy to INEC and restore people's confidence in electoral democracy. Rigged elections disenfranchise the people and set a false agenda for governance. The 2006/2007 voters registration exercise ran into a big hitch, with INEC's insistence on electoral registration machines? The sad part of this is that it confirmed the suspicions of many about the goodwill and neutrality of INEC, and increased the level of apathy among the electorate.

a) Trivialization and bastardization of impeachment provision

The Nigerian constitution is clear on impeachment procedures. But the gale of impeachment that swept across the country under General Obasanjo left doubts about our democracy. Five State Governors were impeached in very controversial circumstances between 2006 and 2007. The affected governors were those of Bayelsa, Anambra, Oyo, Ekiti and Plateau States. The entire exercises were more of political melodramas in which constitutional provisions were easily trivialized and bastardized. Impeachment that was meant to be a way of ensuring accountability of elected leaders became a political weapon used by the presidency to eliminate those perceived to be in the opposing camp. These exercises can best be described as 'removal', if not 'coup'.

A review of all the cases of impeachment show that either members of State Houses of Assembly were cowed to initiate impeachment proceedings based on unsubstantiated allegations of corruption or the panel of inquiry was surreptitiously cornered to give predetermined recommendations. In most cases the Houses of Assembly were factionalized and the leadership controversially changed to favour the 'order from above.' The controversies also bordered on the constitutionality of the quorum (two-third majority), and even venue of sittings of members in virtually all the impeachment cases. It was common that pro-impeachment members carried out their plot outside their States, sometimes in Hotels or residential houses, and sometimes during odd hours of the morning, while enjoying intimidating protection of the Nigeria Police and the State Security Service.

From the cases mentioned, it is clear that the principles of federalism and democracy were violated. The processes of impeachment were not transparent. The electorates were hardly involved in the whole exercise. The rule of law was in abeyance. Above all, justice was perverted. On the other hand, the federal government used its control of police and anti-corruption agencies to intimidate or frivolously incite impeachment processes. In the case of Ekiti, impeachment was conveniently followed with declaration of a state of emergency without due consultation with the National Assembly. All these violations point to the need to revisit the constitution with a view to safeguarding the autonomy of the subnational units and the independence of the judiciary against the might of the federal executive.

It is to the eternal credit of the Judiciary that the impeachment cases in Ekiti, Oyo, Plateau and Anambra States were reversed and declared as unconstitutional.

b) Constitutional violations and democratic deficit

It is true that years of military rule, in part, contributed to the centralization of the Nigerian federation – a far cry from 1965. Candidly, there is need for the revision of the legislative list to give states and local governments more functions. In addition, tax powers of each tier of government should be reviewed to reflect new responsibilities acquired.

Political leaders should be sensitive to constitutional provisions. The Obasanjo administration treated the running of the federation under democracy as if Nigeria was under military rule. His wife, the late first lady, visibly demonstrated such when she sent circulars to wives of governors that she was the only First Lady. This was not a military regime and each governor was elected independent of the President, and was not beholden to him. The constant summoning of the governors to Abuja was also reflective of military rule. The Governors are chief executives of their states, responsible to their electorates, and must therefore be left alone to do their jobs. The use of the National Council of States (NCS) to legitimize government decisions is unconstitutional. Illustrations of these were the announcement made by the Presidency that i) the NCS had approved the 774 Local Government Reforms; ii) NCS had approved the non-inclusion of religion and ethnic group in census exercise; and iii) the raising of pump prices of oil. NCS is an advisory body to the President. The President should relate more actively with the National Assembly, to give the federation and our democracy the proper nudge forward. There were obvious areas of greater inter-governmental relations, which the large egos of some leaders prevented them from exploiting. The third term saga as well as constitutional amendments which nearly threw the whole country into confusion was the best way of throwing away good child with bad water. Most of the demands at the *National Political Reform Conference* (NPRC) were all thrown out with President Obasanjo's demand for term extension which most people including majority in the National Assembly said was unconstitutional and unwarranted.

The Challenge of Distribution of Resources

All federal systems have this problem. In Canada, Ontario, British Columbia and Alberta are the more viable provinces. Through a process of fiscal equalization, funds are transferred to other provinces that are less well to do without necessary robbing the rich provinces of their funds. In Australia, the Australian Lands Grant Commission carries out fiscal equalization among component units of the federation.

It is recommended that Nigeria's Revenue Mobilization, Allocation and Fiscal Commission should collate available data and embark on vertical and horizontal fiscal equalization among the component units of the federation. This should be an annual event, which would still take cognisance of fiscal equalization and transfer of funds to less well-to-do states for the purpose of national development. At the same time, it retains funds in states from where resources are extracted.

At the NPRC (2005), one of the hottest moot-points was the issue of resource distribution. The Niger-Delta had pressed for the control of their resources from 25% but gradually evolving up to 50-60% on the basis of derivation. A number of reactions to this by either members prompted the withdrawal of the South-South delegation from the conference.

Candidly, Nigerians are so concerned with the distribution of resources, they often forget that it is even more important to produce what is to be shared. The argument is like a chicken and egg story, after a point. Some people feel that there is no need to help in the production of resources because those who contributed little gain more. Yet if you do not produce, there is nothing to share. However, as long as you live in the same political community, you need to work out a mechanism for sharing resources through compromise. This is because of the realization that all are equal stakeholders in the process of nation-building.

It does seem that a number of actions need to be taken in the Nigerian federation:-

a) The revision of the legislative list in favour of states and local governments seem to be a political imperative. Similarly, the *tax powers should be correspondingly reviewed.*

b) On the *distribution of oil resources,* it may be suggested that there may be a need to go back to the old dichotomy between *on-shore* and *off-shore* oil. Fifty percent of the on-shore oil revenues should go to the states of origin on the basis of derivation principle. However, fifty percent of the off-shore oil revenues should go into a *stabilization fund* for fiscal equalization among tiers of government and among non-oil producing states. This should be used to relatively close any gaps between oil and non-oil producing states. Ten percent of the off-shore oil revenues should go to the rehabilitation of mining areas (solid minerals and oil). Ten percent of the off-shore oil should go to the social development (education, health, and others) of the oil mineral producing areas while the remaining thirty percent off-shore oil revenue goes to the federation account for the usual distribution.

c) The RMAFC should be tasked with the functions of monitoring and working out formal mechanism for fiscal equalization, vertically and horizontally. This can be periodically reviewed, and should rob the central government of the subjectivity involved in the grants it makes to sub-national units.

d) Greater inter-governmental interaction may reduce the problems associated with inter-tier conflicts. Under the Obasanjo administration, states and local governments were treated as virtual extensions of the federal government. Some of the avoidable conflicts in the federation under the Fourth Republic derive from the hangover of the military regime in which the centre had grown titanic. Curbing the unnecessary adventures of the centre has become a problem. There are many arenas of cooperative inter-governmental relations. Politicians at this stage of Nigeria's development are either ill-equipped to deal with these problems or are unwilling to establish normal inter-governmental relations, even when constitutionally provided.

Like most things in nation-states, there is a need for mutual compromise to enable **fairness, justice** and **relative equity** to lubricate the wheels of the federation. It is hoped that with more discussions and collective experience, the politics of distribution will not be a danger to the federation.

The Nigeria Police, Security Agencies and Federalism

The Nigeria Police and other security agencies have earned themselves bad image when it comes to the discharge of their constitutional responsibilities. The level of personal insecurity and violation of human rights in the country speaks volumes of this image. The failure to perform up to expectation pushed some state governments to establish vigilante groups. Besides, the way the police is used/misused have prompted many to suggest the establishment of State Police Force. In the case of the Anambra saga, the police were found to have acted as the arrow head for the apparent 'coup' against former Governor Chris Ngige, given the role played by the AIG Ige. It is amazing that while the Inspector-General quickly responded to the order of the Enugu High Court judge, that the security around the Governor be withdrawn, it ignored an Appeal Court order which reversed the order of the lower court, supposedly because the Attorney-General of the Federation had advised against the restoration of the police security for the Governor.

Given the Anambra example in which the President was reported to have ordered the withdrawal of federal police protection from the Governor, the call for the establishment of state police became louder. The impeachment cases in Ekiti, Oyo, Plateau, Anambra and Bayelsa, could easily be carried out because of the centre's control of the police and other security agencies. We had argued in the past that the time was not ripe for State Police, based on our past experience of the misuse of state or local police force. However the persistence of brazen misuse of the Nigeria Police by the presidency has made one to revisit this argument. We now strongly suggest that the police should be decentralized such that it can operate efficiently in each State. The Governor of the State should be delegated some powers by the President such that within certain limits, he can operate effectively in collaboration with the Commissioner of Police in the State, referring only very serious matters to the President and the Inspector-General of Police. There should be State Police operating under constitutionally delineated conditions.

Be that as it may, the point is that politicians should not politicize and destroy the credibility of the Nigeria Police Force. Nor should the police force allow itself to be destroyed. The police is the last hope of the ordinary man for rule of law. Political leaders must be careful so that they do not politicize the police to the extent of committing class suicide.

Constitutional Review: Towards a new Legislative List

In the next decade, a number of issues will continue to attract the attention of political leaders. The distribution of powers among the tiers of government and on the horizontal level will continue to engage Nigerian political leaders, irrespective of their party affiliations. It is most likely that the legislative lists will be reviewed in favour of subnational units. The centre may be less powerful than it is now, but it is unlikely that Nigeria will adopt a confederal technique in the management of conflicts arising from its federal association.

In addition, the issue of resource distribution and/or management will continue to dominate the debate in the federation. There may even be violent reactions to the problem. But given the complementarity of the Nigerian economy in the past 80 years, piecemeal compromises are likely to be effected over time. It is hoped that as democratic institutions take their roots, as the political process get routinized, and as intergovernmental relations improve and a new culture of interdependence, healthy competition and cooperation develops among the operators of the federation, Nigerians will develop greater sense of tolerance and accommodation of one another.

There is a continuing process of adjustment and compromise in all federations. No federation has attained a perfect balance between centrifugal pulls (toward self-determination for subnational groups) and centripetal pulls (toward control by and sovereignty of the centre). Adjustment in one area may affect another area on the federal scale. In Nigeria the politics of compromise on the federal context have been complex. Out of the various shocks to the Nigerian political system, only federalism has survived. Both parliamentary and presidential systems have been experimented with federalism. This is a good omen and it is a sign that we can understand ourselves better. Perhaps, the problem is more among Nigerians, not the system.

Attempts at reviewing the constitution were made by both the federal executive and legislative arms. The National Assembly formed a committee on Constitutional Review which collated ideas on the review exercise. In addition, there was also a Presidential Committee on Constitutional Review, comprising members of the three political parties. A Political Reform Conference was also convened in 2005 by the federal executive in order to gather views and opinions on some thorny issues in Nigerian federation. The National Assembly formed another Constitutional Review Committee under pressures from the Presidency in 2006. All these efforts failed. In fact, the last two attempts were grossly abused by the presidency in a bid to achieve tenure elongation for General Obasanjo — popularly called the Third Term Agenda.

Nonetheless, we suggest that the Nigerian federation needs to be demilitarized. The process of demilitarization should begin with reduction of the unitarist streaks in the federation, even though we understand with the patriotic or nationalistic logic behind the centralization of powers over the years. Thus, the **Legislative Lists** should be reviewed:

i) by transferring agriculture, housing and secondary and primary education, water resources (which do not transcend one State boundary) into the residual list of States. Higher education at the level of Universities and Polytechnics can still be in the concurrent list;
ii) the federal government should have departments of agriculture and natural resources which would perform policy coordinating functions, and intervene from time to time to provide funds for particular activities desirable for development; and
iii) federal government should engage in greater *fund transfer* to subnational units as part of competitive – cooperative federation. As an illustration, the federal government does not need to run the Universal Basic Education Commission. It only needs to give persuasive grants to states which abide by some guidelines, to carry out this educational function. Alternatively, the Commission can become an intergovernmental agency for states and local governments, to which the federal government transfers annual bloc grants. This can be done in many areas as a technique for transferring funds from the centre to subnational units as happens in other federations. The Revenue Mobilization Allocation and Fiscal Commission (RMAFC), can, like the Australian Lands Grant Commission, carry out the technical details.

Minority, Citizenship and Indegineity Issues

Any federation that does not *protect its minority groups*, but gives unlimited leverages to the majority groups is bound to have incessant communal violence and instability. In Nigeria, the minority question has been made more complex because of the nature and extent of diversity. While it is very easy to identify Hausa-Fulani, Yoruba and Igbo as the three major ethnic groups at the national level, the majority-minority divide is also visible at the State and local government levels. This is a manifestation of the problem of accommodating over 250 ethnic or 400 lingo-cultural groups in few subnational units. Over the years, states and local governments had been created as a means of coping with the minority-majority conflict. But the various exercises have further created *new majority* and *new minorities* at the subnational levels. Often the new majorities are more vicious than the old majorities.

The issue of *citizenship and indegineity* is related to the problem of minority-majority divide. Reconciling the diverse ethnic groups which make up Nigeria is no doubt a Herculean task. The Nigerian constitutions from 1960 to 1999 recognize the citizenship of every Nigerian. All

Nigerians have the right to settle anywhere in the country to pursue their legitimate businesses and are expected to have equal rights everywhere. But this is not really the correct picture on the ground in the federation. Indegineship-citizenship rights are not well defined and accepted. Many states and communities recognize their indigenes and can easily isolate settlers.

In the political process this has become very controversial and has generated many violent crises. In some cases, the spill over or hang over of this issue have led to electoral violence, because it becomes important who is elected—*indigene or settler*. The Jos-North violence and the Wase case in Plateau State, the Tiv-Jukun conflict in Taraba State and similar other cases of violence, illustrate the explosive nature of this issue in the polity and in the electoral process. State governments may want to make laws stating the residency requirement for indigenship. It may even peg it at 25 years of local residence.

The Economy and Federalism

The Nigerian economy is in a bad shape—the exchange rate is about ₦130 to one USA dollar; inflation still haunts our hopes for a good take home pay; some banks are collapsing; the manufacturing sector has experienced closures; the privatization process appears to be a **personalization** process; there seems to be greater **invasion** of our market by external forces than investment; our infrastructure are dilapidated; our educational system is collapsing and health sector is severely in pains. With all these, one is tempted to ask whether the gloated **economic reforms** of the federal government under Obasanjo are not really causing **economic deforms**?

Political leaders must address these issues urgently because they relate to the sustenance of our democracy, our federation, and our nation. We need to diversify our **monocultural** economy into other sectors. Our **deregulation** and **privatization** policies must be pursued with all sense of patriotism and sincerity, transparency and accountability.

We must not forget that a democratic culture and stability cannot thrive in a society where there is abject poverty. Our poverty alleviation/eradication programmes have so far failed to tackle the problem. We need to work seriously on these in order to save our democracy. With our abundant human and natural resources, we strongly believe that our poverty is related to the ineptitude and inefficiency in the governance of the polity.

So far, the federal government seems to have so much money that it dabbles into any area of its fancy. Candidly, housing, water, agriculture, primary schools and rural development should revert to state and local governments, which should have enough resources to carry out these functions. With regard to the adequacy of fiscal or tax powers, it is clear that all tiers of government have been complacent about generating needed revenues. The over-dependence on the Federation Account by all governments is not conducive to the fiscal autonomy and accountability of the component governments of the Nigerian federation. One wonders if revising the tax powers would make any difference if the appropriate authorities do not collect these taxes. Internally generated revenue and accountability are essential parts of federal autonomy.

Our governments, at federal, state and local levels must summon the courage and will to reverse their current complacent nature in order to achieve economic prosperity for their people. The trend in federal states is generally towards more cooperation among all tiers of government in economic planning and development. A case in which some political appointees at the federal level arrogate to themselves the monopoly of knowledge and expertise of the economic problems and solutions is not helpful. Economic policies need to be streamlined and not imposed on subnational units. This brings to the fore the question of ownership and retainership of the federal government's anointed National Economic Empowerment Strategy (NEEDS) and its derivative at the State and local levels—SEEDS and LEEDS, respectively. Also the federal government should, by virtue of its role in national development, encourage competition among subnational units using incentives, on the one hand, and special grants for the purpose equalization and balancing development, on the other.

Conclusion

We have argued that at the dawn of the 21st century, the Nigerian federation is characterized by strong unitarist streaks as a response to almost three decades of military rule. As a result of over-centralization of the Nigerian federation, there have been numerous demands by subnational groups for a review of the legislative list.

The Nigerian federation faces a number of challenges in the next decade of the new millennium. Among these challenges is the issue of how to decentralize an overly centralized federation. The next few years are likely to witness a constitutional review including a review of the legislative list. It is most likely that the powers of the centre would be reduced in favour of sub-national units.

In similar vein, the distribution of scarce but allocatable resources will continue to dominate the federal debate on the state of the federation in the next decade. As Nigerian groups reassess their benefits from (more often rather than contribution to) the federation, conflicts over distribution of resources will continue to arise. However, given the complementarity and inter-dependence of the Nigerian economy, political leaders are likely to find appropriate forms of compromises, from time to time. The conflicts of distribution may even reach crises proportions, but are unlikely to threaten the existence of the nation-state.

In the new democratic setting, the politics of federalism has led to the emergence of geopolitical bargaining platforms in anticipation of a National Conference. The explosion of sub-national identities and associated aggressive nationalism, are likely to surface from time to time, without destroying the polity.

Ultimately, it is clear that the reasons for the adoption of federalism are very much around. The mutual fears and suspicions of one another by Nigerian groups are likely to continue in the next decade. But it is hoped that as groups interact and establish relative mutual confidence in one another and in the federal system, necessary compromises will be effected and conflicts managed appropriately. For a long while, it does seem that federalism or one federal-type solution or the other will continue to provide the desirable compromise for managing conflicts in Nigeria.

NOTES AND REFERENCES

1. See some other literature on federalism Carl Freiderich, *Trends of Federalism in Theory and Practice* (London: Pall Mall, 1968); Daniel J. Elazar, *The Politics of American Federalism* (Lexington: Mass, -D.C. Heath, 1969); Richard Leach, *American Federalism* (1970); A.B. Akinyemi, P.D. Cole, and W. Ofonagoro (eds.) *Readings on Federalism* (Lagos: Nigerian Institute of International Affairs, 1979); Ronald Watts, *Administration in Federal Systems* (London: Hutchinson Educational, 1970); James Sundquist, *Making Federalism Work* (Washington,

D.C.: The Brooking Institute, 1969) and *Publius: The Journal of Federalism* (Centre for the study of Federalism, Temple University, U.S.A.); Eme Awa, *Issues of Federalism* (Benin: Ethiope Publishers, 1977); Kenneth W. Thompson (ed.) *The U.S. Constitution and Constitutionalism in Africa* (New York: University Press of America, Inc., 1989); Dan J. Elazar, *Exploring Federalism* (Tuscaloosa: The University of Alabama Press, 1987); Vincent Ostrom *The Political Theory of a Compound Republic* (Lincoln: University of Nebraska Press, 1987); D. Elazar, *Governing Peoples and Territories* (Philadelphia: Institute for the Study of Human Issues, 1982); J. Isawa Elaigwu and E.O. Erim, (eds.) *Foundations of Nigerian Federalism: Pre-Colonial Antecedents. Second Edition* (Jos: IGSR, 1996); J. Isawa Elaigwu and G.N. Uzoigwe (eds.) *Foundations of Nigerian Federalism: 1900-1960* (Jos: IGSR, 2001) and J. Isawa Elaigwu and R. Akindele (eds.) *Foundations of Nigerian Federalism: 1960-1995* (Jos: IGSR, 2001).

2. Shridath Ramphal, The Commonwealth Secretary-General, "Keynote Address to the International Conference on Federalism," at the Nigerian Institute of International Affairs, Lagos. Published in A.B. Akinyemi, P. Cole, and W. Ofonagoro (eds) *Readings on Federalism* (Lagos: N.I.I.A., 1979), pp. xiii-xv.

3. K.C. Wheare, *Federal Government* (London: Oxford University Press, 1964), p. 10.

4. *ibid.*

5. Roland Watts, *op.cit.* p.5.

6. Ranjit Sarkaria, *"Foreword"* in S.C. Arora (ed.) *Current Issues and Trends in Centre-State Relations: A Global View* (New Delhi: Mittal Publications, 1991), p.3.

7. See, *The Federalist Government Papers* for interesting discussions on the experience.

8. Ivor Duchacek, *Comparative Federalism: The Territorial Dimension of Politics.* (New York: Holt, Rinehart and Winston, 1970), p. 202.

9. General Obasanjo was a former Military Head of State (1976 - 79). He came to power as an elected President on May 29, 1999. He has not yet shed his military toga. He is fond of taking actions without sensitivity to due process as required in a democratic polity.

10. *The Vanguard* (Lagos), June 24, 2000, p.6.

11. *ibid.; The Vanguard,* May 4, 2000, p.2.

12. There were labour crises all over the country. Many state governments could not pay the new wages, thus negotiations with their labour forces failed. In some states, public servants were on strike for between three to six months. See *Vanguard,* May 4, 2000, p.2. in which Governor Dariye of Plateau State expressed his concern — "Our concern is that we don't want to go back to the ugly past when workers were owed several months arrears of salaries."

13. It has been suggested that the structure of the Nigeria Police Force be decentralized in order to allow the zonal commands to be more responsive to local situations. Quite a number of Nigerians are apprehensive of the wanton

misuse of the local police by local governments, politicians and traditional leaders, in the past.

14. This is the case of Anambra State where the Bakassi Boys became officially recognized *Vigilante* to complement police efforts. Attempts by the Governor of Lagos to use the OPC have been criticized by the Police, especially since the OPC is a banned organization. See *This Day* (Lagos) August 18, 2000, p.13; August 2, 2000, p.1; July 30, 2000, p.1 and July 27, 2000, p.1.

15. Section [8(3)] of the 1999 Constitution states that:

"(3) A bill for a Law of a House of Assembly for the purpose of creating a new local government area shall only be passed if-

(a) a request supported by at least two-thirds majority of members (representing the area demanding the creation of the new local government area) in each of the following, namely-

(i) the House of Assembly in respect of the area, and

(ii) the local government councils in respect of the area, is received by the House of Assembly;

(b) a proposal for the creation of the local government area is thereafter approved in a referendum by at least two-thirds majority of the people of the local government area where the demand for the proposed local government area originated;

(c) the result of the referendum is then approved by a simple majority of the members in each local government council in a majority of all local government councils in the State; and

(d) the result of the referendum is approved by a resolution passed by two-thirds majority of members of the House of Assembly."

16. *The Vanguard* (Lagos), August 23, 1999, pp.1 and 2.

17. *The Vanguard,* March 9, 2001, p.1.

18. *The Punch,* July 7, 2001, pp.1-2.

19. There are many publications on Nigerian federalism, among which are - Frederich Ebert Foundation, *Constitutions and Federalism: Proceedings of the Conference on Constitutions and Federalism* (Lagos: Friedrich Ebert Foundation, 1997); E. E. O. Alemika and Festus Okoye, (ed.), *Constitutional Federalism and Democracy in Nigeria* (Kaduna: Human Rights Monitor, no date); A. Adedeji, *Nigerian Federal Finance* (London: Hutchison Educational, 1969); A. Akanle, *The Power to Tax and Nigerian Federalism* (Lagos: Centre for Business Executives, 1985); E. O. Awa, *Federal Government of Nigeria: A Study of the Development of the Nigeria State* (Berkeley: University of California Press, 1964); Peter P. Ekeh, (ed.) *Nigerian Federalism* (Bufallo: Association of Nigerian Scholars for Dialogue, 1997); *Publius: The Journal of Federalism,* Vol.1, No.1 1994 (on Nigeria); J. Isawa Elaigwu and Erim O. Erim, (eds.) *Foundations of Nigerian Federalism: Pre-Colonial Antecedents,* Vol.1 (Abuja: National Council on Intergovernmental Relations, 1996); J. Isawa Elaigwu and Godfrey Uzoigwe, (eds.) *Foundations of Nigerian Federalism: 1900-1960,* Vol. II (Abuja: National Council on Intergovernmental

Relations, 1996); J. Isawa Elaigwu and R. A Akindele, (eds.), *Foundations of Nigerian Federalism: 1960 -1995, Vol. III* (Abuja: National Council on Intergovernmental Relations, 1996); D. Rothchild and Victor Olorunsola, (eds.) *State Versus Ethnic Claims: African Policy Dilemmas* (Boulder: Westview, 1983).

20. Federal Government of Nigeria, *The Constitutional Conference Containing the Resolutions and Recommendations,* Vol. II, (Lagos: Government Printer, 1995), p.61.

21. The nearest Nigeria went to a Confederal Constitution was crisis period 1966-67, when the Federal Military Government issued Decree No. 8, 1967, of March 17, 1967, in response to the Aburi peace accord in Ghana.

22. There had been Revenue Commissions in the past— i) Philipson Commission (1946); ii) Hicks-Philipson Commission (1951); iii) Chicks Commission (1953); iv) Raisman Commission (1958); v) Binns Commission (1964); vi) Dina Committee (1969); vii) the Military governments issued decrees in 1967, 1970, 1971 and 1975 on revenue allocation matters; viii) Aboyade Commission (1978); and ix) Okigbo Commission (1980). The Okigbo Commission formula was amended by subsequent military regimes, as they deemed fit. See T. Y. Danjuma, "Revenue Sharing in Nigerian Federalism" in J. Isawa Elaigwu, P.C. Logams and H. S. Galadima, (eds.) *Federalism and Nation-Building in Nigeria: The Challenges of the 21st Century* (Abuja: National Council On Intergovernmental Relations, 1994), pp. 87-115.

23. *This Day,* July 28, 2000, p.7.

24. After all, between 1964 and 1969, the percentage of mineral rents and royalties which went back to the States was 45%. It may go up again beyond the current 13%.

25. These political zones are-

North-Central	**North-East**	**North-West**	**South-East**	**South-South**	**South-West**
Benue Kogi Kwara Nasarawa Niger Plateau	Adamawa Bauchi Borno Gombe Taraba Yobe	Jigawa Kaduna Kano Katsina Kebbi Sokoto Zamfara	Abia Anambra Ebonyi Enugu Imo	Akwa-Ibom Bayelsa Cross River Delta Edo Rivers	Ekiti Lagos Ogun Ondo Osun Oyo

26. These states include, Kebbi, Niger, Sokoto, Kano, Yobe, Bauchi, Borno, Kaduna, Jigawa and Katsina.

27. *The Vanguard,* March 27, 2000, p.1.

28. *The Source,* (Lagos) Vol. 6, No.25, April 3, 2000, p.12.

29. *This Day,* (Lagos) August 16, 2000, p.10; *The Vanguard,* September 26, 2001, pp.31 and 33.
30. *The Nigeria Standard,* (Jos) August 17, 2000, p.7.
31. *The Vanguard,* July 19, 2000, p.2.

CHAPTER 2

DIVISION OF POWERS AND RESPONSIBILITIES (INCLUDING TAX POWERS) IN NIGERIA

Habu S. Galadima

Introduction

Federalism has become more popular as a system of government since the Second World War. According to the 2002 *Handbook of Federal Countries*; the citizens of the 25 of the world's 193 countries that have federal political systems comprise 40 per cent of the world's population[1]. Federal countries can be found on all continents and include Australia, Austria, Brazil, Canada, Switzerland, Germany, India, Malaysia, Mexico, Nigeria, Russia, St. Kitts and Nevis, United Arab Emirates and the United States of America among others.

A country belongs to the family of federal states when it is composed of two levels of government or two levels of state, the federation and its federal units (provinces, Länder, cantons, states)[2]. The federal units not only enjoy autonomy or self-rule, but they also determine, at least partially, the policy of their federation (shared-rule).

Federalism thus can be seen as a constitutionally guaranteed balance between self rule and shared-rule of state units within a composed state[3]. Self-rule is the right of the federal units to a limited self-determination on constitutional, legislative, judicial and administrative issues. This may include education, security (police), housing, health, foreign relations, environment, taxes, expenditures, social welfare, private law etc. Shared-rule opens the possibility for the federal units to participate in the decision-making process on the federal level, particularly on issues of constitution making, legislation (second chamber), administrative implementation of federal statutes, etc.

One of the primary features of a federal system of government is the assignment of functions between the various components of government[4]. Division of powers is at the heart of federal arrangements to the extent that without it there is no federalism.

Two types of federalism are commonly identifiable: dual and cooperative.[6] Preceding from this classification and the fact that the nature of dual federalism presupposes the existence of two independent levels of government, autonomous each within its own area, we infer that the legislator on each level produces exclusive legislation in the prescribed sphere. Thus, only two types of legislation are possible: federal exclusive legislation and sub-national exclusive legislation. Analyzing the constitutions, we find more types of the legislation.

According to Dwight Herperger, three general patterns of distribution of powers are discernable in the federal systems.[7] The first type provides for an exclusive list of federal powers, leaving all the other matters as residual to the states. The second pattern presents the three lists of explicit powers: federal, state and concurrent. Canada and Malaysia can serve the example of this type. And the last type is the most common one which provides for two lists of powers: federal exclusive and concurrent. Among the federations which have chosen this type of power distribution are the United States, Australia, Switzerland, Federal Republic of Germany, Russian Federation and some others.

Ron Watts identified the differences in the form of the constitutional distribution of powers.[8]

> a) the extent to which the exclusivity or concurrent jurisdiction of governments has been emphasized,
> b) the assignment of state or provincial powers by a specific listing of jurisdiction or by a general allocation of residual authority,
> c) the extent to which the assignment of executive responsibilities coincides with or is differentiated from legislative jurisdiction,
> d) the symmetry or asymmetry in the powers assigned to different constituent units,
> e) the formal constitutional recognition or not of local governments as a third constitutional order of government guaranteed by their own self-government, and
> f) the extent of federal overriding and emergency powers.

First of all, what is the principle of division of powers between the various levels of authority in a federation? One should distinguish between the principle and the technique for the division of powers and responsibilities.

The Nature of Division of Powers in a Federation

The general principle underlying the division of powers and responsibilities in federal systems is that matters of common interest and concern to the country as a whole should be assigned to the federal government, and matters of a decidedly regional or local character should be assigned to the provincial or state governments.[9] The general pattern which emerges from this principle is that matters such as defence, foreign policy, currency, and external and interstate trade typically fall within the jurisdiction of the federal government, while more regionally or locally oriented matters such as public health, primary and secondary education, social services and municipal government fall within the purview of provincial jurisdictional authority. Where strong national and regional interests coincide, powers have been either concurrent or further subdivided into federal and provincial spheres or aspects. With regard to the principles is the description of aims and functions (peace, order and sound government); opposed to this is the classification of functions according to the general domains of authority of activities. The following broad domains can be identified: foreign affairs, defence, economic affairs, transport, communication, natural resources, administration of justice and law enforcement, the status and rights of citizens, culture, health and welfare, habit and environment. Within these broad domains, more details can be worked out.

A few domains in particular can be described. Economic affairs include trade and commerce (distinguishing between foreign, interstate and intrastate trade), monetary affairs (including foreign exchange, the monetary system and coinage), financial institutions, taxation, public loans, corporations and companies. Cultural affairs include such matters as language arrangements, education, schools, universities, archives, research, exchanges, copyright, books, films, arts, recreation, marriages and divorces, property and civil rights.

When authority functions are described in this way, it should be possible to bestow responsibilities for a particular domain either exclusively on one, or jointly on several levels of authority depending on which level is best equipped for the particular function. Exclusive federal legislative authority means that all powers to legislate in a marked area belong to the federal government and the states may legislate in these fields only to the extent expressly authorized by federal law.

This brings us to the techniques for dividing functions between levels of authority. Three possibilities exist. The first is to define the functions of the central authority and leave the rest (whatever this may include) to the middle-tier authorities, as in the USA, Australia and Switzerland. This method is used to limit the powers of the central authority, to give the individual states or communities more freedom and to bring about a localized federal state. The second is to define the functions of the middle-tier authorities and to leave the rest to the central authority, as in Canada. This method is used to limit the states or communities, to strengthen the central authority and to set up a centralized federal state. The third is to define the functions of both the central and the middle-tier authorities and then compile still another list of functions on which both tiers can take actions, as in India. This method places the state in either category and even brings an end to its federal character, if the list of matters over which both levels have authority is extended to such an extent that there is no terrain over which a single level remains autonomous.

It is generally accepted that the assignment of functions among federating units should be organized in the following ways: functions which can be more efficiently performed by the federal government than lower levels of government should be assigned to it (i.e. be placed in the exclusive legislative list). These include national defence, external relations (including borrowing and external trade), banking, currency, and nuclear energy, among others, (whose benefits are more local than national but with the possibility of spill over effects should be placed in the concurrent list). Such functions include industrial, commercial or agricultural development, post primary institutions, health care, etc. Functions which are purely local in character, in the sense that the benefits accrue, in the main, to limited geographic areas within the country, are usually assigned to local authorities. Such functions would include the establishment and maintenance of markets, car parks and public conveniences, refuse disposal, primary education and the construction and maintenance of local roads and streets.

However, it is difficult, if not impossible, to put most of these functions into watertight departments. This fact underlies the principle of cooperation within federating units in the performance of a number of functions. Although a constitutionally entrenched distribution of powers between two orders of government is considered perhaps the defining characteristic of federalism, not all federal systems have adopted a uniform approach to the general form and enumeration of these powers in their respective constitutions.

An examination of legislative powers in federal constitutions reveals variations relating to the number of lists of powers, the specificity and comprehensiveness of individually enumerated powers, the placement of the residual power, the exclusivity of powers assigned to each tier of government, and provisions for paramount in the case of shared or concurrent powers. As well, various federal systems have adopted arrangements whereby the federal government defines through legislation the broad principles for particular programmes (or entire fields of jurisdiction), and the constituent units are left with the responsibility for execution and administration. Moreover, some federal constitutions provide for a distribution of powers which operates differently in one or more constituent units of a federation (i.e., asymmetry). And, finally, devices such as intergovernmental delegation of legislative power and the constitutional entrenchment of federal-state agreements have been used in some federations to allow greater flexibility and adjustment in the practice of these powers.

Division of Powers and Responsibilities in Nigeria

Essentially, three forms of distribution of powers exist in federal systems. The first is the provision for an exclusive list of federal powers, leaving all other matters as a residual to the states. The second pattern follows an identification of three lists of powers – federal, state and concurrent – along with a residual designation. Finally, the third and most common pattern is to have only two lists – federal and concurrent – with the unspecified residual power going to the states. In Nigeria, however, there are basically two lists, exclusive and the concurrent lists. The exclusive belongs to the federal government and the concurrent list is shared between the federal and the state governments. All other matters not listed belong to the federal government.

The current distribution of responsibilities is provided in the Second and Fourth Schedules of the 1999 Constitution. Part I of the Second Schedule contains the exclusive legislative list on which only the federal government can act; Part II contains the concurrent legislative list on which both the federal and state governments can act; the Fourth

Schedule provides the list of functions of the Local Government Councils. The Exclusive Legislative List has 68 items while the Concurrent List consists of 12 items. Strictly speaking, the Constitution does not really provide the list of functions to be executed by the Federal Government of Nigeria and the states (as it does for the Local Government Councils), but only the subjects upon which they can legislate. However, these legislative lists form the guidelines for other legal decrees and sector policy reports that lay out the specific expenditure responsibilities of the different tiers of government.

The Exclusive Legislative List includes: accounts of the government of the federation; arms, ammunition, and explosives; aviation (including airports); awards of honours and decoration; bankruptcy and insolvency; banks, banking, bills of exchange and promissory notes; borrowing monies within and outside Nigeria for the purposes of the federation or any state; census; citizenship, naturalization and aliens; commercial and industrial monopolies; construction and maintenance of federal trunk roads; control of capital issues; copyrights; creation of states; currency, coinage and legal tender; customs and excise duties; defence; diplomatic, consular and trade representation; drugs and poisons, election to office of president and vice-president, governor or deputy governor; evidence, exchange control; export duties; external affairs; extradition; immigration and emigration; implementation of treaties; insurance; incorporation, regulation and winding up of bodies corporate other than those established by a law enacted by the State Houses of Assembly; labour; maritime shipping and navigation; meteorology; military (Army, Navy and Air Force); mines and minerals; national parks; nuclear energy; passports and visas; patents; trade marks, trade or business names; pensions and gratuities payable out of the public funds of the federation; police and other government security services established by law; posts, telegraphs and telephones; powers of the National Assembly and the privileges and immunities of its members; prisons; public debts; public holidays; public service of the federation; quarantine; railways; regulation of political parties; service and execution in a state of civil and criminal processes, judgements, decrees and other decisions of any court of law within and outside Nigeria, except for laws made by the State; stamp duties; taxation of incomes; profits and capital gains, as provided by the constitution; trade and commerce; traffic on federal trunk roads; water from sources declared by the National Assembly to affect more than one state; weights and measures; wireless, broadcasting and television other than those owned by states; any matter with respect to which the National Assembly has power to make laws under this constitution; and any "matter incidental or supplementary to any matter mentioned elsewhere in this list".

The exclusive responsibilities of the Federal Government of Nigeria are broadly in accordance with standard international practice, including matters of national concern such as defense, foreign affairs, regulation, and monetary policy. The responsibility of service delivery in the areas of education, health, infrastructure, agriculture and industry is concurrently shared with states and Local Government Authorities, with the respective assignments apparently derived from the considerations of inter-jurisdictional spillover effects and economies of scale.

The Concurrent Legislative List comprises— allocation of revenue; antiquities and monuments; archives; collection of taxes; electoral law; electric power; exhibition of cinematography films; industrial, commercial or agricultural development; scientific and technological research; statistics; trigonometric, cadastral, and topographical surveys; universities; technological and post-primary education. Section 4 (5) of the Constitution provides that " if any law enacted by the house of assembly of a state is inconsistent with law validly made by the National Assembly, the law made by the National Assembly shall prevail, and that other law shall to the extent of inconsistency be void."

The logic to the distribution of powers since the civil war has been to strengthen the central government politically and economically to enable it intervenes in essential areas and to keep the country together. The inspiration for this has been the military and its leaders, who in spite of centrifugal forces in the polity have a centrist perception of Nigerian federation, because, for them, survival or security is the first law of the state. Behind the distribution of powers and responsibilities is the principle that each tier of government has political and social obligations. While the federal government has the cardinal function for the security of the state and of lives and property, each tier of government has social welfare and developmental functions. Unfortunately in essential or desirable areas, there have been little intergovernmental relations. Nigeria operates a symmetrical federation, thus even in the sharing of resources in the FA among the states, federal equality of states is a cardinal principle.

Unlike the 1995 Draft Constitution, which tries to specify the state legislative list or residual list, the 1999 Constitution has no state list. All those items not found in the exclusive, concurrent and the local government lists, belong to the states. The residual powers are extensive – health services, rural development, social welfare and others. States, however, complain that the federal government has too much power and that the legislative list should be revised in their favour.

Taxing Powers

The allocation of jurisdiction over financial matters in federal systems is one of the most important features of the distribution of powers. If each tier of government is to deliver properly and effectively the programs and services under its jurisdiction, sufficient fiscal resources must obviously be made available to that government. Two factors have been identified to constitute the major basis for allocating tax-raising powers among the component levels of government in any federal system. These are administrative efficiency and fiscal independence. The efficiency criterion demands that a tax be assigned to the level of government that will administer it efficiently at minimum cost; while fiscal independence requires that each level of government should, as far as possible, raise adequate resources from the revenue sources assigned to it to meet its needs and responsibilities.

In Nigeria, the government's fiscal power is based on a three-tier tax structure divided between the federal, state and local governments, each of which has different tax jurisdictions. The Federal Government's tax powers include - profit tax on petroleum, personal income tax (in respect of members of the Armed Forces of Nigeria, Nigerian Police Force; residents of FCT. Abuja, and staff of the Ministry of Foreign Affairs and non-resident individuals); import and export duties; companies income tax; withholding tax on companies, residents of FCT Abuja and non-resident individuals; Value Added Tax (VAT) shared with other tiers of government; education tax; capital gains tax on Abuja residents and bodies corporate and non-residents individuals; and stamp duties on bodies corporate and residents of Abuja. Presently, VAT's allocation is 35 per cent based on equity of states (50 per cent), population (35 percent) and derivation (2 percent). VAT is imposed on goods only and not services. VAT is applied on each stage of sale.

The most veritable tax handles are under the control of the federal government while the lower tiers are responsible for the less buoyant ones—the federal government taxes corporate bodies while state and local governments' tax individuals.

State tax powers cover-- personal income taxes (Pay-As-You-Earn or direct taxation or assessment); withholding tax (individuals only); capital gains tax (individuals only); stamp duties as instruments executed by individuals; entertainment tax (pools, betting and lotteries, gaming and casino taxes), property tax, market taxes and levies (where state finances are involved) and naming of street registration fees at state capitals.

Local government councils are expected by the constitution to generate their revenues, in part, from - entertainment tax, motor park duties, property tax, trading and marketing licenses; radio and television licenses and rates; shops and kiosks rates, tenement rates; on-and-off liquor licenses; slaughter slab fees; marriages, birth and death registration fees; cattle tax payable by cattle owners only; signboard and advertisement permit fees and customary burial ground permit fees. Local Government taxes are minimal and limit their ability to raise independent revenue, which makes them dependent solely on allocation from the Federation Account.

Nigeria's current revenue-sharing formula gives Federal Government 48.5%, States 24%, Local Governments 20% and Special Funds 7.5%. The special funds consist of the Federal Capital Territory Fund, the Ecology Fund, the Statutory Stabilization Fund, the Mineral Derivation Fund, and the Mineral-Producing Areas Fund. It also provides that such a formula should allow for 13 percent of the Federation Account to be paid to state from where natural resources originate. The horizontal formula is shared as follows: Equality 40%; Population 30%; Social Development Factor 10%; Landmass and Terrain 10% and Internal Generated Revenue Effort 10%. Only federally-collected revenues are subjected to this revenue-sharing arrangement. The states and local governments keep whatever internal revenues they are able to raise themselves, but share from federally-collected revenues. The reason for this is that virtually all the major taxes are federal taxes, and the revenues they collect annually constitute about 90 percent of the total revenues of all the three tiers of government in Nigeria.

Much of the revenue collected by the federal government is distributed among the different tiers of government using the vertical revenue allocation formula. The constitution provides in Section 162 (1), that all revenues of the federation shall go into the Federal Account (FA), except for salaries of the personnel of the Armed Forces of the Federation, the Nigeria Police Force, staff of the Ministry of Foreign Affairs and the FCT Abuja. Section 162 (2) provides that the Revenue Mobilization, Allocation and Fiscal Commission (RMAFC) shall present a revenue formula to the President that shall be placed before the National Assembly for the purposes of distributing resources in the Federation Account among tiers of government.

There has been a high degree of centralization in fiscal federalism in Nigeria. The expenditure requirements of each tier of Nigerian government (particularly local government) have been treated with contempt by the federal government in its allocation of revenue. As a result of this, while other tiers remain pauperized, the federal government has largely remained a surplus-spending unit.

The distribution of financial powers in federal systems are designed not only to meet the task of matching fiscal capacities to jurisdictional responsibilities, but also to provide for a degree of effective control over the functioning of the economy.

Conclusion

In this paper, we have examined division of powers and responsibilities, including tax powers. Although a constitutionally entrenched distribution of powers between two tiers of government is considered perhaps the defining characteristic of federalism, not all federal systems have adopted a uniform approach to the general form and enumeration of these powers in their respective constitutions. We have also noted that there are essentially three forms of distribution of powers. The first is the provision for an exclusive list of federal powers, leaving all other matters as a residual to the states. The second pattern follows an identification of three lists of powers -- federal, state and concurrent -- along with a residual designation. Finally, the third and most common pattern is to have only two lists -- federal and concurrent -- with the unspecified residual power going to the states. We have also examined tax powers and argued that the allocation of jurisdiction over financial matters in federal systems is one of the most important features of the distribution of powers. If each tier of government is to deliver properly and effectively the programs and services under its jurisdiction, sufficient fiscal resources must obviously be made available to that government.

NOTES AND REFERENCES

1. Daniel J. Elazar, *Federal Systems and the World: A Handbook of Federal, Confederal and Autonomy Arrangements*, (Harlow: Longman Current Affairs, 1991).

2. De Villiers, B., *Evaluating Federal Systems*, (Cape Town: Juta & Co, Cape Town, 1994).

3. See Daniel J. Elazar, *Exploring Federalism* (Tuscaloosa: The University of Alabama Press, 1987) and Ronald Watts, *Comparing Federal Systems in the 1990s* (Kingston: Institute of Intergovernmental Relations, 1996).

4. See Carl Joachim Friedrich *Trends of Federalism in Theory and Practice*, (London: Pall Mall Press, 1968); B.M. Sharma, *Federalism in Theory and Practice*, (Chandausi, 1951);

5. Kenneth Wheare, "What Federal Government", *Studies in Federal Planning*, Patrick Ransome (ed.), (London, 1990), pp.23-24. See also Friedrich, Carl J., *Constitutional Government and Democracy and Practice in Europe and America*, (Massachusetts: Blaisdell Publishing, 1950).

6. See Carl Joachim Friedrich, *Trends of Federalism in Theory and Practice* (London: Pall Mall Press, 1968); Tushnet, Mark V., *Comparative Constitutional Federalism: Europe and America*, (New York: Greenwood Press, 1990); Riker, William H., *Federalism: Origin, Operation, Significance*, (Little Brown, Boston, 1964); Kux, S., *Soviet Federalism: A Comparative Prospective*, (Boulder: Institute of East-West Security Studies, 1990); and Herperger, D., *Distribution of Powers and Functions in Federal Systems*, (Canada: Minister of Supply and Services, 1991).

7. Dwight Herperger, *Distribution of Powers and Functions in Federal Systems*, (Canada: Minister of Supply and Services, 1991).

8. Ron Watts "Comparative Reflection" in *A Global Dialogue on Federalism Booklet Series Volume II*, Published by the Forum of Federations, Canada

9. See Bertus De Villiers, *Evaluating Federal Systems*, (Cape Town: Juta & Co, 1994).

10. Herperger, Dwight and Ronald L. Watts, *Looking Forward, Looking Back: Constitutional Proposals of the Past and their Relevance in the Post-Meech Era* (Montreal: Council for Canadian Unity, 1990).

PART II

FISCAL FEDERALISM AND POLITICAL ECONOMY OF DISTRIBUTION

CHAPTER 3
RESOURCE OR REVENUE SHARING IN NIGERIA

Philip Usman

Introduction

Governments all over the world have, as part of their major responsibility, the promotion of the welfare of their citizens. This is done partly through the effective distribution of the nation's resources. Resource distribution in any nation covers a wide variety of issues, including both statuses and revenue as well as distribution of all scarce but allocable resources. Even the location of government projects/offices as well as the pattern of recruitment into political offices and public services constitute an aspect of the distribution process. In this paper, we are concerned strictly with the distribution of revenue.

In multi-level system with fiscal responsibilities vested in both central and lower level governments (federal, state and local) the problem of a decentralized fiscal system (fiscal federalism) becomes paramount. The fiscal roles to be performed by various levels of government and their relationship with one another become issues of serious concern, especially with respect to vertical and horizontal structures of federalism.

The vertical structure deals with the distribution of revenues between the federal, state and local governments. The horizontal structure deals with the equalization factors among states to cater for their needs. The allocation or distribution of resources among the component units of a federation can be quite contentious. As Joseph La Palombara observed "all problems of governance may be considered distribution problems that may or may not reach crisis proportions".[1]

The crisis that emanates from resource distribution is the result of the apparent perception of inequity and unfairness by the leaders of the component units of the federation. Thus distribution must address how allocatable resources are relatively equitably distributed among all members and groups of a state. According to J. Isawa Elaigwu,[2] government decision as to who gets what, where, when and how thus becomes a distribution issue. Equity in the distribution of resources becomes necessary if conflicts are to be avoided. As individuals or groups compete to maximize their share of scarce but allocatable resources, conflicts easily emanate, requiring urgent attention to ensure the smooth operation of the system.

Distribution of resources however must address' two issues; (a) the increase in the production of allocatable resources – the supply side and (b) the nature or basis of the distribution of these resources among groups – the demand side.

Distribution of resources is important because it is a determinant of the pattern and the nature of development among sub-national units. Efforts must be made to avoid over-concentration of resources in few "poles of growth" or "centres of strength" to maximize short run capacity, in order to avoid crises.

Resource distribution issues in a federation, also give rise to a conflict between capacity and equality among the various units which form the federation. As Elaigwu explained the situation, "the conflict between capacity and equality for a federation may' be seen as the overall development of a country on the one hand and even development among sub-national units of a federation for purpose of political stability",[3] on the other.

Fiscal imbalances characterize the nature of modern federation. This development is prevalent because component units of a federation hardly have enough resources to meet their desirable expenditures. Fiscal equilibrium is often difficult to attain. According to Paul Boothe,

> ..."when one order of government collects more revenue than it needs for its own expenditure responsibilities, a vertical imbalance is said to exist. Fiscal transfers from one order of government to another are used to deal with vertical imbalances. In some federations specific transfers are designed to deal with both vertical imbalances and imbalances between provinces, i.e horizontal imbalances.[4]

Federalism implies the acceptance of the existence of differences. Therefore fiscal adjustment in a federation becomes necessary for the following reasons:

1) the problem of resolving the imbalances of resources and need be-

tween the federal and regional or subnational governments.
2) the problem of harmonizing income with needs in different regions.
3) the need to ensure that economic equilibrium is achieved for the federation as a whole.
4) the need to level up so that the poorer regions are raised and the level of services provided in different regions is equalized as possible.

Thus four broad principles have been used over time in Nigeria with regard to resource distribution, namely:

a) The principle of derivation (source)
b) The principle of need (population)
c) The principle of equality (sameness)
d) The principle of national interest (enhanced welfare)

The Theoretical Analysis

In theory, in the examination of the distribution process, two scenarios can be developed.

a. The various state budgets apply their distributional adjustment first and the central adjustment is applied after the state adjustments have been made. As a result the central adjustment will be applied to incomes adjusted by the states. The final distribution position will conform with what is considered proper at the central level. These adjustments at the state level will have a bearing on the required patterns of central revenues but will not affect the final result.
b. The opposite will occur if the central government adjustments come first and that state and local governments adjustments follow. Conflicts arise when both lower levels of governments (states and local) and central governments insist upon their particular pattern of proper distribution. It would lead to a continuous set of adjustments and readjustments without a final equilibrium being reached.

According to Richard A. Musgrave,

since one or the other level of government must be given priority, there is much to be said, in the federal system, for permitting this adjustment to be made at the central level. Unless this is done, distributional adjustments at the State level may come to be nullified by interstate movement and serious barriers to an optimal location of economic activity may be imposed.[5]

In the course of establishing equilibrium in revenue distribution, some imbalances develop which require the function of the stabilization branch. This is best performed at the central level. "while some degree of coordination may be attained between the levels, the compensatory function must be coordinated for the nation as a whole and this requires central action. The heart of fiscal federalism therefore is that the objectives of the distribution and stabilization of accrued revenue require primary responsibility at the central level".[6]

Horizontal equity in the distributive process calls for equalization of income through transfer. This implies that it is the obligation of the federation to see to it that the citizens of each state can enjoy a given minimum level of public services. "if anyone state is too poor to provide this minimum level even though a required minimum degree of tax effort is made, the federation steps in".[7]

This calls for a transfer of funds from wealthy states where the minimum level of public services is provided while tax rates are below the stipulated minimum level. If however a state falls short of the required tax effort, no claim for support can be established. Transfers then are made justifiable only by the basic criteria of fiscal deficiency.

The above approach contains an element of regional equalization of income since transfers are made from wealthy to poor regions and there is also an element of provision for the satisfaction of merit, especially wants since the equalization refers to minimum standards of social rather than private wants. If the concern however is with a minimum level of social wants in general, the appropriate transfer to state budgets is made in a general cash grant.

Fiscal federalism can also address regional income equalization through assuring each citizen of the federation that specific social wants, such as elementary or primary education will be adequately provided in all states. If the social wants in question include those on borderline between nationwide and regional benefit or social wants belonging to the state level but recognized as merit wants at the national level, this calls for earmarked grants or for matching grants from the central to the state level. Thus redistributional elements may be attached to a specific grant. This is very much the same as if the matching ration is rendered a function of state need and fiscal ability.

Grants are also made where there is no intention to interfere with local choice, the objective being one of fiscal equalization. Some jurisdictions (state or local) enjoy a high taxable capacity (ie. the tax rate needed to obtain a given level of revenue is low) and have a relatively low level of need (ie. the amount required to provide certain service levels is small). They are thus in a fiscally strong position, as measured by the ratio of capacity to need. Others are in the reverse position. The central government may then wish to equalize fiscal position through various ways:

1 Equalize the cost in terms of tax effort or tax rate required for providing public services in various jurisdictions, while leaving it to the local jurisdiction to decide what service level it wishes to provide. This calls for matching grants to jurisdictions which are fiscally weak (i.e. which have low taxable capacity and large needs) and these grants would be financed by taxes on the expenditures of strong jurisdiction (i.e. which have a high taxable capacity and low need).
2 The central government on the other hand may wish to equalize actual service levels and for this purpose impose such matching grants (where to raise levels) or taxes (where needed to lower levels) as are required to secure equalization.
3) The central government may wish to secure common minimum levels and adjust its grant policy to secure this objective.

Theoretical Dimension of General Revenue Sharing in Equalization Effort

In a federal set up, general revenue sharing which provides for unrestricted and non-matching grants to states and via a pass–through provision to local governments have come to be used. The grants are used to meet the needs of each tier of government as perceived by that government.

Considerable debate has arisen with respect to the desirability of such grants and their net effect on tax effort of recipient states and local governments. Critics have questioned whether this approach is compatible with a sound system of fiscal federalism. Of particular concern is whether lack of responsibility for raising revenue will not interfere with efficiency in expenditure determination at the state and local levels. The question is: will the political process in determining the use of "gift money", be as prudent as it would be with the use of "own" funds? Economic rationality would answer "yes" since scarce resources are used in both cases; but human nature may respond otherwise. While all states and localities share in the grant money, the funds nevertheless must be raised, leaving some as net contributors and others as net recipients.

To ensure effectiveness, some recognition is given to the need for matching by inclusion of a tax effort variable in the allocation formula, no matter how negligible. With respect to the degree of equalization, the most lively controversy has centred on how the grants should be allocated among states and how much weight should be given to differentials in their fiscal position. Certain criteria with assigned weights are used to arrive at a given formula. As an illustration, one third of the weight could be given each to population, per capita income, and tax effort. The population weight is itself somewhat redistributive since equal per capita grants result in a higher grant/income ratio for states with low per capita income. Moreover, this base helps the densely populated urban states. The use of an inverse income variable (defined as the ratio of per capita income of the country to that of a particular state) directs more funds to the low income states. The tax effort variable is more or less neutral since there is no strong relationship between per capita income and tax effort.

The level of recipient is another issue of major concern in fiscal federalism. Should grants be made to states only or should the federal government deal directly with local jurisdictions. The decentralization thesis favours the latter as does the fact that differentials in fiscal position are frequently more marked among local jurisdiction than among states. Nevertheless, bye-passing the states would be politically unacceptable, and direct federal administration of local grants would pose serious administrative problems. In any case the data base for allocation to location may not be available.

Revenue Distribution in Historical Perspective

The historical antecedent to the issues of revenue sharing in Nigeria has spanned over a long period. The contention over resource distribution as an avenue to ensure development whether for the federation as a whole or its component units beginning from the local government to the states, has spanned over a long historical period.

We shall just list a number of the Revenue Commissions that were established and the basic distribution structure they recommended as a means of ensuring effective revenue distribution. Details can be obtained from various write ups especially the political dimensions.

a) Unitarism to Quasi- Federalism, 1948-53

Under Sir Sydney Phillipson all revenues in the country was centralized under "non-declared" revenue (export duties, import duties, excise duties and companies tax). Two principles were used for distributive purpose: the principles of derivation and of even progress. As a result of lack of data, adequate application was not possible. Population was considered a better option though, never applied.

b) Hicks - Phillipson Commission, 1950

Four principles of revenue distribution were enunciated namely:

(a) independent revenue (regions to impose certain taxes).
(b) derivation
(c) need (based on population density and sparcity)
(d) national interest

Again discontent arising from the application of the above principles led to the next development.

a) Quasi –Federalism, 1954-60

The Louis Chick Commission of 1953 was set up to "assess the effect on the public expenditure of Nigeria as a whole of the re-allocation of functions between the centre and the regions". The attempt was to cater for both vertical and horizontal interests in that the horizontal interests have always been the major factors that have agitated for reviews. This was confirmed by the terms of reference to the commission which stated that it should provide for the regions and the centre an adequate measure of fiscal autonomy within their own sphere of government, and further to ensure that the 'total revenue available to Nigeria are allocated in such a way, that the principle of derivation' is followed to the fullest degree compatible with meeting the reasonable needs of the centre and each of the regions.

The dissatisfaction of the regions with the Chick formula led to the setting up of the Sir Jeremy Raisman Commission. Its terms of reference included, correcting some of the distortions in both vertical and horizontal distribution given the Chick formula defects:

(a) limited range of independent revenue under regional control;
(b) inter-regional imbalance created by emphasis on derivation principle; and
(c) neglect of the relationship between particular needs of a region and its ability to raise revenue within its boundaries.

In order to correct the deficiencies, the commission recommended the establishment of the Distributable Pool. Account (DPA). In an effort to harmonize the principles of need and derivation, four factors were used as basis of allocating funds in the DPA among the three regions. These were:

a) population as index of need
b) an irreducible minimum responsibilities of each regional government'
c) preservation of continuity in government services
d) balanced development throughout the Federation

The operation of the Raisman formula in moving away from derivation and considering other issues, such as, **need and balanced development** moved the country in the direction of greater equity than earlier formula in the distribution of resources.

b) The Binns Commission, 1964

The creation of Mid-West region in 1963 and complaints about regional expenditure based on Raisman formula gave rise to a distortion in the vertical as well as the horizontal set-up requiring a change in revenue sharing. Thus, the Binn Commission under Mr. K.J. Binns was set up.

The commission supported the idea of promoting the welfare of the whole federation. It recommended that each region be placed in a comparable financial position (given allowances for differences in financial policies). The commission rejected the principles of derivation and financial need. The principles of comparability necessitated the following consideration:

a. the general cash position of the regions
b. the recurrent budget proposals
c. the relationship of regional-to-local government finances
d. the effect of regional corporations on regional finances.

The DPA was retained and to be distributed as follows: North 40%, East 30%, West 20% and Mid- West 8%

c)Financial Provision Decree No 15, 1967, May 27, 1967

With the creation of 12 states on May 27, 1967 the Federal Military Government (FMG) made financial payments to the states through the DPA since the states had been empowered to function as the former regions. The distribution of revenue was as follows:

The six states in the North 7/100 each

Lagos	2/100
Western State	18/100
Central Eastern State	7/40
South-Eastern State	3/40
Rivers State	1/20
Midwest State	2/25

The deficiency of the DPA above failed to meet the yearnings of most of the states with regard to the issue of revenue sharing, Given the new states structure, the disparities and inadequacies of the formula necessitated the review of the Binns formula.

d) The Dina Commission, 1968

The Dina Commission emphasized cooperative federalism in revenue sharing. This promoted the concept of a working partnership between the centre, and the states on one hand, and among the states on the other. The report showed another desire to maintain both vertical and horizontal equilibrium. '

It changed the DPA which was the main bone of contention in Nigeria's fiscal system, to States Joint Account (SJA). The Commission used ten possible principles of revenue allocation which were collapsed into three main principles:

a. basic needs
b. minimum national standards
c. balanced development

A Special Grants Account (SGA) was also established for the purposes of fiscal equalization. The commission clearly showed concern for the general economic development of the country and balanced development of its component political units. But discontent still arose leading to the establishment of the next commission.

e) The Aboyade Commission, 1977

The commission recommended resource distribution along vertical and horizontal levels. For the first time, the Local Governments were recognized as a "guaranteed tier of government entitled to statutory allocation from federally collected funds".

The following categories of vertical distribution were suggested:

Level of Government	**Share %**
Federal Government	57
State Government	30
Local Government	10
Special Grants Account	03

To ensure effective horizontal distribution the commission suggested five criteria for the sharing of revenue among states and local governments.

Principle	**Share %**
Access to development	25
Minimum standard for national integration	22
Absorptive capacity	20
Independent revenue and minimum tax effort	18
Fiscal efficiency	15
	100

The complexity in the application of the above recommendations led to its rejection by the Shagari government. This gave rise to the Okigbo Commission of 1979.

f) The Okigbo Commission, 1979

This Commission recommended the vertical sharing of the Federal Account as:

Level of Government	Share %
Federal Government	53
State Government	30
Local Government	10
Special Fund	07

The special fund account was distributed as follows: Initial development of FCT 2.5%; mineral producing areas 2.0%; ecological and other disasters 1.0% and revenue equalization fund 1.5%.

As for the horizontal allocation, the commission used four principles for the distribution of resources.

Principle	Share %
Minimum responsibilities of government	40
Population	40
Social development Primary school enrolment	
- direct enrolment	11.5
- inverse enrolment	3.5
Internal Revenue Effort	5.0
	100

Conflicts arising from the vertical and horizontal allocations continued to hamper the smooth operation of the revenue allocation formula. In spite of all the tinkering with the system through the 1981 Revenue Allocation Act and the establishment of the States Joint Local Government Account (SJLGA) to ensure some horizontal equalization of distribution, the conflict between states and the federal government continued.

Thus by 1988 the National Revenue Mobilization Allocation and Fiscal Commission (1988) was established.

g) The National Revenue Mobilization Allocation and Fiscal Commission, 1988 (NRMAFC)

Among the terms of reference of the above commission were principal ones dealing with vertical and horizontal distribution namely:

a. carry out periodic review of allocation principles and formulae
b. ensure revenue sharing arrangements

This gave rise to the following vertical and horizontal revenue allocation recommended by the Commission. For vertical allocation it recommended:

Tier of Government	**Share %**
Federal Government	47
State Government	30
Local Government	15
Special Fund	8
	100

The special funds to cover the following activities; F.C.T 1.0%; stabilization 0.5% savings 2.0%; derivation 2.0%; development of oil mineral producing areas 1.5%, development of non-oil mineral producing area 0.5%; general ecology 0.5%.

On the horizontal plane, the commission recommended the following:

Principle	**Share %**
Equality of State	40.0
Population	30.0
Social development factor (including education, health, water, land/mass and terrain)	10.0
Internal Revenue Effort	20.0
	100

h) Revenue Allocation: May 1999 to date

From the recommendations submitted by RMAFC in 2001 to 2004

many decisions were made and revised depending on the volume of clamor against it especially with regard to vertical distribution. The following vertical distribution was agreed to in 2004.

Tier of Government	Share %
Federal Government	47
State Government	30
Local Government	15
	100

The constant clamour about the inadequacies of the allocation process at both vertical and horizontal level, led to the widening of the horizontal allocation determinants over time. The number of principles used for horizontal allocation has increased from about two to three at the beginning to ten principles by the 2004 position. These are as follows:

Principle	Share %
Equality of State	45.23
Population	25.60
Population density	1.45
Internal Revenue Generation Effort	8.31
Landmass	5.35
Terrain	5.35
Rural Roads/Internal Waterways	1.21
Potable water	1.50
Education	3.00
Health	3.00
	100.00

From the above historical analysis, the issue of vertical and horizontal distribution of revenue in the country has gone through various changes over the years. The underlining reasons for the changes are:

a) the various changes in the federal structure (changes in number of States and Local Governments)
b) the military experience
c) increase in oil revenue and the politics of derivation
d) the desire for fiscal equalization

e) the persistent demand for the review of the legislative list and the expansion in the tax powers of states/local governments
f) the necessity for equity and national development.

With regard to vertical and horizontal distribution there have been demands for changes, especially since the introduction of local governments as a statutory tier of government in revenue distribution. The various commissions have sought to address the distribution structure with some measure of success. However the need to constantly revisit the recommendation of the various commissions have continued. On the horizontal level, new principles of allocation continue to increase especially with specific agitations being introduced into the distribution issues. Thus at present there are ten principles associated with the horizontal distribution. With time these number is be expected to increase, in search for greater equity and development.

The Future Challenges

As long as the Nigerian federation continues to survive, resource sharing adjustments will continue to feature as an important fiscal arrangement in the federation. This will continue to play a vital role in the operation and structural interplay of the federation.

Moreover as increased pressures are exerted on the limited resources of the nation, how these resources are shared among competing components of the federation will continue to be called to question. All tiers of government need resources to survive. As demands are placed on each tier of government the struggle for more equitable resource sharing formulae will continue.

The principle of derivation as a basis for revenue sharing will increasingly be emphasized because of the needs of the various components of the federation and the desire to have greater control over resources by the various components of the federation.

The various principles for sharing resources will invariably change as some of these principles that are currently used become obsolete. As an incentive to ensure greater generation of revenue by the various tiers of government, derivation will be given more emphasis. This can augur well for the nation as each component of the federation will work hard to generate more internally derived revenue, thus reducing the over dependence on Federation Account. This is a very probable positive development in the future. The over-concentration on Federation Account will need to be reduced as a matter of necessity. In fact the measure of development of the states would be determined by how much revenue they are able to raise internally. The current unhealthy situation of overdependence on Federation Account cannot continue to be allowed or be encouraged.

Moreover, for grassroots development to take place, it would be necessary to pass on more resources to the local government tier of the federal structure. But this will require more stringent measures and increased accountability in the use of funds at that level. The current situation where most local governments are hardly involved in capital projects which give rise to development at the grassroots levels must be addressed.

The local governments must be able to generate resources from cottage industries and other productive activities rather than depending on market levies as the principal source of revenue. The weakness of this strategy is that a local government with few markets cannot raise much revenue. Alternatively the local people get overtaxed in an effort to raise revenue level.

Thus, resource sharing must address the necessity for rapid development at the grassroots level. As development gets entrenched at the grassroots level the federal government will invariably relinquish some of her activities. This will necessitate reorganizing the resource sharing structure.

Development consequent on effective resources sharing will minimize the clamour for constant changes in the formula. But the most important future challenge is the necessity to widen the bases of revenue generation such that each state or zone can have resources it can derive revenue from. This will call for concerted effort by every state to develop its available resources. States must no more look to the centre for survival but can survive without the centre. How to develop this will be the main challenge of resource sharing in the future. Thus, derivation and all the acrimony it has generated can be minimized and in fact rendered insignificant.

The hope is that by developing various resource bases, derivation is rendered of no effect and that engenders development.

Conclusion

Resource distribution in any nation has always been an issue especially in a federal set up. This is so because of the need to ensure adequate and effective flow of funds to various tiers of government to meet the perceived needs at various levels,

Government's needs also vary over time because of many factors – some unique, some general depending on the country. These varying needs, over time, necessitate the need to vary the allocation process, both vertical and horizontal.

For the desired effect of enhancing the welfare of the citizens, however, the production aspect must be given the due attention.

For development to take place especially at the grassroots level, horizontal distribution is very crucial. The efficiency in the use of funds at the local level of government must be increasingly monitored and effected in order to move the nation forward. The clamour for development, especially in the area of poverty reduction can best be achieved through a combination of effective vertical and horizontal distribution of revenue.

Conflicts are inevitable if a measure of inequity is perceived to exist whether at vertical or horizontal level. Government must work towards eliminating such possibilities. The political process has a major role to play in ensuring that an equitable level is arrived at in both vertical and horizontal distributive processes. The .political development of the country will significantly depend on how effective it has been in revenue sharing in the years to come.

NOTES

1. *Problems and Prospects* (London: Hutchison Educational, 1968).
2. Adebayo Adedeji, *Nigerian Federal Finance: Its Development Pr*Harod D. Lasswell as quoted in J. Isawa Elaigwu, *The Politics of Federalism in Nigeria* (Jos; Aha Publishing House Ltd; 2005), pp. 243-333.
3. J. Isawa Elaigwu, *Nigeria Yesterday and Today for Tomorrow: Essays in Governance and Society* (Jos: Aha Publishing House Ltd, 2005), pp. 256-68.
4. Richard A. Musgrave, *The Theory of Public Finance. A Study in Public Economy* (International Student Education) (New York: McGraw-Hill Book Company Inc. 1959), p. 179.

5. Richard A. Musgrave and Peggy B. Musgrave, *Public Finance in Theory and Practice* (Second Edition) (New York: McGraw-Hill Book company Inc. 1973), pp. 625-30.
6. Selma J. Mushkin and John F. Cotton, *Functional Federation* (Washington: George Washington University, 1968).
7. Wallace R. Oates, *Fiscal Federalism* (New York: Harcourt Brace, 1972).
8. A.R Prest, *Public Finance in Theory and Practice* (London: Weidenfeld Nicolson, 1970).
9. Carl S. Shoup, *Public Finance* (London: G. Weidenfeld and Nicholson Ltd, 1970).

CHAPTER 4
FISCAL FEDERALISM IN NIGERIA: THE CHALLENGES OF THE NEXT DECADE

Akpan H. Ekpo

Introduction

Nigeria's fiscal federalism is anchored on economic, political, constitutional, local and cultural developments. The country runs a federal structure but during the period of military rule, the structure of governance was more unitary than federal in practice. The country's federal structure grew from three regions in 1960 to four regions in 1963. Between 1967 and 1970, twelve States were created and by 1976 the number of States stood at nineteen. It increased to twenty-one in 1987 and further increased to thirty in 1991 with a separate Federal Capital Territory, Abuja. Presently, there are thirty-six States, a federal capital territory and seven hundred and seventy-four local governments. Consequently, the structure is a three tier or level of government: the centre (federal), states and local governments, within a presidential system of government.

The increased number of sub-national governments (states and local governments) has been driven more by agitation and attempt to reduce ethnic tension rather than economic viability. Ironically, the lower centres of government, particularly the local governments, have been centres of economic development. This is not to suggest that development was not considered as a variable but it was a secondary consideration.

The fiscal inter-relationship between the three tiers of government has been contentious over the years.[1] In recent times, the revenue allocation matter became heated when minority states from the oil producing areas demanded additional revenue based on derivation. This resulted in the 'resource control' crisis as a result of the re-introduction of the on/off-shore oil dichotomy. In recent times minority states (of south-south) zone at the National Political Reform Conference staged a walk-out as a result of disagreements over the derivation principle. The crisis in the Niger-Delta area of the country hinges on the revenue-sharing issue. Hence, the next decade will pose challenges for the leadership of the Nigerian state and her policy-makers as they tackle the fiscal relationship among the three levels of government.[2]

The objective of this chapter is to examine the challenges of the next decade as Nigeria's leadership, policy-makers and stakeholders attempt to practice fiscal federalism in the country.

Structure of Government and Fiscal Powers

Nigeria operates a federal structure of government under the 1999 Constitution, which guarantees the existence of the federating units. The functions of the Federal Government are contained in the Exclusive List, that of States in the Concurrent List; where conflict exists, the exclusive functions of the federal government dominate. The constitution spells out the assignment of functions and areas of fiscal jurisdiction among the various units of the federal system.

The 1999 Constitution, Section 4 (Second Schedule), shows the Exclusive Legislative List, comprising the responsibilities on which only the federal government can act, and the Concurrent Legislative List on which both the federal and the state governments can act. In addition, Section 4 (7a) assigns the so-called residual functions to state governments. These are functions not indicated either in the Exclusive List or the Concurrent Legislative List. Section 7 (5) (Fourth Schedule) of the Constitution provides for the creation of local government councils with responsibilities set out in the Fourth Schedule of the Constitution.

Within the structure of government as defined in the constitution the following issues appear important:

i) the constitution combines expenditure responsibilities and revenue-sharing functions in its assignment of responsibilities;
ii) the assignment of powers and responsibilities is derived from several constitutional conferences held over the years;
the assignment of revenue-raising functions were often left to be determined by the various fiscal commissions, which usually followed each constitutional conference;
iii) the assignment of functions has not changed significantly since independence in 1960, beginning from the 1963 Constitution to the present 1999 Constitution; and
iv) it is important to examine the underlying principles behind the assignment of functions in the Nigerian system.

It is also usual to discuss the assignment of powers and responsibilities in a federal system within the context of the major functions of government, namely, allocation, distribution and stabilization. At the theoretical level, the distribution and stabilization functions of government are better performed by the central government. The allocation function depends on a number of factors such as the division of functions between the private and the public sectors of the economy. In the assignment of revenue, it is necessary to understand the basis of the allocation of tax powers by reviewing the evolution of the division of tax powers in the Nigerian federal system. This is beyond the scope of this chapter.[3] Suffice it to state, that the lucrative taxes are under the jurisdiction of the federal government on grounds of administrative efficiency particularly as it relates to the collection of taxes.

Theoretical Framework

There are political and economic rationales for the practice of fiscal system in an economy. The political arguments centre on the heterogeneous characteristics of the different regions making up the federation. The economic justification is derived from the need to promote efficiency in the use of national resources. Therefore, in examining fiscal federalism and macroeconomic management, the roles of the various tiers of government as they relate to each other with regard to how the economy is managed are usually the focus.[4]

Federalism has been defined as the amalgam of sub-units of a national sovereign government that operate independently within a constitutionally defined sphere of functional competence. The federating units often give up sovereignty in certain aspects of their operations in order to achieve the benefits of national unity in some areas of government activities while retaining some measure of autonomy in other areas. Inter-governmental fiscal relations can be situated within the concept of federalism. Therefore, federalism connotes a system of government where revenue and expenditure functions are divided among the different levels of government. This is done to enhance the delivery of services at all levels of government. It is generally agreed that revenue generation and spending responsibilities, inter-governmental transfer and the administrative aspects of fiscal decentralization remain the real issues in inter-governmental fiscal relations or fiscal federalism. Therefore, Nigeria's fiscal federalism involves the allocation of expenditure and tax-raising powers among the federal, state and local governments. The argument is that fiscal federalism/decentralization is good for any economy since it enhances better service delivery and stimulates growth and development. It is important to state that contrary views do exist.[5]

Some fundamental principles of fiscal federalism have been evolved to guide inter-governmental fiscal relations in practice. These are:

- Diversity
- Equivalence
- Centralized stabilization
- Correction of spillover effects
- Minimum provision of essential public goods and services
- Fiscal equalization
- Efficiency
- Derivation
- Locational neutrality
- Centralized redistribution

These principles have guided, to some extent, the practice of fiscal federalism in Nigeria.

The Practice of Fiscal Federalism in Nigeria: Selected Issues

It is clear that fiscal arrangements are a consequence of a federal structure. The types of fiscal arrangements ought to affect the nature of the federal structure. The main problem centers around how to put in place, a federal structure that would be conducive to national and equitable allocation of the country's resources among the different subnational governments in order to reduce intergovernmental and intergroup tensions. In addition, other problems in Nigeria's fiscal arrangement include power sharing and the apparent imbalance between the expenditure responsibilities assigned to the different levels of government and the tax powers available to them, state and local government dependence on federal sources of funding, and the concentration of spending power on the part of the federal government.

The allocation of functions among federating units is more of a political than an economic exercise, and there may be no stated principles underlying such allocation in the Nigerian federation. However, allocation follows some of the principles discussed above. As illustration, those functions whose benefit covers the entire country and/or that can be more efficiently performed at a national level have been assigned to the federal government. These include national defence, external relationships, banking, currency, coinage and legal tender, and weights and measures. Those functions whose benefit areas are more local than national but with the possibility of spillover effects such as antiquities and archives, scientific and technological research, and university are on the concurrent list. Functions that are purely local in character (in the sense that benefits accrue to limited geographic areas) are often assigned to local authorities. These include the establishment and maintenance of cemeteries, markets, motor parks, public conveniences, refuse disposal, and construction and maintenance of local roads and streets. Table 1 below provides a summary of the assignment of expenditure responsibilities in Nigeria.

Table 1: Assignment of Expenditure Responsibilities in Nigeria

Levels of Government	Expenditure Category
Federal Only (Exclusive List)	Aviation including airports Award of national titles of honour, decorations and other dignitaries Bankruptcy and insolvency exchange and currency, coinage and legal tender Construction and maintenance of federal trunk roads Defense Deportation of non-citizens Diplomatic, consular and trade representation Drugs and Poison

	Elections (excluding elections to Local Government Councils) **External Affairs** **Fingerprints, identification and criminal records** **Immigration into and emigration from Nigeria** **Meteorology** **Military (Army, Navy and Air Force)** **Mining and Minerals, including oil fields, oil mining, geological surveys and natural gas** **National Parks** **Nuclear energy** **Pension, gratuities and other benefits payable out of the Consolidated Revenue Funds of the Federation** **Police and other government security services established by law** **Posts, telegraphs and telephones** **Prisons** **Public services of the Federation** **Railways** **Price control of goods designated as essential by the National Assembly** **Traffic and Federal Trunk Roads**

Federal-State (Concurrent List)	Antiquities and monuments Archives Electoral Law Electric Power Exhibition of cinematograph films Industrial, commercial or agricultural development Scientific and technological research Statistics Trigonometrically, cadastral topographical surveys University, technological and post-primary education
State (only) (so-called Residual Powers)	Any matters not included in the Exclusive Legislative List
Local Government	Participation with the State in economic planning and development Establishment and maintenance of cemeteries, burial grounds and homes for the destitute or infirm Establishment, maintenance and regulation of slaughter houses, markets and motor parks. Construction and maintenance of roads, streets, street lightings, drains and other public highways, parks and gardens Provision and maintenance of public conveniences, sewage and refuse disposal Participation with State in: • The provision and maintenance of primary,

	adult and vocational education • The development of agriculture and natural resources other than the exploitation of minerals • The provision and maintenance of health services

Note: 1. *For a comprehensive listing of the functions, see Section 4 and the Second Schedule and Section 7 and the Fourth Schedule of the 1999 Constitution.*
Source: *The 1999 Nigerian Constitution.*

The practice of inter-governmental fiscal relations in Nigeria presents important issues:

1. *Imbalance between assigned responsibilities and tax powers.*

The fiscal arrangement in the country heavily concentrates fiscal powers at the centre. The lucrative taxes are under the federal government either due to administrative efficiency and/or fiscal independence (see Table 2). Hence, there is an over-dependence of states and local governments on federal sources of funding; this is often confused with dependence on the centre. The federal government should be seen as administering those lucrative taxes on behalf of all the governments of the federation. Hence, the federal government has no more right over the moneys collected by it than the state and local governments. The federal government is not constitutionally assigned to collect such revenues.[7]

The current fiscal arrangement is characterized by weak fiscal capacity of both the state and local governments. Thus, solid mineral development, ports, defense and security, and aviation are assigned to the federal government while the responsibilities of primary education, town planning and urban and rural water lie with the state governments. For each level of government to execute the responsibilities assigned to it, it needs to access funds through assigned tax bases. However, internally generated revenue of state and local governments compared with their shared revenue remains very low. Between 1991 and 2002, internally generated revenue of state governments averaged 6.8 percent. The low internal revenue base resulted from the types of taxes assigned to the sub-national governments. These taxes such as property and personal income taxes have low yields and high cost of administration.[8]

It appears, therefore, reasonable to adjust the revenue sharing formula in order to address the problem of imbalance between the functions and the tax powers assigned to the different tiers of government. The tax powers of the federal government need to be re-examined so as to move certain taxes to the lower levels of government. In addition, the issue of conditional grants and/or fiscal equalization ought to be part of the menu of options to be considered.

2. *The Federation Account.*

The question to address, among others, is whether the federal government's retention of the lion's share of the Federation Account can be justified on the basis of the relative *weight* of functions assigned to it? If the policy is to grow a viable private sector then one wonders the justification of the centre in ascribing to itself more revenue. For example, with the Global Service Mobile System and Private Courier Services, who needs NITEL and the Post Office? This borders also on the matter of vertical revenue allocation and the ability of the inherent allocation formula to minimize inter-group tension.

In addition, it is not still very clear whether all collected revenues are put in the pool before sharing despite the ruling of the Supreme Court on the Resources Control suit. In addition, the amount set aside as 'Special Fund' within the Federation Account is still controversial. It should be noted that a presidential order merely transferred the special funds to the Federal Government's share, thereby increasing it from 48.5 percent to 56 percent. The states were unsuccessful in challenging the presidential order in the Supreme Court in January, 2003.

3. *Horizontal Revenue Allocation.*

This is supposed to correct horizontal imbalances caused by the fact that some jurisdictions have higher tax bases and/or extra-ordinary expenditure needs than others. This type of fiscal transfer is meant to close the gap between fiscal capacities and fiscal needs of the lower units. It is not surprising therefore that in Nigeria, horizontal revenue allocation is a kind of unconditional block grant to states and local governments to correct horizontal fiscal imbalances among them. A proper application of the horizontal allocation formula requires the need to ascertain the fiscal needs of the lower levels of government.

It follows, therefore, that in examining the principles applied in horizontal revenue sharing, population, internal revenue effort, landmass and derivation ought to be considered. Each of these variables remains controversial in Nigeria's fiscal federalism.[9] The attempt to make the population census figures acceptable has been a matter of debate. Recently, the Lagos State Government sued the federal government over the census figures. It has become extremely difficult to determine internal revenue effort of lower governments while the appropriate weight on derivation resulted in the resource control crisis. It is thus crucial that the horizontal revenue allocation formula ought to be re-examined in the context of fairness and equity.

4. *Niger-Delta Area and Resource Control.*

The crude oil produced in the Niger-Delta drives the economy of the country yet the area remains highly underdeveloped. The area suffers from near total neglect by both the Federal Government which claims ownership of the oil and the multi-national companies which actually exploits the oil reserves. The wanton devastation and degradation suffered by the oil producing Niger-Delta States ought to be corrected by large inter-governmental transfer. The area needs a special attention beyond that of the Niger-Delta Development Commission (NDDC). It is pertinent to reconsider increasing the weight attached to derivation; increasing the derivation variable will partially address the resource control issue. At present, stakeholders in the area have complained that the 13 percent for derivation is too low.

5. *Allocation to Local Governments.*

The 1999 Constitution (Section 162(5) and (6)) provides for the channeling of local government share of the Federation Account to local government councils by stating that the amount standing to the credit of local government councils in the federation account shall be allocated to the states for the benefit of their local government councils. In addition, each state shall maintain a special account to be called 'State Joint Local Government Account' into which shall be paid all allocations to the local governments of the state from the Federation Account as well as from the government of the state.

In reality most states are reluctant in releasing funds due to local government councils. State governments find all sorts of excuses not to channel funds to local governments. It would be more interesting if the refusal to channel funds is based on lack of satisfactory performance by local government councils. Under this scenario, it would be necessary to devise benchmarks for measuring performance. Otherwise, state governments ought to implement the constitutional requirements of transferring funds from the Federation Account and from state governments to local government councils. It is important to state that most local governments have used the non-receipt of funds as the reason for lack of adequate development projects in their jurisdictions.

6. Fiscal Federalism and Macroeconomic Management.

Inter-governmental fiscal relations if not properly coordinated can create problems for the wider economy. For example, if budget deficits are persistent at the sub-national levels then it becomes difficult to implement sound fiscal policy for the entire economy. Hence, it is crucial that fiscal co-ordination among the three tiers of government be pursued vigorously and not legalized. It is, therefore, questionable why fiscal co-ordination needs to be legalized through the Fiscal Responsibility Act. The Act itself negates the very spirit of fiscal federalism and calls to question the ability of the centre to challenge the expenditure needs of the lower levels of government.

It is important that all the levels of government see the need and be committed to effective, disciplined, and coordinated budgetary planning, implementation and reporting. Lower levels of government ought to understand the need to stabilize the economy, controls borrowing and generate revenue through innovative mechanisms to finance their expenditure requirements. Thus the importance of co-ordination must be stressed if monetary and fiscal policies are to be effective for the wider economy.[10]

7. Decentralization, Democracy and Good Governance.

The dynamics of decentralization suggest that good governance and democracy can be sustained under federalism; proper devolution of powers to sub-national governments have inherent democratic values. Decentralization itself connotes some form of democracy. If good governance is practised at the lower levels then democracy and for that matter inter-governmental fiscal relations, can be sustained. The implication of this is that transparency, accountability and probity are necessary arguments for sustaining democracy. Lower levels of government are closer to the people than the centre hence if good governance is confirmed at the lower levels then the wider economy stands to benefit. Furthermore, prudent fiscal management at the lower levels exerts positive pressure on the centre to properly manage the economy; these are aspects of good governance with better implications for democracy.

It is, thus, pertinent that the fight against corruption be intensified. Corruption denies the lower levels of government the needed resources for development. Anti-corruption agencies need to direct more attention at policy-makers at the state and local government levels so as to ensure that funds are used for development purposes. This is an important challenge for the Nigerian state because available evidence shows that funds allocated to local governments have not resulted in the meaningful economic development of such areas. In addition, lower levels of government particularly local governments lack the capacity to enforce due process in the economic management of their jurisdictions. In order to ensure good governance and benefit from decentralization, the quality of leadership must be addressed at all levels of government. This can be achieved through training and re-training

Table 2: Disposition of Major Tax Powers among the Three Tiers of Government

S/N	Federal Government of Nigeria	State Government	Local Government
1.	Import Duties	Personal Income Tax (Administration and Collection)	Property Taxes and Ratings (Tenement Rate)
2.	Companies Income Tax	Withholding Tax (on individuals)	Market and Trading Licenses and Fees
3.	Withholding Tax on Companies	Capital Gain Tax (Administration and on individuals)	Motor Park Dues
4.	Petroleum Profit Tax	Stamp Duties on Individuals	Radio and Television Licenses (other than radio and television transmitters)
5.	Capital Gains Tax (legal basis)	Entertainment Tax	Marriage, Birth and Death Registration Fees
6.	Mining Rents and Royalties	Road Taxes (motor Vehicle and Driver's Licenses	Bicycles, Trunk, Canoe and Wheel barrow fees
7.	Stamp duties on Corporate Body	Pools Betting and Lotteries and gaming Taxes	Public Convenience, sewage and Refuse Disposal fees
8.	Value Added Tax (VAT)	Land Registration and Survey Fees	Signboard and Advertisement Permit fees
9.	Education Tax	Development Levy	

10.	Personal Income Tax (except in respect of members of the Armed Forces of the Federation, members of the Nigerian Police Force; residents of the Federal Capital Territory, Abuja and staff of the Ministry of Foreign Affairs and non-resident individuals)		

Source: Nigerian Constitutions, Fiscal commissions, Revenue Mobilization Allocation and Fiscal Commission, and Value Added Tax (VAT) Decree of 1993 and subsequent amendment of 1996.

Challenges of the Next Decade

The challenges of the next decade include, among others:

a) The need to review the division of functions among the various tiers of government. This is to ensure that the country's fiscal system conforms to best practices without sacrificing the essentials of Nigeria's peculiarities.
b) The percentage ascribed to the derivation principle ought to be increased in order to reduce tension. In adjusting the derivation weight, fairness and equity should be considered. An increased share based on derivation will partly resolve the resource control matter.
c) The custodian of the Federation Account. The federal government behaves as both the custodian and owner of the Federation Account despite the Supreme Court decision against it. The continued illegal and unconstitutional deductions, dedicated accounts of public institutions such as the Nigerian National Petroleum Corporation (NNPC) will continue to generate controversies on the distributable pool account.
d) Coordination of fiscal policy among the tiers of government. Unguided expenditure at the lower levels of government could generate distortions in the wider economy. The ability to domesticate the due process methodology as well as the commitment by all tiers of government to fiscal discipline will result in a more robust macroeconomic management of the economy. Consequently, the implementation of the Fiscal Responsibility Act will remain a challenge.
e) Oil producing areas and resource control. This will involve the participation of indigenes of the areas in the exploitation of mineral re-

sources not just crude oil. There is the need to review the ownership structure particularly as regards participation in both the downstream and upstream sub-sectors of the oil industry. Policy-makers must pay attention to the economic development of the natural resources producing areas.

f) Another challenge will be the need to decentralize tax administrations in the country. This will enhance the fiscal capacity of the federating units to be able to carry out their constitutional responsibilities. Tax decentralization will restore private sector confidence in lending to local government hence sharing the risks and rewards of such lending.

g) The issue of internally generated revenue effort as one of the variables for allocating revenue allocation among states. There is the issue of its measurement as well as how to reward states that show effort or lead others in internally generated revenue drive. It may be necessary to examine the matter of unconditional grants and fiscal equalization to support the development projects at the lower levels of government.

Conclusion

We have attempted to analyse fiscal federalism in Nigeria by highlighting the inherent challenges. It is clear that fiscal federalism in Nigeria is based on several factors – economic, political, cultural and constitutional. Furthermore, the practice of fiscal federalism has generated a lot of controversies over the years particularly on the formula and/or weight attached to both horizontal and vertical sharing formulae. Fiscal federalism in Nigeria poses series of challenges which have been discussed in this chapter.

However, reforms are necessary if some of the challenges derived from the practice of fiscal federalism are to be addressed. The recommended reforms include:

a) the establishment of an Independent Inter-governmental Committee to promote a framework of fiscal discipline and fiscal policy coordination. Such a framework will incorporate the adoption of fiscal rules;

b) an amendment to the 1999 Constitution to provide for the devolution of more powers to lower levels of government; and

c) lower levels of government require relative autonomy in economic matters. The bureaucracy for economic policy and decisions are over centralized. For example, a state interested in establishing a power plant requires several approvals from agencies at the centre.

The issues examined in this chapter suggest that the practice of fiscal federalism in Nigeria should stress revenue generation more than allocation. In addition, there is need to continuously fine-tune the process of inter-governmental fiscal relations through dialogue, fairness and equity.

NOTES

1. Several studies on Nigeria's fiscal federalism confirm this position. See Adedotun O. Philips, "Four Decades of Fiscal Federalism in Nigeria" *Publius: The Journal of Federalism* 21 (1991): pp. 103-11; B. O. Nwabueze, *Federalism in Nigeria Under the Presidential Constitution*; Akpan H. Ekpo, "Fiscal Federalism: Nigeria's Post-Independence Experience, 1960-90" *World Development* 22 (8): pp. 1129-46.

2. The Presidential system also faces the challenges of the introduction of Sharia law by some Muslim States in the North; the rise in ethnic/sectional militant groups such as the Odu'a People's Congress in the South-west, the Movement for the Actualization of the Sovereign State of Biafra (MASSOB) in the South-east.

3. Ekpo, Akpan and Enamidem Ubok-Udom. *Issues in Fiscal Federalism and Revenue Allocation in Nigeria,* (Ibadan: Future Publishing, 2003).

4. Oates, Wallace. *Fiscal Federalism,* (New York: Harcourt Brace, 1972)

5. Prud-Homme, R. "On the Dangers of Decentralization". *The World Bank Research Observer*, 1995.

6. Agiobenebo, T. "Issues in Fiscal Management:

Implications for Monetary Policy in Nigeria". Central Bank Annual Conference 2003. See also: Ekpo and Englama forthcoming 2007.

7. Mbanefoh, G. F. "Unsettled Issues in Nigeria's Fiscal Federalism and the National Question". *Nigerian Economy Society,* (Ibadan, 1993).

8. Ekpo, A. H. and Englama A. "Fiscal Federalism in Nigeria: Issues, Challenges and Agenda for Reform" Processed, 2007.

9. Ekpo, A. H. and E. Ubok-Udom (2003).*op.cit*

10. Ekpo, A. H. "The Practice of Fiscal Federalism in Nigeria: Comparative Perspective" (forthcoming), 2007.

REFERENCES

Adedeji, A.: *Nigerian Federal Finance*: (Hutchinson Educational, London, 1969).

Agiobenebo, T. T. "Issues in Fiscal Management: Implications for Monetary Policy in Nigeria" 3rd Annual Central Bank of Nigeria Conference, 2003.

Bahl, R. S. *Fiscal Decentralization as Developmental Policy*. Public Budgeting and Finance, 1999.

Central Bank of Nigeria (2005): *Annual Reports and Statement of Accounts*, Abuja.

Ekpo, Akpan H.: Fiscal Federalism: Nigeria's Post-Independence Experience, 1960-90, *World Development*, vol. 22, No. 8 1994, pp. 1129-1146.

Ekpo, Akpan H.: "Fiscal Federalism and Local Government Finances in Nigeria" in, *Fiscal Federalism and Nigeria's Economic Development*,(Ibadan: Nigerian Economy Society, 1999).

Ekpo, Akpan H. and Enamidem Ubok-Udom: *Issues in Fiscal Federalism and Revenue Allocation in Nigeria*, (Ibadan: Future Publishing, 2003).

Ekpo, Akpan H.: *Fiscal Theory and Policy*: Selected Essays, (Lagos: Somaprint, 2005).

Ekpo, Akpan H. and A. Englama "Fiscal Federalism in Nigeria: Issues, Challenges and Agenda for Reform" (Processed, 2007).

Ekpo, Akpan H. "The Practice of Fiscal Federalism in Nigeria: Comparative Perspective" (Forthcoming, 2007).

Ekpo, Udeme: *The Niger Delta and Oil Politics*, (Lagos: International Energy Communications, 2004).

Emenuga, Chidozie: "Nigeria: In Search of Acceptance Revenue Allocation Formula". in *The National Question and Economic Development in Nigeria* (Ibadan: Nigerian Economic Society, 1993).

Federal Republic of Nigeria *Report of the Presidential Commission on Revenue Allocation, Vol. 1*. Main Report. (Lagos: Government Press, 1977).

Federal Republic of Nigeria *Constitution of the Federal Republic of Nigeria 1999*. (Lagos: Federal Government Press, 1999).

James, E. K.. *Fiscal Decentralization: Theory as Reform*, 2003.

Mbanefoh, G. F. and Akpan H. Ekpo: *Review of Constitutional Provisions on Fiscal Federation in Nigeria Processed*. (Abuja: World Bank, 2005).

Mbanefoh, G. F. "Unsettled Issues in Nigeria's Fiscal Federalism and the National Question". In *The National Question and Economic Development in Nigeria* (Ibadan: Nigerian Economic Society, 1993).

Mbanefoh, G. F. "Federalism and Common Property". *The Guardian*, Saturday, February 20, 1993b: 13.

Mbanefoh, G. F.: *Military Presence and the Future of Nigerian Fiscal Federalism*, Faculty Lecture Series No. 1. Faculty of the Social Sciences, University of Ibadan, Ibadan, 1986.

Mbanefoh, G. F.: *Nigerian Fiscal Federalism: Assignment of Functions and Tax Powers.* Paper presented at the National Seminar on Revenue Mobilization, organized by the Revenue Mobilization, Allocation and Fiscal Commission, Enugu, April 21-23, 1992.

Musgrave, R. A. and Musgrave, P. B. : *Public Finance in Theory and Practice*: (Singapore: n.d., 1984).

Nwabueze, B. O.: *Federalism in Nigeria under the Presidential Constitution,* (Lagos State Ministry of Justice, Lagos, 2002).

Nyong, M. O.: *Fiscal Federalism, Revenue Allocation Formula and Economic Development in Nigeria* in Ekpo, Akpan H. and Enamidem Ubok-Udom: *Issues in Fiscal Federalism and Revenue Allocation in Nigeria,* (Ibadan: Future Publishing, 2003)

Oates, Wallace. *Fiscal Federalism,* (New York: Harcourt Brace, 1972).

Okigbo, P. N. C. *Nigerian Public Finance,* (London: Longmans, 1965).

Osayinwese, Izevbuwa and Sunday Iyare. The Economics of Nigerian Federalism: Selected Issues in Economic Management" *Publius: The Journal of Federalism* 21, (Fall, 1991), p. 89-101.

Phillips, Adedotun O. "Four Decades of Fiscal Federalism in Nigeria" *Publius: The Journal of Federalism,* 21, (Fall, 1991) p. 103-111.

Prud-Homme, R."On the Dangers of Decentralization" *The World Bank Research Observer,* 1995.

Shah, A. Fiscal Decentralization: An Elusive Goal? A case study of Indonesia and Pakistan Experience. (International Conference on Fiscal Decentralization on Developing Countries, 1998).

CHAPTER 5
REVENUE SHARING
(VERTICAL AND HORIZONTAL)

Eghosa Osagie

Introduction

After two terms of the Obasanjo presidency, it is appropriate and timely to assess the performance of Nigeria in the practice of fiscal federalism. Indeed the objectives of this workshop highlight the identification of the major issues and challenges, practical solutions to emerging problems and the specification of recommendations that ensure that the favoured framework of fiscal federalism promotes national peace and security, and reflects genuine federalist arrangements between the three tiers of government.

During the constitutional debates and conferences of the 1950s immediately preceding the attainment of independence in 1960, Nigerian political leaders agreed that federalism provided a solid foundation for national stability and peace as it recognized and presumably promoted cultural diversity, in the process ensuring that all parts would have a genuine sense of belonging, and that no part, no matter how large and powerful would be able to dominate the others. Incidentally, the former Northern Region with the distinct advantage of size and the former Western Region (then the most developed part of Nigeria), were the leading exponents of federalism.

It is ironic that the greatest threats to the idea and practice of federalism have come from leaders from these former Regions in recent years; specifically the North during military regimes (1966–1979) and the South-West during the quasi-military or pseudo-civilian Administrations during the Fourth Republic.

The negative impact of military regimes on federalism is expected and logical. The highly centralized command structure of the military invariably resulted in having a centralizing impact on the structure of government and distribution of power in the polity. It was, therefore, not surprising that under military regimes, the so-called Federal Military Government (a misnomer) made laws applicable in all the regions/states, and more importantly, appointed military governors for the states.

It is disappointing to politicians who struggled for the return of civilian politics to realize that what emerged in 1999 was not normal civilian policies and governance but a quasi-military regime where the most important political actors were former military political leaders whose attitude to the idea and practice of federalism in Nigeria never changed from what they were during full military regimes. The result is the disenchantment with Nigeria as a political entity by Nigerians in parts of the country who felt marginalized in the exercise of power and authority at the federal level. This feeling of alienation and exploitation is more observable in mineral-producing areas where decades of neglect by federal and state governments have produced militant youths, either demanding a drastic re-negotiation of the structure of government or promoting the break-up of the country. Today, it is the Niger-Delta Region; tomorrow, it may be parts of the Middle Belt and the far North with their abundant natural endowment of precious stones and solid minerals. A country with multiple disintegrative forces deliberately working for the break-up of the polity, cannot survive.

Nigeria would survive as a political entity if it returns to the original federalist idea of the founding fathers. This would be achieved by providing for a considerably loose federation where powers that were inappropriately taken over by the centre since 1966 are returned to the federating units. This desirable restructuring would be impossible if the government that assumes power on May 29, 2007 resists the convocation of a constitution revision conference among Nigerian ethnic groups, or if it seeks to teleguide the conference to produce another inappropriate constitution with a strong centre, or if former military politicians employ their considerable influence to impose their idea of a unitary system on the country.

Taking into consideration the analysis so far, the following challenges are relevant:

a) how does Nigeria survive as a single political entity?
b) how does Nigeria address the disintegrative tendencies of militants agitating against extreme centralization of power and their marginalization?

c) how does Nigeria make former military politicians to realize that their preference for, and promotion of a unitary system of government is a sure recipe for disintegration?
d) how does Nigeria organize a constitutional conference of the constituent ethnic groups providing for a loose federation?

These are the crucial political challenges before Nigeria in 2007. Until they are satisfactorily resolved, we cannot meaningfully consider fiscal federalism as a framework for fiscal relations between the three tiers of government. To prepare the ground for conclusions and recommendations, the following sections will discuss issues and factors that have been at play right from pre-independence years.

Relevant Issues

Revenue Allocation, Fiscal Commissions and Decrees

The issue of revenue allocation has always generated controversy in Nigeria's experience as a political entity since 1946 when the Phillipson Commission introduced a revenue-sharing formula which placed emphasis on the principle of derivation. Succeeding Commissions such as the Hicks-Phillipson (1951), Chick (1953), Raisman (1958), Binns (1964), Dina (1969), Aboyade (1977), and Okigbo (1980) have come up with different revenue allocation formulae which the members felt suited the times. As Nigerian economic and political environments changed in the years leading to independence and in the turbulent era of the 1960s, new formulae replaced old ones which were felt to have been rendered inappropriate by changing conditions. In the 1970s, a battery of military Decrees which had far-reaching implications on federal-state fiscal relations were introduced, and indeed imposed by the Federal Military Government. During that period, The Constitution (Distributable Pool Account) Decree 13 of April 1970, Decree No. 9 of 1971, Decree No. 6 of 1975 and Decree No. 7 of 1975 steadily increased the fiscal power of the Federal Government viz-a-viz the States, and deliberately reduced revenue shared out to States on the basis of derivation.

The "predictable" climax was reached in 1977 when the Aboyade Commission neatly removed that criterion which was replaced by a new set of revenue-sharing criteria. The subsequent Okigbo Commission somewhat reversed this trend, and introduced a new tendency providing room for the principle of derivation – a development which was followed by the Allocation of Revenue (Federation Account) Act 1981 and subsequent legislations on revenue allocation by military regimes in the 1980s and in June 1992.

An important innovation in revenue allocation was introduced in 1989 when the National Revenue Mobilization Allocation and Fiscal Commission (NRMAFC) was established as a permanent institution. Unlike all previous revenue allocation commissions which were *ad hoc* in nature and whose recommendations formed the basis for intergovernmental fiscal relations, the new Commission was to be permanent and its scope went beyond revenue allocation to include revenue mobilization and fiscal matters. Specifically, the Commission was "to monitor the environment and fine-tune continuously the principles and formula for revenue allocation".[1]

The Constitution provides for regions as federating units to have powers and responsibilities some of which are currently exercised by the Federal Government. The debate featured disagreement over the derivation principle. While there was general agreement that derivation should be accepted as one of the criteria for revenue allocation, there was however disagreement regarding the percentage of revenue distributed using the derivation principle going to producing States. The range is between the current 13 per cent and 100 percent demanded by exponents of full resource control. It is expected that skillful negotiation would produce a compromise between the two extremes.

The other issue considered during the constitution review in 2006 project was extension of the presidential term from two to three. In view of the military antecedent of the sitting president, the passage of that proposal would have sounded the death knell of federalism in Nigeria. Perhaps, if the powers and authority of the presidency were not so excessively attractive, President Obasanjo would not have engaged in the *third term project.*

An appropriate revenue allocation formula for any particular period in a properly functioning federation should take into consideration a number of socio-economic and political developments which have impact on the nature and health of federal arrangements. Periods of military regimes, largely due to the centralized nature of military organizations, tend to weaken federal arrangements and move the country in the direction of a unitary political system with a strong centre. This development has its fiscal counterpart in disproportionately large percentages of government revenues going to the federal government largely at the expense of the States.

This section presents recent changes in the political and economic life of Nigeria on the basis of which suggested changes in the revenue allocation formula are made in following sections. Failure to consider this recent development exposes the revenue-sharing process to subjective biases and crude parochial self-interest. We now proceed to discuss briefly these developments.

1999 Constitution and Attempt at Reviews

The 1999 Constitution though espousing federalism on paper, largely continued the tradition of an imperial president provided for in the 1979 Constitution. Attempts at revising the 1999 Constitution during the Obasanjo regime largely missed the point by considering the creation of new states, a development that would have strengthened the centre at the expense of the states. A desirable proposal would feature constitutional amendment efforts. The term of the president should be limited to a single term of five years to prevent a growing ambition of a sitting president from undermining federalist principles entrenched in the constitution.

The Structural Adjustment Programme (SAP)

Since 1986, Nigeria has been implementing a macroeconomic Structural Adjustment Programme which gives ample scope to market forces in national economic management. Important features of the programme include elimination or reduction in subsidies, privatization and commercialization of parastatals, staff rationalization in the public sector and devaluation of the exchange rate of the naira. The elimination or reduction of subsidies, commercialization and staff rationalization have resulted in a significant reduction in some traditional areas of Federal Government expenditure. The devaluation of the naira exchange rate has substantially increased the naira value of foreign exchange earnings managed by the federal government and the Central Bank.

In these circumstances, it is rational to reduce the shares of the Federation Account allocated to the Federal Government. The failure to do this has, in recent times, been marked by the federal government playing the role of *Father Christmas* at home and abroad and by the proliferation of non-productive federal institutions duplicating the functions of the ministries. Although the federal government reduced the number of ministries in 2007, there is the possibility that a new regime after May 29, 2007 may be tempted to reverse this decision in an effort to reward party members that worked to secure electoral victory.

The new federal government should resist this temptation. Similarly, the process of limiting bureaucracy should be promoted at state and local government levels so as to make financial resources available for people-oriented capital projects. There is another reason for limiting the percentage of the Federation Account allocated to the federal government. Copious evidence of massive mismanagement and misallocation of funds exposed by the federal government itself after investigation of the Petroleum Technology Development Fund (PTDF) in 2006 and 2007 indicate a considerable level of corruption at the centre. This fact should be taken into consideration in reducing the share of the federal government in the Federation Account.

Census Figures

Census figures have since 1962 been politicized in Nigeria. This attitude to a supposedly technical operation is due to the fact that population is taken into account in the distribution of seats in the National Assembly as well as in the horizontal sharing of the Federation Account among the states. Before the 1991 census, Nigeria's population was estimated at about 110 million, based on extrapulation of the 1963 figure. To the surprise of many Nigerians, the provisional census results gave the population as above 80 million. Besides, wide disparities in population between local government areas raise questions about the equality factor in the distribution of revenue among local governments and the viability of certain local government areas in the country. These issues have to be handled with care to avoid social and political unrest in the future.

The creation of 9 additional states and a relatively large number of local government areas in 1991 have significantly affected the distribution of power within the Nigerian federation. The states are expected to provide financially for specific basic minimum facilities and institutions required by the status of statehood. The new states had to build from scratch. To compound the fiscal problems confronting the states and local governments, responsibility for the financing of SAP relief measures, greater burdens in the health, education and other key sectors have been placed on the States whose existence and proper functioning guarantee the federal structure of government. On the basis of these considerations, it is clear that the 25 per cent of the Federation Account allocated for distribution among the states before June 1992 and the 24 per cent since June 1992 were grossly inadequate and hostile to the keeping of campaign promises made by civilian state governors. A fair and appropriate revenue sharing formula must raise the share of the states in the Federation Account if Nigeria is not to degenerate to the status of an excessively centralized polity. In view of the ethnic diversity of our country, that would be an undesirable development.

Provisional figures released by the Federal Government after the 2006 Census put the population of Nigeria at 140 million. Again, this result is being subjected to critical comments in certain parts of the country. The Government of Lagos State and Ndigbo stakeholders, for example, have completely rejected the census results. In future constitutional review exercises, the population criterion will feature once again as a criterion in horizontal allocation of revenue to the states. It is bound to generate controversy as different stakeholders argue for or against its use.

Complaints of Oil-Producing States and Local Governments

Nigerians living in oil-producing areas, for a long time, have voiced their disillusionment over the neglect and insensitivity they have experienced. Oil-prospecting and production activities systematically destroy the environment of the producing areas: pollution and continuous flaring of associated gas create health hazards and render farming and fishing almost impossible. This disillusionment takes an ominously political complexion as the nationality groups concerned are minority ethnic groups who are, more often than not, unrepresented in federal organs of state and in the oil companies where decisions regarding their plight are taken. In the 1970s when successive military decrees progressively reduced the share of oil-producing states in the Federation Account, one of the implicit reasons for such decisions was to prevent a situation where two out of 12 states enjoying large amounts of oil revenue develop much faster than the others, thus introducing widening disparities in standards of living within the same country. Between the 1990s and 2000s, the situation changed remarkably as the federal government decided to make up for the hardship experienced by oil-producing states. In addition, there are now about six oil-producing states, and other valuable minerals have been discovered in a growing number of other states. An appropriate revenue-allocation formula which fairly rewards the locality would encourage states and local governments to provide conditions conducive to production activities in areas where valuable minerals have been discovered.

Increasing Clannishness

A development that has taken on frighteningly ominous proportion is the surprising rise of clannishness and ethnic antagonism since the early 1980s. In some parts of the country, the situation is compounded by religious unrest. This sad development has been attributed partly to difficult economic conditions and partly to the mischievous intrigues of highly placed anti-social elements bent on realizing narrowly focused selfish ends. Whatever the reasons for recent social upheavals, they have had far-reaching implications for the integration and long-term survival of the country. Nigerians who have lived for long periods in parts of the country other than their ethnic traditional areas have returned to their ethnic areas. These developments tend to poison inter-ethnic relations and make our ethnic nationalities inward-looking.

It is ironic that Nigerians became increasingly clannish at a time when power was being concentrated at the centre. A centralizing polity is expected to demonstrate the spirit of ethnic collaboration and tolerance to encourage different ethnic groups to have a sense of belonging. But an attitude of winner-takes-all as exhibited by the so-called majority ethnic nationality groups generates an expected response of alienation and oppression on the part of the so-called ethnic minorities, leading to calls for a loose federation where those who wish to be clannish are free to do so within their own federating units. Even then, other minorities within federating units would feel alienated, and so the slide continues to possible armed conflict and eventual disintegration. Even within a loose Nigerian federation, there should be no room for clannishness in all its ramifications.

Return of Derivation Principle

As stated earlier. The derivation principle was de-emphasized in the 1970s. In the 1980s, the Okigbo Commission made a special plea for the criterion as it argued:

> In line with the current practice, we propose that some fund be set aside to be shared by the mineral-producing States on the basis of derivation. We are persuaded in this direction by our conviction that it is only fair and proper that the special contributions from these States to the resources of the nation be recognized. Besides, unlike manufacturing where the impact of location is immediate and substantial, the case of oil exploration is minimal.[2]

Current De-emphasis of Politics of Cake-Sharing

Before the establishment of the *National Revenue Mobilization, Allocation and Fiscal Commission* in 1989, revenue-sharing exercises were largely preoccupied with the sharing of the national cake syndrome. It is to be expected that the Commission devotes a substantial part of its time and effort at revenue mobilization. Hence, there should be no room for spurious criteria for revenue allocation which encourage fraudulent claims by states and discourage revenue mobilization effort. Indeed, Federal Government gave vent to the new spirit of fiscal responsibility when it argued at the inaugural ceremony of the Commission as follows:

> Specifically, the Commission will be expected to emphasize national self-reliance as a basic for sustainable development. Our basic idea of self-reliant development is that individuals, households, enterprises, all tiers of government, and indeed all Nigerians must live within their means and that the means be legitimately acquired".[3]

Vertical Allocation

In this section, we consider the composition of the Federation Account, the percentage distribution of the account between the three tiers of government, the share allocated on the basis of derivation standing on its own as an autonomous criterion for vertical allocation of revenue, and provisions made for such nationally important items as research, science and technology; ecology; and national emergency and contingency.

Before proposing a new revenue allocation formula which takes into consideration developments presented above, it is necessary to have, as points of reference, the formulae suggested by the *National Revenue Mobilization, Allocation and Fiscal Commission* in 1989, that adopted by the Federal Government between 1989 and June 6, 1992, and the new sharing formula introduced "with immediate effect" on June 6, 1992. Table 1 presents the 3 formulae referred to above.

The Revenue Commission's 1989 report was competently put together. Its allocation of 47 per cent of the Federation Account to the federal government was rather on the generous side, though the Government White Paper on that aspect raised the share to 50 per cent. The reduction of the federal government's share of the Federation Account from 50 per cent to 48.5 per cent in June 6 1992 did not go far enough if our plans for the future include a sustainable and development oriented federal system. The Revenue Commission's recommended allocation of 30 per cent of the Federation Account to the states in 1989 was perceptive and far-sighted. In view of recent developments, it would be advisable to implement that recommendation and reverse the downward trend in allocations to the states observed since 1989.

Table 1 Vertical Allocation of the Federation Account

	Report of National Revenue-Revenue Mobilization	Revenue-sharing	Revenue-sharing		
	Recipients	Allocation and Fiscal Commission	Formula before June 6	Formula after June 6 1992	Revenue sharing Formula in the Fourth Republic

		(1989)			(1999)
		%	%	%	%
Fed-eral Govt.		47.0	50.0	48.5	48.5
State Govt.		30.0	25.0	24.0	24.0
Local Govt.		15.0	20.0	20.0	20.0
Spe-cial Fund s		(2.0)	(1.5)	(3.0)	13.0
(a)	Derivation (% of the mineral Revenue) (% of Total Reve-nue)				
(b)	Ecology	(0.5)	(1.0)	(2.0)	2.0
(c)	Special Funds	-	(2.5)	(2.5)	
(d)	Federal Capital Territory	(1.0)	-	-	1.0
(e)	Stabilization	(0.5)	-	-	0.5
(f)	Savings	(2.0)	-	-	
(g)	Development of oil producing areas	(1.5) of oil	-		
	mineral revenue	-	-		
(h)	Development of oil mineral	of non-oil	(0.5) of non-oil		Mineral pro-oil mineral
	Producing areas	Revenue	-		-

Sources

(a) *National Revenue Mobilization Allocation and Fiscal Commission, Main Reports,* Vol. I, May 1989, p. iii;

(b) *National Concord,* Monday, June 8, 1992, p. 21.

(c) Federal Ministry of Finance, *Summary of Gross Revenue Allocation by Federation Account Allocation Committee.* (1999 and after).

Again, the Commission's recommended allocation of 15 per cent of the Federation Account to the local governments was fair and realistic under conditions prevailing in 1989. The recent transfer of responsibility over primary education funding justifies the raising of local governments' share of the Federation Account to 20 per cent. It is doubtful if many local governments can meet their statutory obligations if they depend heavily on allocations from the Federation Account and do not receive additional funds from the derivation criterion and if they fail to make effective efforts at generating substantial revenue from internal sources.

Interestingly, the four arrangements presented in Table 1 completely ignore the requirements of research, science and technology. It is important to note here that all developed countries of the Northern Hemisphere and the rapidly industrializing ones in East Asia (the so-called Asian Tigers) commit substantial percentages of national resources to research and the application of science and technology to productive effort as they strive to remain competitive in the gradually evolving global economy. If Nigeria expects to be taken seriously by other countries in the twenty-first century, and consciously seeks to avoid marginalization in international economic relations, she should provide adequately for research, science and technology in her revenue allocation arrangements.

We now come to the potentially contentious issue of the composition of the Federation Account. First, we consider ways of increasing the size of the Account and improving the presentation of the components of the Account. It is expected that in a few years time, gas production and export will overtake crude oil as the most important source of foreign exchange and government revenue in Nigeria. In agreement with the Revenue Commission's recommendation in 1989, the sale of gas should be accounted for separately from crude oil sales, and the same principles applied to both in the allocation of the Federation Account. Second, surpluses or profits recorded by the Central Bank, other parastatals (e.g., NNPC), and dividends accruing from public sector investments should be paid into the Federation Account. Third, the Federation Account should be properly credited when the federal government uses oil to pay for capital projects executed by foreign contractors. When such transactions take place, they are equivalent to the federal government making crude oil sales and spending the whole proceeds without subjecting it to the revenue-sharing formula of the Federation Account. When such transactions occur, the federal government should appropriately augment the Federation Account by an amount equivalent to the spot market value of the oil involved.

Fourth, the treatment of mining rents and royalties needs to be reconsidered. The Chick Commission Report of 1953, in the true spirit of federalism, allocated mineral royalties "in full to the region from which the mineral was extracted"[4]. In 1958, the Raisman Commission recommended that "revenue from mining rents and royalties was to be allocated between the regions in whose areas the minerals existed, the Centre, and the distributable pool in the ratios of 50%, 20% and 30% respectively"[5]. The *Dina Report* recommended that rents from on-shore mining activities should go to the states of origin, a recommendation with which the Okigbo Commission agreed. On the issue of royalties, both Commissions were rather ambivalent. In the 1970s, various military governments worked to reduce by decrees, the share of mining rents and royalties going to the producing states.

Specifically, the *Constitution (Distributable Pool Account) Decree 13 of April 1970* ensured that the lion's share of revenue collected by the federal government was retained by it. Regarding rents and royalties, the Decree transferred 5 per cent out of the 50 per cent allocated to producing states by Raisman (1958) and Binns (1964) to the centre. In 1971, Decree No. 9 transferred rents and royalties derived from off-shore petroleum production from producing states to the centre. The process of unilaterally depriving producing states of their share of mining rents and royalties was brought to its culmination by Decree No. 6 of 1975 which reserved 20 per cent of on-shore mining rents and royalties to the producing states "on the principle of derivation" and by the Aboyade Commission which recommended that all mining rents and royalties should go to the Federation Account [6].

It is important to note here that (unlike the situation in other federations), mining rents and royalties have been taken away from producing states in Nigeria without the people's consent. This is one area that has to be adjusted and amended in our revenue sharing arrangements. Specifically, the point being made here is that the whole of mining rents and royalties without making any distinction between on-shore and off-shore production should not go to the Federation Account. An agreed percentage should go to producing states, and the balance to the Federation Account.

On the basis of these considerations, the following recommendations are made for the vertical allocation of revenue between the three tiers of government and carefully selected national programmes:

1. 30 per cent of mining rents and royalties without making any distinction between on-shore and off-shore petroleum production should go to producing areas, and 70 per cent allocated to the Federation Account. In addition, mining rents and royalties should be split on a ratio of 50:50 between the state and local governments where the minerals are produced, and earmarked for appropriate capital projects.
2. proceeds derived from sale of gas should be accounted for separately and treated in the same way as revenue from crude oil sales.
3. surplus from the operations of the Central Bank, NNPC, and other public sector commercialized enterprises should be paid into the Federation Account.
4. when the federal government uses crude oil to pay for capital projects executed by foreign contractors, the value of such oil swaps should be calculated at current spot prices and the federal government should pay an amount into the Federation Account equivalent to the spot market value.
5. the share of the federal government in the Federation Account should decrease from 48:5 per cent to 40 per cent.
6. the share of the states in the Federation Account should rise from 24 per cent to 30 per cent in agreement with recommendations of the National Revenue Mobilization, Allocation and Fiscal Commission in 1989.
7. the share of the local governments in the Federation Account should remain at 20 per cent.
8. 10 per cent of the Federation Account should be allocated to Special Funds as follows:
9) Research, Science and Technology:
a) 7.0 per cent
b) Ecology 1.0 per cent
c) National Emergency and Contingency 2.0 per cent

Horizontal Allocation

Horizontal allocation of revenue among the states appears on the surface to be straight-forward and not as contentious as vertical allocation. However, the introduction of new criteria by the Revenue Commission in 1989 created a land mine for future fiscal controversy. These new criteria have to be carefully reconsidered by the federal government, the Commission, the democratic representatives of the states and the local governments. The formulae for the horizontal distribution of revenue among the states and the local governments are presented in Table 2. The aim of revenue allocation is to provide adequately for the administration of states and local governments and at the same time induce them to generate internal revenue for their use. Due to the increase in the number of states to 36, the percentages of 40 assigned to equality of states factor by the Commission's 1989 Report seems on the low side. On the other hand, the weight of 50 per cent assigned this factor in horizontal allocation is too high if we are to expect states to make concerted efforts to raise internal revenues. The weight of 30 per cent assigned to population is rather high given unreliability of population figures in Nigeria and the controversy that traditionally accompanied the release of census figures over time.

Table 2
Horizontal Revenue Allocation (Among States) Allocation 1992

Criterion by Nat. Revenue	Commission (1989)	**FORMULA (1992)**
	%	%
Equality of States	40	50
Population	30	30
Social Development	10	10
Internal Revenue		
Effort	20	10
Land Mass and Terrain	-	10

Source: *National Revenue Mobilization, Allocation and Fiscal Commission, Main Report,* Vol. I. May 1989. pp. iii-iv.

The weight of 10 per cent assigned to social development factor is on the low side. This criterion should be taken as proxy for direct enrolment in educational institutions. No room should be provided for inverse enrolment unless we want to create the impression that Nigeria places premium on illiteracy and educational underdevelopment. Other proxies for social development factor such as health and water should not be entertained as states are normally expected to provide for these amenities from all their revenue sources including internally generated revenue. Similarly, the criterion of landmass and its two aspects of size of land and difficulty of terrain are spurious, politically motivated and not normally considered in revenue allocation arrangements in other parts of the world. The weight of 10 per cent assigned by the military regime to this criterion was and remains untenable. Finally, our commitment to self-sufficiency should lead to the raising of the weight attached to internal revenue effort.

In view of the considerations discussed above, this paper recommends a horizontal allocation formula applicable to revenue to be shared among states as follows:

	Percentage
Equality of States	45
Population:	20
Social Development Factor:	15
Internal Revenue Effort:	20

The same formula may be applied in the distribution of revenue from the Federation Account among the local governments. However, the current practice requiring the states to allocate 10 per cent of internally generated revenue to local governments opens the relations between states and local governments to crisis. First, the requirement that state assemblies should legislate on the distribution formula for sharing the 10 per cent internally generated state revenue to the local governments unduly politicizes the exercise. Second, the precarious fiscal position of some states suggests that many states cannot fulfil this responsibility to local governments. To avoid this problem, local governments should be empowered to assist state governments collect revenue and to retain an agreed percentage.

Policy Issues and Recommendations

This paper considered the problems of coping with and resolving future challenges of fiscal federalism in Nigeria. It identifies the current unitary system of government as the product of the long period of military rule in Nigeria, and the operation of a quasi-military regime since 1999. The centralized system is inconsistent with the idea of federalism favoured by the Founding Fathers who predicated political stability on the practice of a loose federal framework. We can discuss federalism only if past and present military politicians desist from further manipulating the constitutional framework to favour a unitary system of government.

In a truly federal system, fiscal federalism is implemented partly through revenue allocation formulae. It also considered recent developments in Nigeria which have implications on horizontal and vertical aspects of revenue allocation. The overriding consideration should be given to stability of civilian regimes in the twenty-first century which largely depends on agreement on key political issues by the numerous nationality groups that make up Nigeria. The preferred recommended revenue allocation arrangement is conditioned by our commitment to development from below, avoidance of waste, congruence between constitutional division of functions between the three tiers of government and the provision of adequate funds to each tier to guarantee constitutional responsibilities, self-reliance, fairness and national integration. The paper contains a number of controversial suggestions such as adding surpluses of public sector enterprises to the Federation Account and the recognition of the derivation principle as an autonomous criterion for vertical revenue allocation. We also recommend a drastic reduction in the share of the federal government in the Federation Account from 48.5 per cent to 40 per cent to curb the *Santa Claus* and *Ali Baba* propensities of the centre and to allow for transfer of more funds to the states. In addition, we call for 30 per cent of mining rents and royalties to be returned to producing states in line with the practice in other successful federal systems in the world. With regard to horizontal revenue allocation, the weights assigned to equality of states and population were reduced and the landmass criterion was dismissed as spurious and politically motivated. Weights attached to social development factor and internal revenue efforts were raised to stimulate development and fiscal self-reliance.

With fairness and objectivity on all sides, it is possible for Nigeria to discuss new ideas and suggestions and come up with a realistic and generally acceptable revenue allocation formula. As Nigeria engages in more mature negotiations on revenue allocation in 2007 and beyond, the leaders should bring to the exercise scientific objectivity, fairness and equality of esteem. Anything short of these is bound to generate disintegrative stress for the country.

NOTES

1. National Revenue Mobilization Allocation and Fiscal Commission, Main Report, Vol. I, May, 1989.
2 .Ibid., p. 32.
3 .Ibid., p. 61.
4. Ibid., p. 16.
5. Ibid., p. 17.
6. Ibid., pp. 20-21.

REFERENCES

Central Bank of Nigeria, *Economic and Financial Review.* (Several issues).

Federal Republic of Nigeria, (May 1989, *Official Gazette* containing Decree No. 12 – The Constitution of the Federal Republic of Nigeria (Promulgation) Decree 1989.

Federal Ministry of Finance, Summary of Gross Revenue Allocation by Federation Account Committee (Several Issues).

National Concord, Monday June 8, 1992, p. 21.

National Revenue Mobilization, Allocation and Fiscal Commission, 1989, *Main Report*, Vols. 1 and II.

Osagie, E. (ed.), *Structural Adjustment in Nigeria* (Kuru: National Institute, 1992).

Osagie, E. *The New Nigerian Economy: From Poverty to Prosperity.* (Benin City: AFBSN Publishers, 2007).

Sanusi, H.U. *Public Policy Coordination in Nigeria.* (Kuru: National Institute, 1992).

PART III

INTERGOVERNMENTAL FISCAL RELATIONS: FINANCING NATIONAL DEVELOPMENT

CHAPTER 6

INTERGOVERNMENTAL RELATIONS IN NIGERIA: FINANCING NATIONAL DEVELOPMENT

Mike I. Obadan and I. B. Bello-Imam

Introduction

In the view of Kenneth C. Wheare,[1] Federalism presupposes the conglomeration of sub-units of a national sovereign government that operate independently within statutory or constitutionally defined spheres of functional competence. It also assumes that although the different component units within such a federal structure are relatively independent, yet because they operate within a single national sovereign state, (being themselves infra-sovereign units), they are co-ordinated with one another.

Theoretically, and also largely in practice, Nigeria operates a federal system of government with a federal government at the centre (Abuja), 36 state governments and 774 local government units (as at 2007). The number of local governments includes six area councils located at the Federal Capital Territory, Abuja. Each of these levels of government has its sphere of influence and functional competence. The Constitution of the Federal Republic of Nigeria has also assigned sources of revenue to the three levels of government. For instance, the federal government has exclusive constitutional responsibility for some functional subjects under the "Exclusive Legislative List", while it has joint responsibility with the state governments for the concurrent legislative list of functional subjects. Relatedly, the Fourth Schedule of the 1979, 1989, 1995 (Draft) and 1999 Constitutions outlined the functions that should be performed by the Local Governments. Some of the listed functions are exclusive to the local governments while others are concurrent, i.e. they could be executed in conjunction with state governments or state/private agencies.

Irrespective of these constitutional delineation of responsibilities among the three levels of government, the dynamics of our federal structure often subordinate the local government to the other tiers of government.[2] Ironically, but in line with the experiences of virtually all federations the world over, there is hardly any congruence between the functions and responsibilities assigned to the levels of government and their financial resources to execute them. Consequently, the apparently weaker tiers of government within such federations end up depending on the stronger tier(s) for financial assistance in order to provide public goods and services to the people. The challenge facing such a country then is to evolve acceptable tax assignment/revenue sharing arrangements in relation to expenditure assignments in such a way that the essence of federalism is not undermined enough for it to degenerate into a unitary system.

It is against this backdrop that this paper first defines the concept of fiscal federalism and addresses the issues of Tax and Expenditure assignments both theoretically and practically within the context of fiscal federalism in Nigeria. The paper also addresses the issues of sources and legal basis of government revenue as well as the problems of vertical and horizontal fiscal transfers in Nigeria. The revenue profiles of the three levels of government are our next focus. This is followed by a discussion of the issues of fiscal imbalances, the system of matching grants and resource control for mutually acceptable intergovernmental relations. The final section concludes the discussion.

Fiscal Federalism

Fiscal Federalism is an off-shoot of federalism. Fiscal federalism refers to the statutory defined financial transactions between the different tiers of government within a federation. It could be seen as the existence, in one nation-state, of more than one level of government having responsibility for both taxation and expenditure[2,3]. Essentially, the principles of fiscal federalism deal with theoretical (and institutional) issues of intergovernmental fiscal relations and how these relations impinge on sound macroeconomic management[4]. Within a fiscally federated state, a citizen can be subjected to the influence of fiscal operation of different levels of government. Such a development is what economists tag "economics of the multi-level"[5]. However, Wheare aptly argued that each level of government should have adequate resources to perform its functions without appealing to the other level of government for financial assistance. He emphasized this view when he said that:

> If state authorities, for example, find that the services allotted them are too expensive for them to perform, and (hence) they call upon the federal

> authority for grants and subsidies to assist them, they are no longer co-ordinate with the federal government but subordinate to it. Financial subordination (marks) an end of federalism in fact, no matter how carefully the legal forms may be preserved. It follows therefore that both state and federal authorities in a federation must be given the power in the constitution, each to have access to and to control, its own sufficient financial resources. Each must have power to tax and to borrow for the financing of its own services by itself[6].

Nigeria has since 1946, accepted the principles of federalism and its concurrent concept of fiscal federalism. Today, there are three distinct levels of government in the country – each with its constitutionally assigned functions and responsibilities as well as their respective financial resources to execute their assigned functions. Unfortunately, in Nigeria, federalism ceased to operate in practical terms as from January 1966 with the incursion of the military into governance. Except for a civilian interregnum of four years (1979 - 1983), Nigeria was ruled by military dictators between 1966 and May 1999. For all practical purposes, military governments tend to be unitary, regardless of whether the country is constitutionally a federation. Military governments in Nigeria have not been exceptions. Besides, even when a civilian government succeeds a military government, some of the practices and styles (if not structures) of a military administration continue under the civilian government. Thus, under the current democratic dispensation some of the practices and styles of the military have subsisted. Additionally, the centripetal forces that characterise military regimes are significantly reinforced in the structure of revenue generation such that the bulk of revenue is collected by the national government, as has been the case in Nigeria since the early 1970s owing largely to oil resources[7].

Nevertheless, three critical issues are the central focus of intergovernmental fiscal relations. These are first, what taxes and other related revenues should be collected by each of the levels of government within the nation-state. The second is how whatever is collected is shared among the different levels of government within the nation-state. The third and final issue is what criteria should guide the sharing of whatever revenue is collected among the sub-national entities within the country. These issues are addressed in the subsequent sections of this chapter.

Assignment of Functions and Tax Powers

Basis for Assignment of Functions

There is no consensus anywhere in the world on "who gets what, when and how" in a nation-state. This lack of consensus is very pronounced in Nigeria. As an illustration, the fiscal relationship between the three levels of government has remained a controversial issue. Successive governments in the country have set up several fiscal Commissions/Committees to review the fiscal relationship that would tally with constitutional and functional roles of the various tiers of government. Nine of such commissions/committees have been set up to date. Irrespective of this number of Commissions/Committees that have been set up to review the fiscal relationship in Nigeria, the issue has remained unresolved[8]. And, indeed, the revenue allocation system in the country has been described as being neither efficient nor equitable.[9]

Nevertheless, each of the three levels/tiers of government has assigned revenue generation powers and expenditure responsibilities. Theoretically, the revenue generating power allotted to each tier of government varies and depends on the magnitude of expenditure responsibilities. This is because the decentralisation of taxing or revenue generation power(s) provides the conceptual basis of expenditure assignment among the three tiers of government in Nigeria. See Table 1.1 for conceptual basis of tax assignment. From this table, it is evident that the macro services that touch on the lives of all the citizens of the country are assigned to the federal government, while the state governments provide services that are of equi-distance utility. Micro services that touch on the lives of the citizens are assigned to the local governments. Thus, in line with the geographic range of benefits principle, the central government provides public goods whose benefits cut across the country or population (e.g., defence, central banking, macroeconomic stabilisation, external relations). On the other hand, states and local governments provide those public goods and services that are susceptible to division among sub-units and whose benefits are concentrated geographically. In addition, while certain revenues are best collected by the central government on account of economies of scale, or because a particular tax is easy to evade at the local level but not at the national level, there are certain services that are best performed at lower levels of government but produce spill over effects. Transfers of revenue are made from the central to lower levels of government to redress the effects. Besides, in line with the principle of economies of scale, the federal government tends to find it cheaper to provide certain services, for example, those related to a national army as opposed to those produced by sub-national governments having their army units.[10]

Table 1.1: Conceptual Basis of Tax Assignment.

Expenditure Category	Service Responsibility	Provision of Service	Comment
Defence	F	F	Benefits/Costs are National
Foreign Affairs	F	F	Benefits/Costs are National
International Trade	F	F	Benefits/Costs are National
Environment	F	F	Benefits/Costs are National
Banking and Currency	F	F	Benefits/Costs are National
Internal Commerce	F	F	Benefits/Costs are National
Immigration	F	F	Benefits/Costs are National
Airways/Railways	F,S,L	F	Benefits/Costs are National
Industry and Agriculture	F,S,L	S,L	Significant Interest Spill over
Education	F,S,L	S,L	Transfer in Kind
Health	F,S,L	S,L	Transfer in Kind
Social Welfare	S,L	S,L	Transfer in Kind
Police	F,S,L	S,L	Primary Local Benefits
Highways	F,S,L	S,L	Some Roads have Interstate spill over, others are Primarily Local.
Natural Resources	F,S,L	S,L	Promotes a Common Market

Note: F= Federal, S=State, L= Local

Source: Olomola and Adewuyi (2001) (End-note 12)

Allocation of Tax Powers and Expenditure Responsibilities

Tax powers or jurisdiction among the different levels of government within a nation-state are determined by a number of factors. These are essentially *administrative efficiency* and *fiscal independence.* The *efficiency criterion* demands that a tax be assigned to that level of government that will administer it efficiently at minimum cost while *fiscal independence* requires that each level of government is permitted, as much as possible, to raise adequate resources from the revenue sources assigned to it to meet its needs and responsibilities.

However, in reality, the efficiency criterion tends to conflict with the principle of independence. This is because, whereas the efficiency criterion calls for a great deal of concentration of tax powers at the higher levels of government due to limited administrative capacity of the lower tiers of government, the fiscal independence criterion demands the devolution of additional tax powers to the lower units of government to match the functions assigned to them. But as was observed earlier on in this chapter, the weight of the two criteria have always tilted in favour of the efficiency criterion hence the Federation Account has a towering status in Nigeria's fiscal federalism. Table 1.2 shows the pattern of revenue/tax jurisdiction in Nigeria's fiscal federalism.

Table 1.2: Nigeria's Tax System, 1997

Federal Government	State Governments	Local Governments
1. Companies Income Tax	Personal Income Tax (on residents of the State)	Tenement Rate
2. Petroleum Profits Tax	Capital Gains Tax (on individuals only)	Shop and Kiosk Rates
3. Value Added Tax	Stamp Duties (on individuals only)	Liquor Licence Fees
4. Education Tax (on Companies only)	Road Taxes e.g. vehicle licences	Slaughter Slab fees
5. Capital Gains Tax	Betting and Gaming	Marriage, Birth and

(on Corporate Bodies and Abuja Residents)	Taxes	Death Registration Fees
6. Stamp Duties (on Corporate Bodies)	Business Premises and Registration Levy	Street Name Registration Fees (excluding State and Capital)
7. With-holding Tax (on Companies)	Development Levy (max. of N100 per annum on taxable individuals only)	Market/Motor Park Fees (excluding State-owned Markets)
8. Personal Income Tax (on Personnel of the Armed Forces, Police, External Affairs Ministry, and Residents of Abuja.	Street Name Registration Fees (State Capital only)	Domestic Animal Licence Fees
9. Mining, Rents and Royalties	Right of Occupancy Fees (State Capital only)	Bicycle, Trucks, Canoe, Wheelbarrows, Carts and Canoe Fees.
10. Customs Duties (i.e. Import Duties and Export Duties	Market fees (where market is financed by State Government)	Right of Occupancy Fees (excluding State Capital)
11. Excise Duties	Miscellaneous Revenues (e.g. rents on property)	Cattle Tax
12.Miscellaneous Revenues (e.g. Earnings from Oil Sales, rents on property, etc.)		Merriment Fees
13.		Radio and TV Licence Fees
14.		Vehicle Parking fees
15.		Public Convenience, Sewage and Refuse

		Disposal Fees
16.		Burial Ground and Religious Places permit fees
17.		Signboard and Billboard Advertisement Permit Fees

Source: Federal Ministry of Finance

Since there is only little room for manoeuvring on the pattern, only marginal changes have been effected on it over the years. The notable changes have been the transfers of the legal aspects of Capital Gains tax, Personal Income tax, Stamp Duties, and lately the Value Added Tax (VAT), which replaced Sales Tax, from state governments to the federal government. The federal government rationalised the action on the basis that these taxes do not fully satisfy the conditions required of them to be declared truly State taxes. In 1994 too, the Education Tax was introduced by the Federal Government which the federal level of government also retained it as its tax. From Table 1.2, the broad but various sources of revenue/taxes open to the three tiers of government in Nigeria are clearly evident. From the Table too, it is obvious that the buoyant revenue sources like import and excise duties, petroleum profit tax, mining rents and royalties, and company income tax, are under the jurisdiction of the federal government. Their placement under federal jurisdiction is largely a function of the preference of the fiscal efficiency criterion.

It is also evident from the Table that apart from personal income and sales taxes, both of which were originally assigned to the state governments, and property rates which belongs to the local governments but largely under-deployed, both the states and local governments have jurisdiction over minor and yet miscellaneous sources such as football pools and other betting taxes, entertainment tax, motor vehicle and drivers licence fees, land ground rent, market and trading licences and fees, and motor park dues which can hardly justify their collection as a result of their very poor yield.

The federal government does not only have jurisdiction over the major and lucrative sources of revenue but also accounts for the bulk of overall government revenue collected in Nigeria. For example, in 2004 out of ₦2, 813.8 billion collected by the three tiers of government, the federal government alone collected 94.4 per cent while state and local governments collected 4.8 and 0.8 per cent, respectively. Although a sizable proportion of the federal collection is shared with the lower tiers of government, fiscal federalism experience shows that fiscal concentration at the centre always threatens the stability of the federal system.[11] In Nigeria, the major source of this possibility is the rather excessive dependence of the lower levels of government on the centrally-collected funds.

Considering expenditure responsibilities, Table 1.3 shows that the arrangement tallies with the theoretical formulation which states that macro-services which indeed are the highest responsibilities should be borne by the federal government. The expenditure responsibilities of the various tiers of government derive from the constitution, which spells out functions of governments such as the maintenance of law and order as well as a range of functions connected with sectors of the economy.

Accordingly, the federal government has exclusive legislative responsibility with regard to 65 substantive functions including defence, banking, insurance, currency and immigration. The 12 items on the Concurrent List include allocation of revenue, antiquities and monument, archives and collection of taxes. These are functions over which the federal and state governments have shared or parallel responsibility. The local governments equally have their responsibilities spelt out. Thus, the federal government has overwhelming expenditure powers as it has over revenue jurisdiction. But as Olomola and Adewuyi [12] have observed, "the major problem in the discharge of the assigned responsibilities is the lack of coordination in the concurrent responsibilities leading to duplications, deprivations, discontinuities and wastage of resources".

Another problem is the contravention of the constitution concerning the inter-governmental disbursements of funds for meeting the expenditure responsibilities. One example is the maintenance by the federal government, until recently, of Special Funds and funding of priority projects. And very important, the domination of both revenue and expenditure by the federal government put the lower tiers of government in precarious financial conditions as they were unable to provide basic goods and services because of grossly inadequate financial resources, particularly at the times successively federal administrations were inclined to interpret the right to administer and collect revenue as synonymous with the right to appropriate it.

Table 1.3: Allocation of Expenditure Responsibilities in Nigeria

Responsible Level of Government	Expenditure Category
Federal Only	Defence Foreign Affairs International Trade include export marketing Currency, banking, borrowing, exchange control Use of water resources, shipping, federal trunk roads Elections Aviations, railways, postal service Police, and other security services Regulation of labour, interstate commerce, telecommunications, immigration Mines and minerals, nuclear energy, citizenship and naturalisation rights Social security, insurance, national statistical system (census, births, deaths, etc.) Guidelines and basis for minimum education, Business registration Price control
Federal-State (Shared)	Health, Social Welfare Education(post primary/technology) Culture Antiquities Monuments, archives Statistics, stamp duties Commerce, industry Electricity (generation, transmission, distribution) Research surveys
State Only	Residual power i.e. any subject not assigned to Federal or Local Government level by the consti-

	tution
Local Government	Economic planning and development Health Services Land Use Control and regulation of advertisement, pets, small businesses Markets, public conveniences Social welfare, sewage and refuse disposal, registration of births, deaths Marriages Primary, adult and vocational education Development of agriculture and natural resources

Sources: Adapted from Anyanwu, 1995

Vertical and Horizontal Financial Transfers

Vertical financial transfer refers to the transfer of funds from the central government to all the levels of government within a nation-state. It could be from a central pool. Viewed in terms of allocation, vertical revenue allocation focuses on how centrally pooled revenues are shared between the different levels of government. On the other hand, horizontal fiscal transfer or allocation refers to the sharing of the centrally allocated funds to each level of government among its constituents, e.g. among states or local governments. Vertical and horizontal revenue allocations have remained the centre-piece of inter-governmental fiscal relations; they have equally been a veritable source of long-standing controversy in the various attempts to establish a generally acceptable revenue sharing arrangement in the country. [13]

Evolution of Fiscal Transfers Principles

Over the years, in Nigeria, several commissions and committees have been set up to examine issues relating to appropriate strategies and formula for vertical and horizontal fiscal transfers. The various commissions/committees on revenue allocation, ranging from the Phillipson Commission (1946) to Okigbo (1980), Danjuma (1989) and Revenue Mobilisation, Allocation and Fiscal Commission (RMAFC) (2001), have articulated various principles for revenue allocation in the country. These principles have generally followed a common pattern with the notable exception of the Aboyade Commission's (1977) recommendations which marked a radical departure from the others.[14] For example, the principles with respect to horizontal fiscal transfers are as contained in Table 1.4 and grouped into equity and efficiency principles (Appendix 1 further shows the developments in horizontal revenue allocation in Nigeria). The equity principles range from derivation, population, need to even development and land mass. Their definitions tended to differ in the various reports. And according to Phillips,[15] many of the principles are defined in a rather vague manner. The imperative of competition over sharing national wealth in the context of a plural society has tended to prevent any meaningful operational definitions. The result has been either equal allocations or occasional arbitrary allocations in response to some specific pressures.

On the other hand, the efficiency principles have been more clearly defined. For instance, *"independent revenues"* refers to internally generated revenues while *"absorptive capacity"* refers to the ability of state governments to effectively utilise the resources made available to them. *"Tax efforts"* refers to the tax revenues raised by each state while *"fiscal efficiency"* refers to the efficient use of fiscal resources by each state. Our observation however, shows that since 1946, these efficiency principles have not really exceeded 30-35 percent of the allocation formula as government (both civilian and military) have been inclined to distrust the measurement criteria proposed by experts for the sharing. Most disturbing in this regard are the principles of *"absorptive capacity"* and *"fiscal efficiency"*. Thus, generally, since the early 1980s, the principles that have provided guidance to horizontal revenue allocation are equality of states (minimum responsibility of government), population, social development factor and internal revenue effort. These contrast, to some extent, with the earlier principles which emphasised derivation. Indeed, the derivation principle was applied fully up to the mid-1960s, perhaps, because as has been argued, the major tribes in the country benefited from it and the defunct Western Region was the major beneficiary.[16] The following summary shows the evolution of the various principles.

In 1946, the Phillipson Commission recommended *Derivation, Even progress* and *Population* as the key variables to determine allocation amongst the different regions. In 1951, the Hicks-Phillipson Commission emphasised *Derivation, Need* and *National Interest* as the key determinants for the sharing of the national cake. The Binns Commission of 1964 recommended *Basic Needs, Financial Comparability* (Need), *Even Development* and *Tax Effort* as the variables to be used, while in 1968, Dina recommended *Basic Needs, Minimum National Standard, Balanced Development* and *Derivation*. Aboyade in 1977 recommended *Equality of access to Development Opportunities; National Minimum Standards; Absorptive Capacity; Independent Revenue* and *Tax Effort; Fiscal Efficiency* as the variables to fall upon. In close sequence, Okigbo, in 1979, recommended *Minimum Responsibility of Government; Population; Social Development* and *Internal Revenue Effort* while Danjuma's permanent Commission of 1989 emphasised *Equality of States; Population; Social Development Factor; Tax Effort;* and *Land Mass*. Table 1.5 shows the status of the various principles from 1981. In the same way, Table 1.6 shows the evolution of the vertical revenue allocation formula with the federal government dominating the revenue allocation. Sometimes, during the military rule, a number of changes, courtesy of executive fiat, were introduced into the principles governing vertical revenue allocation. However, in 1988, in order to discontinue the ad hoc approaches to the unending dynamic problems of revenue allocation in Nigeria, a permanent Commission was created to monitor, review and advise the government on revenue allocation. This Commission is the National Revenue Mobilisation, Allocation and Fiscal Commission.

Table 1.4: Principles Determining Horizontal Fiscal Transfer in Nigeria

	Equity Principles	**Efficiency Principles**
i.	Derivation	Independent Revenue
ii	Population	Absorptive Capacity
iii	Equality of States	Tax Effort
iv	Need	Fiscal Efficiency
v	Even Development	
vi	Continuity of Government Services	
vii	Minimum Responsibility of Government	
viii	Equality of Access to Development	
ix	Minimum National Standard	
x	Financial Comparability	
xi	National Interest/Geographical Spread	
xii	Land Mass	
xiii	Ecological Problems	

Source: Adedotun A. Philips, "Managing Fiscal Federalism: Revenue Allocation Issues". In: Publius – The Journal of Federalism, Vol. 21, No 4, 1991 and updated by the authors.

Table 1.5: Horizontal Revenue Allocation Formula in Nigeria: 1981-1999

Principle	1981	1984	Jan. 1990	Jan. 1992	June 1992 - Dec. 1999
Equality of States	40%	40%	40%	40%	40%
Population	40%	40%	30%	30%	30%
Social Development Factor	15%	15%	20%	10%	10%
Internal Revenue Effort	5%	5%	10%	10%	10%
Land Mass and Terrain	=	=	=	10%	10%
Total	100	100	100	100	100

Source: Compiled by the authors from various Federal Government records for the respective years.

Table 1.6: Vertical Revenue Allocation Formula in Nigeria: 1981-1999

Levels of Government	1981	1984	Jan. 1990	Jan. 1992	June 1992 - Dec. 1999
Federal	55%	55%	50%	50%	48.5%
State	32.5%	32.5%	30%	25%	24%
Local	10%	10%	15%	20%	20%
*Special Fund	2.5%	2.5%	5%	5%	7.5%
Total	**100**	**100**	**100**	**100**	**100**

* **Note:** The Special Fund, administered by the President, takes care of ecological problems, funds to mineral producing areas as well as stabilisation of the economy

How Acceptable are the Revenue Sharing Principles?

What is clear is that the efforts of the various Commissions notwithstanding, an acceptable revenue allocation formula has yet to evolve, particularly with respect to the revenue allocation among the three tiers. The lower tiers of government, particularly the states have continued to express dissatisfaction, with the existing formula, which gives over 50 per cent of revenue to the federal government, about 26 per cent to the states and 20 per cent to local governments. Under the conditions in which the federal government's dominance of both tax jurisdiction, revenue and expenditure has resulted in only limited effectiveness of its expenditures, in terms of development outcomes, the case can be made for a downward review of the federal government's share of the Federation Account while the share of state governments is enhanced. Although this is not implying that state governments' expenditures are more effective, enhanced revenue allocation is one way to ensure equity and a viable fiscal federalism. The situation in which the federal government poses as *Father Christmas* and doles out matching grants and other forms of transfers to the lower tiers of government seriously undermines the evolution of true federalism.

Very importantly, the revenue allocation formula and principles have not given adequate incentives to the states and local governments to fully exploit their own internal sources of revenue. The principles have encouraged the sub-national governments to see their shares of the Federation Account as a "primary source" rather than as a supplement to whatever independent revenues they would have mobilised[17]. Indeed, some states and local governments found it more rewarding to concentrate their energies on attempting to obtain large grants from the federal government than attempting to raise more internal revenue[18]. The principles of equality of states and population, although related to equity, have not encouraged internal revenue efforts. Essentially, the observation made one and a half decades ago remains pertinent. It is that "the principles of horizontal revenue sharing are far from being economically optimum in the sense that they do not have any in-built mechanisms to propel any significant effort in internal/independent revenue mobilisation"[19]. This is worrisome more especially as, against the background of daily rising expectations and inadequate statutory fiscal transfers from the centre, many sub-national governments have experienced varying forms of fiscal stress and inability to meet their statutory responsibilities.

Revenue Profiles of the Governments

Available data show that all the tiers of government have continued to depend delicately and heavily on oil revenue which is passed through the instrumentality of statutory allocation to them from the Federation Account. Oil revenue accounted for 26 per cent of federally-collected revenue in 1970. But since the mid-1970s, it has accounted for over 70 per cent, being 86.0 per cent in 2004. All the levels of government depend on statutory allocation to the tune of over 70 per cent. In 2004, the federal government's dependence on the Federation Account was to the tune of 91.5 per cent. In that same year, state governments depended on statutory allocation from the Federation Account to the tune of 70 per cent having declined from 79.4 per cent in 1991.

A detailed consideration of the case of local governments reveals a number of features. (See Table 1.7 for the structure of local government revenue). It comprises all the sources of revenue into five distinct sources for a number of years, (i.e, 1993 to 2004). These sources are federal statutory allocation, state statutory allocation, VAT, internally generated revenue and grants. VAT was introduced and made a federally collected revenue source in 1994. Since then, the source has become the second highest income earner for Nigerian local governments. As shown in Table 1.7, the federal statutory allocation still occupied the primus place in their revenue sources. In 1993 and 1994, before the introduction of VAT, the federal statutory allocation accounted for 92.2 per cent and 90.1 per cent, respectively, in the revenue profile of local governments in Nigeria. But since the introduction of VAT, the tempo of this source of revenue in local government finances had reduced. As an illustration, in 1995, federal statutory allocation went down to 73.2 per cent. In 1996, it further went down to 71.9 per cent, 64.6 per cent in 1997 and 68.0 in 1998. By 2004, it stood at 80.2 per cent.

Trailing in the second position, the newly introduced VAT contributed 14.6 per cent to the revenue of Nigerian local governments in 1995. This percentage has risen steadily from year to year. In 1996, it rose to 19.8 per cent, 24.4 per cent in 1997, 22.6 per cent in 1998 and 25.0 per cent in 1999. It, however, declined to 9.8 per cent in 2004 to the advantage of federal statutory allocation.

Of note is the dwindling contribution of the state statutory allocation element of the revenue sources of local governments. Out of the eight years covered by Table 1.7, there was no single year it contributed up to 3 per cent to the total revenue. The highest it contributed was in 1996 when it contributed about 2.9 per cent to the local governments' revenue. The only plausible explanation for this trend is the persistent refusal of some state governments to honour this element of revenue to local governments. Even in states that manage to pay, they usually tie it to services performed for local governments whether such services are needed or demanded by them or not.

One other disturbing trend in the revenue pattern of Nigerian local governments is the dwindling contribution of the internally generated revenue element. Whereas this revenue source accounts for more than 50 per cent of the revenue of local governments in United Kingdom and United States of America, it only contributes between 4.8 per cent and 8.8 per cent to the revenue of local governments in Nigeria. Such a trend does not enhance local autonomy nor meaningful democracy at the grassroots.

The fifth element and, indeed, final element of the revenue sources is "grants and other sources". As shown in Table 1.7, the performance of this element is nothing to write home about except, perhaps, in 2004. It contributes between 0.2 per cent and 3.1 per cent to the revenue sources of Nigerian local governments. This trend is perhaps explained by the reluctance of the federal and state governments to give discretionary grants to local governments. It is believed that if they change their attitude in this regard, this source has immense potential for local government revenues.

Table 1.7: Summary of Local Government Revenue in Nigeria: 1993–2004 (₦ million)

	i	ii	iii	iv	V	
Revenue source	Federal Statutory allocation	State Statutory allocation	Value Added Tax (VAT)	Internally Generated Revenue	Grants and others	Total Current Revenue
1993 **(₦)**	18,316.4	253.1	0.0	1,035.6	269.4	19,874.5
%	92.2	1.3	0.0	5.2	1.3	100
1994 **(₦)**	17,321.3	466.4	0.0	1,205.9	229.5	19,223.1
%	90.1	2.4	0.0	6.3	1.2	100
1995 **(₦)**	17,875.5	625.4	3,558.1	2,110.8	242.9	24,412.7
%	73.2	2.6	14.6	5.6	1.0	100
1996 **(₦)**	16,569.7	691.1	4,581.7	2,027.1	72.5	23,042.1
%	71.9	2.9	19.8	5.5	0.3	100
1997 **(₦)**	20,066.3	688.3	7,586.1	2,515.6	202.0	31,058.3
%	64.6	2.2	24.4	5.00	0.6	100
1998 **(₦)**	30,620.9	750.4	10,170.8	3,331.6	94.5	44,968.2
%	65.0	1.7	22.6	7.4	0.2	100
1999 **(₦)**	36,746.9	719.2	13,903.9	4,047.8	594.2	56,012.0
%	66.0	1.3	25.0	7.2	1.0	100
2004 **(₦)**	375,656.3	3,625.7	45,985.2	22,407.5	14,537.5	468,295.2
%	80.2	0.9	9.8	4.8	3.1	100

Source: Central Bank of Nigeria (CBN): *Statistical Bulletin, and Annual Report and Statement of Accounts* (Various Issues).

Table 1.8 shows the formula for sharing VAT proceeds among the three tiers of government in Nigeria's federal set up. As for within the tiers of government, VAT is shared on the basis of three criteria: equality (50%); population (30%) and derivation (20%).

VAT has been immensely successful since it replaced Sales Tax, a state government tax. Should the VAT not therefore return to the states for equity reasons and if not, should the federal government charge such a high administrative fee for its collection? Secondly, the Government should consider, seriously, the exclusion of some essential services and public goods from the purview of the tax. Thirdly and finally, there are tongues wagging in our society that all possible avoidance and evasion holes have not been adequately blocked. All these issues need to be seriously addressed in order to achieve maximum results from this viable revenue source as well as improving on its efficiency and equity.

Table 1.8: Formula for Sharing VAT Revenue over Time

Tier of Government	Percentage Share				
	1994	1995	1996-97	1998	1999
Federal	20	50	35	25	15
Government	80	30	40	45	50
State Governments	-	20	25	30	35
Local Governments					
Total	100%	100%	100%	100%	100%

Source: Compiled by the authors from the records of the various years.

Fiscal Imbalances, System of Matching Grants and Resource Control

Dimensions of Fiscal Imbalances

Imbalances manifest in different forms in Nigeria's fiscal system. First, is the heavy and precarious dependence of the government budget on crude oil revenue and the instability of the international oil market. Second, are huge vertical imbalances reflecting the dominance of the federation's revenue by the federal government, both in terms of mobilisation and appropriation. This fiscal centralisation and the resultant financial incapacity of the sub-national governments have had two notable effects, one of which is the reinforcement of structural vulnerabilities of the states and local governments and their quest for federal economic patronage. The other is that the vertical imbalances in revenue allocation in favour of the central government encouraged the past governments, particularly the military, to usurp most of the normal functions of the lower tiers in the name of national unity. In this regard, the military governments assumed greater responsibilities through the states in the areas of education, health, housing, agriculture and water supply.

Besides the above, the outcomes of both the vertical and horizontal revenue allocation formulae applied over the years have shown gross imbalances between assigned functions and tax powers. Further analysis of fiscal imbalances underscores the federal government's dominant role in incurring expenditure besides its role in appropriating revenue. In the 1990s, the federal government accounted for about 75 per cent of total government expenditure, while state governments accounted for only 18 per cent and local governments about 7 per cent. And the share of expenditure followed an upward trend. Of course, as the federal share increased, the shares at the state level witnessed considerable decline. The lower expenditure shares of the lower tiers of government are incompatible with their actual and expected responsibilities[20].

A further consideration of even the lower expenditure shares with the shares of revenues reveals considerable fiscal deficits most of the time, over the years. Even the fiscal operations of the federal government that had the largest shares of total revenue have been characterised by huge deficits. The fiscal deficits of the lower tiers of government which have no access to Central Bank financing support the case for more revenue opportunities through control of more tax handles such as the VAT. Finally, with the current state of dissatisfaction with the level of development of the country, it appears that the concentration of fiscal responsibilities at the centre has been counterproductive. This again underscores the need to review tax jurisdiction and expenditure assignments in favour of the lower tiers of government.

Towards Redressing the Fiscal Imbalances

As stated above, although there is no where in the world where there is complete congruence between assigned functions and tax powers to deal with them, vigorous efforts need to be made by Nigeria's political leaders to search for an acceptable revenue allocation formula that would hopefully address the problems posed by the fiscal imbalances with a view to minimising the inevitable intergovernmental tension inherent in the trend. Towards this end, the following are suggestive.

a. Realignment of functions and Tax Powers

Realignment of functions and tax powers involves the shifting of functions to the level of government with "surplus revenue". However, a strict application of this method is always unsuccessful as it is antithetical to the principles that guide the allocation of expenditure functions and tax jurisdiction especially as the two roles are generally guided by different criteria. For instance, whereas geographical range of benefits and scale economies loom largely in functional allocation, administrative efficiency is primus in the assignment of tax powers. Thus, the suggestion being made concerning the realignment of functions and tax powers is that in order to redress the financial problems of the lower tiers of government arising from their structurally weak revenue bases, the VAT should be collected by the state governments with the accruing revenue shared with the local governments according to agreed criteria. And, in general, in order to ensure the stability of the Nigerian federation, the inter-tier distribution of jurisdiction over revenue sources, as Phillips has similarly argued,[21] should be adjusted in favour of state and local governments. This will put more money into their coffers and lessen the dominance of the fiscal structure by the federal government. Besides, greater financial empowerment of the lower tiers of government may also moderate the existing 'do or die' attitudes often associated with elections or appointment to federal positions of power.

b. Revenue Sharing Arrangement/Revenue Allocation

The assignment of responsibilities to each level of government on the basis of the level that is best suited to administer each revenue source most efficiently, rather than revenue powers being assigned on the basis of the responsibilities assigned to each level, has occasioned the non-correspondence problem between revenue sources and the responsibilities assigned to each tier. But then, it is undesirable for the federal government to arrogate to itself the role of *father christmas*. Therefore, there is the need for a review of the revenue allocation formula in favour of the lower levels of government so that they should not be waiting or 'begging' for hand-outs. The revenue allocation formula should be reviewed in such a way that the state governments receive not less than 33 – 35 per cent of the Federation Account.

Matching Grants and Issue of Fiscal Equalisation

In the light of the observed imbalances and inequalities in the distribution of resources in Nigeria's fiscal federalism, the need has been expressed by concerned stakeholders for a greater focus on equalisation. A suggestion made in this direction is the use of matching grants. The argument is that the system of matching grants can serve as an instrument to stimulate uniform development across the country. For this purpose, block grants can be made from the central government to the sub-national governments for equalisation. Specific matching grants can also be made to implement programmes and projects in the various sectors – education, health, infrastructure, water supply, etc.

Some of the Revenue Allocation Commissions recommended special funds are geared towards equalisation through grants. For example, the Dina Committee of 1968 recommended the establishment of a Special Grants Account to be disbursed to states on their application to a Planning and Fiscal Commission (to be established) based on the principles of tax effort, balanced development and national interest. But the Report upon which this recommendation was made, was not accepted by the Federal Military Government. Also, the Aboyade Commission Report of 1977, recommended the creation of a special grants account (3% from federal government's revenue share) to be administered by the federal government for the benefit of mineral producing areas and areas in need of rehabilitation from emergencies and disasters. Similarly, the Okigbo Commission Report (1980) recommended a revenue equalisation fund of 1.5 per cent among the revenue sharing formula. But the approved formula by the government sidelined this recommendation.

Nevertheless, in practice, there is evidence of specific grants from the federal government to the sub-national governments. In the early 1970s, when the reform of the Marketing Board System led to the reduction of the independent revenues of the state governments, they were compensated for the loss of revenue through grants. Thereafter, matching grants featured prominently, particularly during the military regimes, in the implementation of various sectoral projects. However, the system of matching grants in Nigeria tended to reflect arbitrariness, abuses and poor administration and poor outcomes. It was seen as an instrument of doling out economic patronages by the federal government on a discretionary basis and hence, it featured gross abuses and inefficiency. It was hardly formula-based; it was not output/performance-oriented. Also, the system did not provide national fora to build consensus on objectives and design of programmes. Besides, the system tended to increase the financial dependence of the sub-national governments on the federal government and aided fiscal centralisation. And very importantly, it portrayed the federal government as a *father christmas*, having too much financial resources at its disposal, thus revealing weaknesses in the basic revenue allocation formula.

The implication of this is that the importance of the system of matching grants will reduce in significance if the official revenue allocation formula provides for adequate financial resources to each tier of government and such resources are distributed equitably horizontally. Nevertheless, where matching grants have to be used, they must be based on objective criteria and guidelines in the context of transparency and accountability. The system of grants should be built into the revenue allocation formula and objectively and transparently implemented to achieve the objectives of reduced inequalities and balanced development.

Resource Control for Mutually Acceptable Intergovernmental Relations

Since 1999, when Nigeria again returned to democratic rule, the issue of resource control has assumed a significant dimension in national political discourse. Resource control arguments favour greater emphasis on the principles of derivation in revenue sharing. It is predicated on the need for those states/areas which account for the bulk of the revenues accruing to the Federation Account and which bear the "effluents" of baking the national cake to be given a larger piece of the cake. But arguments of equity and even development, among others, have been advanced to counter those of resource control. It is argued that unbridled use of derivation as a criterion for sharing out the economic fortunes of a nation accentuates regional inequalities[22]. Besides, it is contended that the principle of derivation has little or no place in a cohesive fiscal system for national and social development[23].

However, there are some merits in the resource control arguments, particularly as it relates to areas/regions where the extraction of natural resources leads to huge external costs in terms of environmental pollution, degradation, loss of farmland, water resources, and other means of livelihood, as is the case in the Niger-Delta region. However, the derivation principle in revenue allocation should not be stretched up to a point where it results in islands of affluence in some areas and islands of poverty in other areas. It needs to be applied up to the extent where it will not compromise the national goal of relatively even development. This is the development which will guarantee the provision of minimum development infrastructure and public goods to the different parts of the country. Generally, however, in revenue allocation, emphasis should be on the indices that emphasise tax/revenue generation efforts in order to encourage hard work and competition in revenue generation[24, 25].

The oil producing states had, for quite sometime, perhaps, until recently, always been out-manoeuvred in the politics of 'who gets what, when and how' in the revenue arrangement of the country. But conscious efforts need to be made to address the recurring problem of the oil producing Niger-Delta region. To this end, the restiveness in this region can be largely addressed if the percentage of derivation in the revenue accruing to them is significantly beefed up from the current 13 per cent. In this direction, the 25 per cent derivation revenue demanded by the representatives of the Niger-Delta region at the National Political Reform Conference in Abuja in 2005 is not out of place. This, of course, presumes the existence of good governance in the region to ensure judicious use of the enhanced revenue.

Concluding Remarks

Although federalism implies the sharing of the three "Ms", (i.e. men, money and material) among the various tiers of government for the purposes of pursuing the objectives of the nation-state, the problematics of the sharing are that equity and fairness are usually strange concepts in reality. In an improperly managed federal system, as the apparently higher/superior tier of government which is usually the central government takes the lion's share of everything, it tends to leave only the crumbs for the state and local governments. An outcome of this development is that peace and stability of the nation-state are threatened. Because of this pervasive development in most federations of the world, their sub-national entities have unconsciously transformed into deconcentrated units of the federal government at the periphery. If this trend continues unabated, the prospects of federalism anywhere become very bleak. One way out of this is effective co-ordination of the activities of the various tiers of government through mutually beneficial negotiations, compromise and mutual respect of the constitutional provisions setting up the various tiers of government. The trend in most federations is for a neutral agency comprising all the tiers of government to be set up to oversee such negotiation and co-ordination.

In order that Nigeria can adequately face the developmental challenges of the future, she must take certain fundamental but initial steps. Most critical in this regard is that Nigeria must be quickly returned to a truly democratic and true federal arrangement where every level of government will be free within the constitution to do its own thing, in its own way and at its own pace. Within this context, the country should evolve a revenue allocation formula that substantially rewards revenue generation efforts of the sub-national entities and by extension unconsciously eliminate the present cut-throat competition for political power in the country. Specifically, there is the need to realign functions and tax powers among the tiers of government such that the VAT, for example, reverts to the states. Also, the revenue allocation formula should be reviewed to provide more financial resources to the sub-national governments. Besides, matching grants may be used for purposes of fiscal equalisation and reduction of inequalities but under objective criteria and transparent conditions. Finally, fiscal federalism should ensure the financing of national development in such a way that weak and impoverished sub-national governments are not produced alongside a very strong and central government with surplus revenue.

NOTES AND REFERENCES

1. Wheare, K. C. *Federal Government* (4th ed.; London: Oxford University Press, 1963), p. 183.
2. Okigbo, P. N. C. *Nigerian Public Finance* (London: Longmans, 1965).
3. Anyanwu, J. C. "Revenue Allocation and Stable Fiscal Federalism in Nigeria" *Journal of Economic Management,* (Ibadan, 2: Oct. 1995).
4. Onimode, Bade, "Fiscal Federalism in Nigeria: Options for the 21st Century". *A Research Report,* (Ibadan: NISER, 2000), p. 15.
5. Gbayesola, T. O. and Uga, E. O. "Sources and Structure of Government Revenue". In: Komolafe, Oluranti,S., Jalilian, H. and Hiley, M. (ed.) *Fiscal Policy Planning and Management in Nigeria,* (Ibadan: NCEMA, 1999) p. 72 and Buchanan, J. M. "An Economic Theory of Clubs", *Economica* (February, 1965).
6. Wheare, K. C. *op. cit.*
7. Phillips, Adedotun O. "Managing Fiscal Federalism: Revenue Allocation

Issues" in *Publius, The Journal of Federalism*, Volume 21, No. 4, on *Federalism in Nigeria: Towards Federal Democracy*, edited by Ladipo Adamolekun; (Philadelphia: Bar Ilan University and Temple University, 1991).

8. A number of books and articles attest to the controversial nature of the issue. Some of them are Adebayo Adedeji, *Nigerian Federal Finance*, (London: Hutchinson Education, 1969), Adedotun Phillips, "Nigeria's Federal Financial Experience", *Journal of Modern African Studies*, 9,(October 1971), pp. 389 - 408; Adedotun Phillips, "Revenue Allocation in Nigeria, 1970-1990", *Nigerian Journal of Economic and Social Studies*, 17, (July 1975), pp. 1-28; Adedotun Phillips, "State Creation, Revenue Allocation and Nigeria's Development", *Management Development in Nigeria*, Vol.2, (Akure: Nigerian Institute of Management, 1984).

9. Olowononi, G. S. "The Political Economy of Revenue Allocation in Nigeria": In: Taiwo, I. O and A. A. Fajingbesi, ed. *Fiscal Federalism and Democratic Governance in Nigeria* (Ibadan: NCEMA, 2004).

10. Mbanefoh, Gini F. "An Unsettled Issue in Vertical Fiscal Adjustment in Nigeria: The Non-Correspondence Problem", *Annals of the Social Science Council of Nigeria*, (SSCN, Ibadan, Vol. 1, No. 4, 1994).

11. Phillips, A. O, *Nigeria's Fiscal Policy, 1998-2010*. NISER Monograph Series, No. 17, 1997.

12. Olomola, A. S and A. O. Adewuyi, "Public Spending Assignments in Nigeria". *Report of a Research Project, 2001.*

13. Abubakar, H. I. "Financial Transfers: Vertical and Horizontal Revenue Allocation". A Paper Presented at the National Seminar on Revenue Mobilisation, Organised by RMFAC in Enugu, April 21-23, 1992.

14. Abubakar, H. I. *op. cit.* p. 8.

15 Phillips, A. O, 1991, *op. cit.*

16. Olowononi, G. D. 2004, *op. cit.*

17. Abubakar, H. I, 1992, *op. cit.*

18. Olowononi, G. D, 2004, *op. cit.* p. 164.

19. Abubakar, H. I, 1992, *op. cit*, p.16.

20. Olomola and Adewuyi, 2001, *op. cit.*

21. Phillips. A. O, 1997, *op. cit.*

22. Abubakar, H. I, 1992, *op. cit*, p. 9.

23. Aboyade, O, *Report of the Technical Committee on Revenue Allocation* (Lagos: Federal Government Printer).

24. Bello-Imam, I. B. and Agba, A. V. "Fiscal Federalism, the National Question and Resource Control: Practice and Prospect" in Bello-Imam, I. B. and Obadan,M. I. (eds.) *Democratic Governance and Development Management in Nigeria's Fourth Republic, 1999-2003* (Ibadan: CLGARDS, 2004).

25. Obadan M. I (2006), "Fiscal Policy and Government Finances in Nigeria". Chapter 14 in a proposed book on the Nigerian Economy (unpublished).

Appendix I
Developments in Horizontal Revenue Allocation in Nigeria: 1946 – 2002

SN	Commission /Committee	Recommended Principles	Other Basic Features of Recommendation/Formula
1.	Phillipson, 1946	(i) Derivation (ii) Even progress	Balance after meeting Central Government budgetary needs allocated to Regions.
2.	Hicks-Philipson, 1951	(i) Derivation (ii) Fiscal autonomy (iii) Need (iv) National interest	Proportions of specified duties and taxes allocated to regions on the basis of derivation, special grants - capacitation, education and police.
3.	Chick, 1953	(i) Derivation (ii) Fiscal autonomy	Bulk of revenues from import duties and excises to the Regions on the basis of consumption and derivation.
4.	Raisman, 1958	(i) Derivation (ii) Fiscal autonomy (iii)Balanced development	Proportions of specified revenues distributed on the basis of derivation. Creation of distributable pool account (DPA) with fixed Regional proportional shares: North, 40 percent; West, 31 per cent; East, 24 per cent and Southern Cameroons, 5 per cent.
5.	Binns, 1964	Same as (4) above plus financial comparability	Composition of DPA relative shares slightly altered: North 40 per cent; East, 30 per cent; West 20 per cent and Mid-West 8 per cent.
6.	Decree No. 15, 1967	Same as (5) above.	Regional proportional shares of the DPA split among the 12 new states. 6 Northern States received 7 per cent each. East and Western States shared in accordance with relative populations.
7.	Dina, 1968	(i) Even development (ii) Derivation (iii) Need (iv) Minimum responsibility of government	Special Grants Accounts introduced, recommended the establishment of a permanent Planning and Fiscal Commission. Recommendations rejected.
8.	Decree No. 13, 1970	(i) Population (50%) (ii) Equality of States (50%)	Export duties to States reduced from 100% to 30%; duty on fuel to States reduced from 100% to 50% mining rents and royalties to States reduced from 50% to 45%.
9.	Decree No. 9, 1971	(i) Same as (8) above	Transferred rents and royalties of off-shore petroleum mines from the States to

SN	Commission /Committee	Recommended Principles	Other Basic Features of Recommendation/Formula
			the Federal Government.
10.	Decree No. 6, 1975	Same as above	On-shore mining rents and royalties to States reduced from 45 to 20 per cent. Remaining 80% go to the DPA. Import duties on motor spirit and tobacco to be paid 100% into DPA. 50% of the excise duties retained by Federal Government, 10% to DPA.
11.	Aboyade, 1977	(i) Equality of access 0.52% (ii) National minimum standards 0.22% (iii) Absorptive capacity 0.20% (iv) Independent revenue 0.18% (v) Fiscal efficiency 0.15	Replaced DPA with federation account. Fixed proportional share out of this account between Federal, 75%; State 30%, Local Governments, 10% and Special Fund 3%. State Joint Accounts and Local Government Joint Account created.
12.	Okigbo, 1980	(i) Population 40% (ii) National minimum standards 40% (iii) Social development 15%, Internal revenue 5%	Federation Account to be shared; Federal Government, 53%; State Governments, 30%; Local Governments, 10%, Special Fund, 7%.
13.	1981 Act	Same as (12) above	Federation Account shares: Federal Government, 55%; State Governments, 30.5%; Local Government, 10%; ecological problems 1%, development of mineral producing areas, 1.5% derivation, 2%
14.	Decrees No. 36, 1984	Same as (13 above but social development (primary school enrolment: direct, 11.25%, inverse, 3.75%).	Federation account to be shared: Federal Government, 55%; State Governments, 32.5%; (out of which 2% went for derivation); Local Governments, 10%; ecological problems 1%; development of mineral producing areas, 1.5% (Special Funds: 2.5%).
15.	Danjuma, 1989	(i) Equality of States 40% (ii) Population 30%	Federation Account to be shared: Federal Government, 47%; State Governments, 30%; Local Governments 15%; Special Fund (8%); FCT, 10%; Stabilization 0.5%;

SN	Commission /Committee	Recommended Principles	Other Basic Features of Recommendation/Formula
		(iii) Social development 10% (iv) Internal revenue effort 20%	savings, 2%; derivation, 2%; development of non-oil mineral producing areas, 0.5%; general ecology, 0.5%
16.	AFRC Approval, Jan. 1990	(i) Equality of States 40%, Population 30% (ii) Social development (iii) 10% (Education 4%; Health 3%; Water 3%) (iv) Landmass and terrain 10% (v) Internal revenue effort 10%	Federation Account shared: Federal Government 50%; State Governments 30%; Local Governments, 15%, Special Fund (5%). FCT 1%; stabilization, 0.5%; derivation, 1%; development of oil mineral-producing areas, 1.5%; general ecology, 1%.
17.	AFRC Approval, Jan. 1992	Same as (16) above	Same as (16) above except that State Governments (25%) and Local Governments (20%).
18.	AFRC Approval, Jan. 1992	Same as (17) above	Federation Account Shared: Federal Government, 48.5%; State Government, 24%; Local Governments (20%); special fund (7.5%): FCT, 1%; stabilization 0.5%; derivation, 1%; development of oil mineral producing areas, 3%; general ecology, 2%.
19.	NRMAFC /President Obasanjo, 2001*	Not available	Federation Account Sharing Federal Government 41.5% State Governments 31.0% Local Governments 16.0% Others 11.5% The 11.5% i.e. others was to be shared as follows Basic Education 7% Agriculture & Solid Minerals 1% Ecology 1% Scientific Research & Development 1% Federal Capital Territory 0.5% National Reserve Fund 1.0%

Source: Compiled by the authors from the various revenue allocation formulae published by the Federal Government

* This revenue allocation bill was not approved and was overtaken by the Resource Control suit. Even the second one proposed by President Obasanjo as a fence mending exercise became mired by the fall-outs of the Supreme Court verdict. Thus at as December, 2003 the country does not have a revenue allocation formula.

CHAPTER 7

INTERGOVERNMENTAL RELATIONS IN NIGERIA: IMPROVING SERVICE DELIVERY IN CORE SECTORS

Lev Freinkman

Introduction

Nigeria's model of fiscal federalism represents a fundamental legal and institutional framework for policymaking in the country. As in other federations, it defines the core rules for resource allocation, distribution of responsibilities for service delivery, and mechanisms for interaction between different tiers of government.

Nigeria's fiscal federalism arrangements are currently attracting increasing attention from both policymakers and analysts. This is a reflection of the fact that longer term perspectives of economic policy reform in the country are critically dependent upon improvements in the organization of inter-governmental arrangements. Such arrangements have direct implications for achieving national growth and poverty reduction targets. Simply put, there is a major need to strengthen the incentives of government agencies at all levels of authority to improve cooperation in designing of their policies and delivery of services. At the same time, capacity will have to be built to support such future inter-governmental cooperation.

The need for stronger cooperation and other reforms in federalism is driven by several factors such as the following:

a) According to the Nigerian constitution, main public sector responsibilities are split across various government levels. Thus, no sole government could deliver radical improvements in service delivery on its own, which means that *coordination and cooperation* are pre-requisites. However, the existing mechanisms and institutions for inter-governmental policy coordination are weak and need strengthening.
b) Significant fiscal decentralization of the public finance system have taken place since 1999. Given the existing resource allocation rules, such decentralization poses the risk of emphasizing–rather than taming - fiscal inequalities across the states. But the extent and trends in

horizontal inequality remains undocumented, and no mitigation mechanism has been proposed as yet.
c) Reforms undertaken in Nigeria since 2003 appear to have been more profound at the federal level than in the states. The benefits of drastic improvements in macroeconomic policies and fiscal discipline at the Federal Government of Nigeria (FGN) level are severely constrained by lagging reforms in the states. The FGN is actively exploring options for setting up—within its existing legal and institutional remits—new mechanisms to encourage states to accelerate reforms and to improve intergovernmental coordination in key service areas under joint responsibility.
d) the reform of federal arrangements is politically sensitive. Reforms of the Federal system are likely to be gradual and based on broad political consensus. This underlines a need for broadening a public debate on key challenges in the existing model of fiscal federalism. The post-2007 election period may present a window of opportunity for addressing some of these issues, and it is important to inform policy makers in advance about existing challenges and available choices.

This paper intends to discuss some of these issues from the perspective of improvements in the quality of service delivery in core sectors, such as education and health.

Insufficient Coordination in the Environment of Growing Inequality

Nigeria's constitution provides for the participation of all three tiers of government in the delivery of core public services, such as education and health. This makes policy coordination an important precondition for effective and efficient service delivery. Several factors can be adduced as justification for building workable inter-governmental coordination mechanisms. As an illustration:

a. in the environment of shared responsibility for service delivery, non-coordinated interventions of different government levels create a risk for duplication of efforts and sub-optimal allocation of resources.
b. when there is an agreement on common national priorities and development objectives, such as those reflected in the National Economic Empowerment and Development Strategy (NEEDS), it is sensible for all government levels to align their actions with such priorities and thus complement each other's efforts. This is because, as in common complex social systems, there is significant potential for synergies between coordinated policies and actions.

c. finally, there is a case for the standard efficiency argument. Coordination could lead to better overall resource utilization through economy of scale, quicker project completion, and more efficient use of limited resources (such as specialized technical expertise). It also helps to facilitate dissemination of best management practices.

What are the policy parameters that may be of special interest for governments that are interested in better policy coordination? The following list, while far from being comprehensive, presents some important components:

i.level and structure of government spending in a particular sector.
ii.technical and quality standards of service delivery, such as curricular and educational standards, as well as immunization rules.
iii.expected levels of service delivery, such as the availability of health services (measured for instance through number of health personnel per 10,000 residents).
iv.management practices (e.g. parameters used for cost-benefit analysis of proposed public projects).
v.reporting and accountability formats to ensure comparability of outcomes across different locations, which would support monitoring of progress towards achieving national policy priorities.

The issue of intergovernmental policy coordination has become increasingly important in Nigeria in recent times. This is primarily because since 1999 the Nigerian fiscal system has gone through rapid decentralization (Figure 1). Compared to the recent past, a much larger portion of public funds today is spent on the basis of independent, non-coordinated decisions of individual state and local governments. The share of sub-national budget spending in the consolidated budget doubled, increasing from 23 percent in 1999 to 46 percent in 2005. Total sub-national budget expenditure in 2005 was almost four times higher in real terms than the 1999 level. Moreover, spending by local government authorities (LGAs) has been growing even faster than state government spending, which means that sub-national budget systems have become increasingly decentralized.

Figure 1. Real growth in government expenditure, 1999-2005, 1999=100%

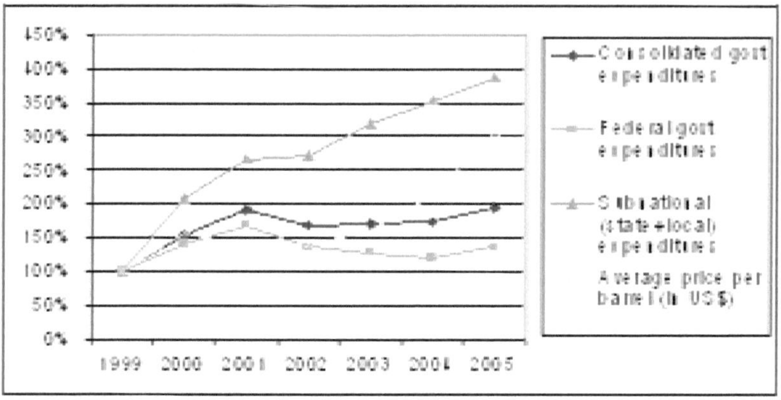

Note: Includes off-budget spending, such as cash calls and excess crude account.
Source: World Bank (2007)

The main drivers of such rapid decentralization can be summarized as follows: (*World Bank*, 2007):

a. stricter enforcement of constitutional requirements; in particular, since the return to the civilian rule, the FGN has been much more disciplined in enforcing the existing revenue sharing rules than was the case in the 90s;
b. restoration of the derivation principle in the 1999 Constitution;
c. Supreme Court decisions of 2002 that reduced the size of the first line deductions from the Federation Account (FA); and
d. some adjustment in FA allocation shares since 2002 that favored sub-national governments.

Rapid expenditure decentralization has created both new opportunities and challenges for public service delivery in Nigeria. Given that Nigerian sub-national governments are mainly responsible for financing basic public services such as primary health and education, decentralization creates the potential for further improvements in the financing of these priority sectors. At the same time, due to well-known capacity constraints at the sub-national level, this expansion in financing creates a substantial risk of a decline in spending efficiency. It also increases the risk of misuse of funds due to slower pace of public finance management (PFM) reforms in states. So far, fiscal decentralization in

Nigeria has not been accompanied by strengthened accountability of sub-national governments for efficient utilization of resources they have now in their disposal. This complicates progress in improving service delivery.

The costs of non-coordinated policies are further aggravated by Nigeria's rather rapid fiscal expansion and by the favorable oil prices of the world market. It is estimated that in 2005-07 total expenditures of the consolidated government in Nigeria (that includes spending of all government levels and extra-budgetary government accounts) in real terms will be growing at an average rate that exceeds 12% a year.

Existing arrangements for Intergovernmental Policy Coordination

Technically, Nigeria has the full set of institutions necessary to support policy coordination at both the macro and sector levels. Such existing structures are set up at four different administrative levels and these include:

a)National Council for Economic Planning that has state governors as members
b)National Council on Development Planning with a membership of State Commissioners for Planning
c)Joint Planning Board, in which states are represented at the level of Permanent Secretaries from respective planning ministries
d)National Sectoral Councils in all key sectors, representing respective state sectoral ministers and in which the National Planning Commission (NPC) is also represented
e)In addition, NPC has a statutory mandate for monitoring state economic performance and inter-governmental policy coordination.

Overall, these existing arrangements for policy coordination between the federal and state governments remain quite weak. While there have been regular meetings of various councils and due preparation of joint plans, to large extent, the prevailing coordination effort remains at the level of coordination of plans, but not of actual implementation activities. As such, coordination has been often seen as a "paper exercise", which does not have a real impact on either actual project selection or budget spending patterns of state governments. Effectiveness of national sectoral councils is low, and they are seen by many as just "talking shops" for participating officials.

The key indication of existing weaknesses in current coordination arrangements relates to the fact that Nigeria does not have an established system for production of consolidated national reports on performance in individual sectors. At the moment, due to lack of the most basic information on performance of individual governments, nobody can tell, for example, how much money the consolidated Nigerian government spends on primary education, what the structure of this spending is, and what is achieved with these expenditures. A lack of information on outcomes and outputs undermines the whole concept of planning and coordination. Planning without monitoring and evaluation cannot be productive. If actual behavior is not monitored, participants will not take seriously the commitments they make in the course of the planning and coordination phase.

Insufficient information sharing across various governments represents a fundamental weakness of the existing inter-governmental arrangements in Nigeria. Many state governments interpret the concept of state autonomy in a way that complicates information sharing and coordination with the federal government, while the FGN currently has inadequate capacity and policy instruments to encourage states to engage in federal initiatives. This seriously complicates the development of modern evidence-based national policies, in particular in the Millennium Development Goals (MDGs)-related sectors.

The following list points to several specific examples of economic losses due to weak inter-governmental coordination:

> *i) Primary Health:* Federal Government has been investing in construction of new primary health centers (PHCs), but states do not provide adequate financing for their operations. As a result, these facilities are heavily underutilized. At the same time, states spend an increasingly large portion of their health budgets on construction and operation of hospitals, which the Constitution defines as federal responsibility.
> *ii) Water:* All three government levels have been engaged in uncoordinated activity to drill new boreholes, and this frequently resulted in duplication of efforts. At the same time, there has not been much interest in the development of local water systems.
> *iii) Roads:* The national road network has been developed in an uncoordinated way, with too much political influence over technical decisions on priority road projects. Moreover, the lack of an agreed strategic vision resulted in under-financing of maintenance of the existing

roads, their over-use, and the poor quality of roads which drive up the costs of domestic transportation.

Issues of Intergovernmental Coordination in Education

Primary education represents an important and interesting example of the status of inter-government coordination in Nigeria. Sectoral analysis reveals nine out of 12 key management functions in the sector are concurrent, i.e. expected to be delivered by more than one government level. Thus, the sector has enormous needs for effective coordination arrangements. This challenge has been taken quite seriously by the sector leadership. According to a recent Department for International Development (DFID) report, based on cross-sectoral analysis, the existing arrangements in primary education currently represent the best example of vertical inter-government coordination *(Improving Intergovernmental Collaboration…, 2005).*

Still, there is a major need for further improvement. In education, similar to other sectors, more attention is paid to coordination of plans than to coordination of their execution. Moreover, the coordination effort is unevenly distributed across various management functions, with some functions being more popular than others. As a result, on one side, there is a noticeable duplication of efforts in some areas (school construction, school supervision) while insufficient attention to others (pre-school education, analysis/evaluation of sector performance).

Another weakness of the current arrangements in education relates to lack of clarity in the accountability framework. It is unclear which government level is responsible for achieving key educational outcomes. There are also major concerns about interactions between the Universal Basic Education Commission (UBEC), a federal structure created to support primary education nationwide, and state ministries of education. There has been a common claim that instead of supporting state efforts to upgrade primary education, UBEC has been trying to run the primary school network without showing much interest in building state capacity to manage its primary education *(World Bank, 2003)*. This undermines longer-term sustainability of the recent reform efforts.

An important function of UBEC relates to the administration of federal matching grants to states in support of primary education. This specific grant scheme has been an important innovation in Nigeria's system of intergovernmental fiscal arrangements. The analysis suggests, however, that the UBE grant program has serious challenges that led in recent years to under-utilization of available program funding. The reasons for such difficulties could be summarized as following:

a) insufficiently strong interest of state governments to improve service delivery undermines their incentives to participate effectively in the program;
b) state governors' concern of becoming dependent on unpredictable sources of federal financing. Governors require greater assurance that a transfer program of this nature is protected from potential political manipulation;
c) the way UBEC runs its business, similar to many other federal parastatals, antagonizes many state government officials. There is insufficient consultation, reflection of local priorities in project selection, and no real desire to engage local officials in implementation and monitoring;
d) insufficient availability of information on actual performance of the UBE program, which limits opportunities for its reform.

Moreover, there is a sign of inadequate policy coordination even among federal entities operating in the education sector, such as the Federal Ministry of Education on one side, and UBEC and Education Trust Fund (ETF) on the other. An example is the latest government strategy document in the sector, the 2007-9 Education MTSS, which did not cover funding administered by the UBEC or ETF. These organizations continue to claim their policy independence from the federal government.

Finally, an additional area where there is clear need for strengthening inter-governmental coordination in education relates to the framework for resource allocation in the sector. The World Bank (2003) points to an absence of transparent rules for resource allocation based on clear national guidelines and recommended norms of per student spending, differentiated by type of educational facility. Lack of such rules leads to major horizontal expenditure inequalities within the education system, at the level of both individual schools and states. Within the current system, there is no clear strategy to address horizontal inequalities in education financing.

Summary: Institutional Challenges in the area of Intergovernmental Coordination

Overall, the institutional challenges for more efficient intergovernmental coordination can be summarized as follows:

> a) federal government entities do not have capacity and an effective mandate to monitor and coordinate state performance. It does not have practical instruments at its disposal to influence states' project and spending choices.
> b) states' leaders perceive themselves as "independent to the extreme", with rather weak interest in information sharing and participation in joint projects. Broad powers guaranteed to states by the Constitution in policy making and expenditure allocation policy are seen as a mandate for non-cooperation. This is aggravated by generally weak accountability of sub-national governments.
> c) there is a critical lack of information on governments' performance. However, without adequate information, it is impossible to design and operate an efficient coordination mechanism. Three types of informational problems should be highlighted in this context:
> *i) Critical information is not produced on a regular basis.* It is worth noting that this challenge is broadly recognized by the government, and major effort has been underway to build capacity of the National Bureau of Statistics (NBS). Major recent achievements include the completion of the population census and national poverty survey. However, less progress has been made so far to improve quality and availability of information on expenditure pattern and quality of service delivery.
> *ii) Information is available, but it is of poor quality and does not meet recognized international standards.* For instance, Nigeria's budget data are largely incomparable with those from other countries because of fundamental weaknesses in the existing budget classification.
> *iii) Information is produced, but not made publicly available.* In part, due to the legacy of military rule, there is considerable reluctance to share information on government performance. As an illustration, the reports of Auditors-General are commonly seen to be "too sensitive" to be made publicly available. The recently prepared Freedom of Information Bill is expected to improve the situation in this area.

Insufficient availability of good social and fiscal information has major implications for government policy. It greatly undermines efficiency of policymaking in general by isolating policy deliberation from realities on the ground. It has particularly grave implications for a design of the system of inter-governmental fiscal arrangements. International experience suggests that quality information is a key precondition for establishing a transparent and mutually acceptable system of sharing a common pool of fiscal resources across different government levels.

Moreover, lack of comparative information on state performance greatly limits inter-state competitive pressures to improve service delivery. In Nigeria, state authorities do not face much of competitive pressure to perform, and this represents under-utilization of a major potential advantage of federal system – competitive federalism.

Risk of growing Fiscal Inequality

The benefits of recent fiscal decentralization have been distributed rather unevenly across sub-national governments. This is because, in keeping with the constitutional requirements, about a third of all allocations from the Federation Account to states reflects derivation oil payments, which are heavily concentrated. The four main oil-producing states (Rivers, Bayelsa, Delta, and Akwa Ibom) jointly received about 90 percent of all derivation oil payments, or about ₦265 billion (US$2 billion) in 2005. The fact that despite all these additional revenues, the oil producing states of Nigeria did not perform much better than the rest of the country in terms of service delivery and human development indicators suggests that major efficiency gains still remain available through improvements in the expenditure management and accountability systems of these states.

The existing level of inequality in the Nigeria's fiscal system is rather high and has been growing recently due to high oil prices. Table 1 presents some estimates of cross-state inequality in the distribution of funds collected by the federal government, (i.e. what is usually called "federal transfers" in other federal systems). Since such transfers form about 90% of all revenues in most states, these inequalities reflect rather accurately overall inequality in per capita budget expenditures at the state level.

Table 1. Cross-state variation in total statutory allocation per capita,
(Naira thousand, a sum of allocations from the Federation Account and VAT)

	2001	2005
Average allocation per capita	3.11	8.28
Coeff. of variation	62.4%	105.3%
Max/Min ratio	8.80	17.38
Share of 4 oil states in total	25.5%	34.0%

Source: *CBN, Population Census*
Note: Based on the 2006 population data as reported by the National Population Commission.

As Table 1 shows, the difference in per capita transfers between the wealthiest and poorest states increased from about 9 times in 2001 to more than 17 times in 2005. While four richest states, which collectively host only about 11% of Nigerian population, received a quarter of all transfers in 2001, their share increased to more than a third in 2005. Figure 2 presents the full scale of variation in per capita transfers in 2005.

Figure 2. Variation in the level of per capita transfers, 2005,
(N thousand, a sum of Federation Account allocations and VAT)

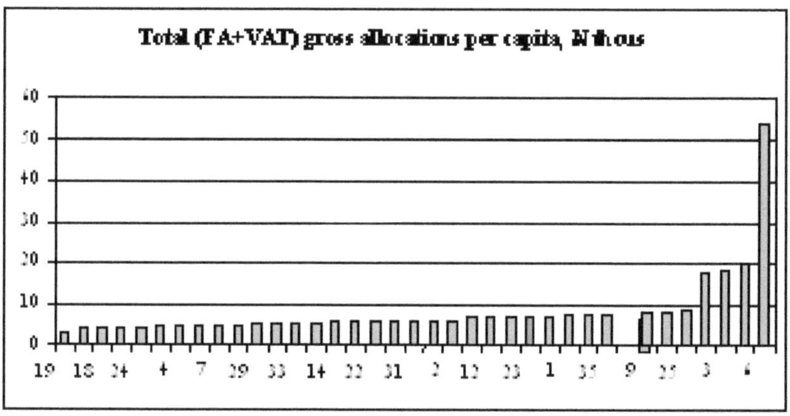

Note: The Red column indicates a national average level of per capita allocation.

The reasons for such a high level of inequality are quite clear. It is because the existing formula for horizontal allocation of revenues pays insufficient attention to equity considerations. The following features of the existing federal allocation arrangements are important to mention in this context:

a. 54% of federation account funds are distributed equally across states, which works against more populous states
b. huge derivation premium, as discussed above, which primarily benefit only four states
c. no attention to local revenue capacity of individual states
d. small share (2.5%) of funds is distributed proportionally to local revenue effort, which usually works as a penalty on poor states that have less opportunities to increase their revenue collections

Overall, rapid expenditure decentralization poses a risk of growing inequality across the states, especially with respect to the quality and availability of social services. Moreover, as international experience suggests, high level of horizontal inequality may bring additional political risks. To be able to achieve its national development targets, in particular with respect to MDGs, the federal government will need to develop its capacity for monitoring cross-state differences in access to core social services and at some point expand federal equalization programs to provide additional opportunities to citizens in less developed states.

Reform Directions to Strengthen Inter-Governmental Policy Coordination

Our analysis so far suggests that without better inter-governmental coordination it would be difficult for Nigeria to make sustainable progress in the attainment of the MDGs. This is primarily because, while states and local governments have major responsibilities for MDG-related sectors, without closer cooperation with the federal government, they would not be able to secure adequate funding and necessary improvements in the quality of service delivery. Some states are just too poor and do not have enough resources to provide adequate funding for MDG-related activities due to the inequality in the existing system of resource distribution. At the same time, many states, including those that have a better funding base, do not use their resources in line with national priorities, in particular in such areas as primary education, health, and rural development. Moreover, overall nationwide progress is affected by the loss of efficiency due to duplication of efforts by different governments.

To address these challenges, Nigeria's inter-governmental arrangements may require a thorough review and comprehensive reform in line with the international best practices and Nigeria's own experiences. So far, there has been considerable imbalance in discussions on what is necessary to make Nigeria's fiscal federalism more effective. Discussions focus on issues of resource control and on arguments in favor of further re-distribution of resources from the federal to state governments rather than on better utilization of available resources. Similarly, there is surprisingly little interest in the equity dimension of the resource control problem.

New more Cooperative Models of Service Delivery

There is a need to build a broader consensus around the idea that a new, more cooperative model of inter-governmental relations is necessary to ensure better utilization of available resources. Such a model should include the following key elements:

a) jointly developed policies in the sectors of recurrent responsibility;
b) real coordination in implementation, including project selection and spending levels;
c) joint monitoring and evaluation;
d) disclosure of results;
e) encouragement of competition in service delivery.

The new model would also suggest that the FGN should gradually withdraw from the actual delivery of services and instead play a more active role in setting national policy, in co-financing of service delivery undertaken by lower government levels, and in monitoring and evaluation of actual performance.

Two directions for reform

To ensure progress towards a new model, reforms should be undertaken simultaneously in two inter-related directions:

(i) inter-governmental finance, and (ii) improved institutional framework.

With respect to *inter-governmental finance*, the existing system of sharing the common pool of funds may need careful and gradual transformation to provide for (i) more equalization of the system, and (ii) introduction of new financing mechanisms, such as federal matching, conditional, and specific grants to states. The latter are necessary to encourage states to align their interests in line with national priorities, influence states' choices, and strengthen their accountability for spending public money.

With respect to the institutional framework, the immediate priority is to strengthen the effectiveness of existing coordinating institutions, based on their functional review. The recent report sponsored by the DFID *(Improving Intergovernmental Collaboration…, 2005)* could be used as a starting point in this work. A possible strategy could be based on (i) consolidating/rationalizing the existing set of institutions, and (ii) providing the NPC with a bigger and clearly defined mandate for intergovernmental policy coordination. The latter may include responsibility for design and execution of different federal grant schemes, monitoring and evaluation of performance of such schemes, support for sector-specific coordination structures, as well as coordination of various federal efforts to accelerate state level reforms linked to state capacity building and dissemination of best local practices and others. The NPC should also lead the work on developing a set of requirements for effective implementation of joint expenditure programs, including administrative, legal, financial and reporting requirements.

There is also a need for a critical review of governments' expenditure mandates under the current arrangements. Its purpose would be the development of options for their gradual adjustment in light of international experience. As an illustration, in the health sector, the analysis suggests a need for a larger role of the federal government in primary health, health insurance, and disease prevention.

Another priority direction for institutional strengthening relates to improvements in the accountability framework, based on better information on how public money are used and data on quality of service delivery. As emphasized by Paul Collier (2006), a preferable institutional arrangement in ethnically diverse societies with resource rents, such as Nigeria, is a democracy with decentralized public spending and unusually strong checks and balances. So far, Nigeria has been doing pretty well with respect to expenditure decentralization, but accountability of government officials remains generally weak, despite the reform efforts of the last few years.

Overall, the transition to the new model of inter-governmental arrangements would require strong federal agencies capable of performing *inter alia* the following functions:

a) participatory development of sectoral strategies, establishment of clear regulatory framework for service delivery
b) establishment of national targets for service delivery
c) costing national strategies and their main components
d)drafting model state-level laws and regulations (where appropriate) and encourage states to adopt them (such as disclosure, reporting, and monitoring rules)
e) designing and delivery of federal technical assistance programs for states, helping states to develop their own efficient strategies and implementation arrangements
f) monitoring of progress in the key sectors, including support for independent evaluation of state performance and spending of FA allocations in the context of SEEDS benchmarking

A separate important federal function within the new model, which would be relatively new for Nigeria, relates to federal support to states with implementation of their sectoral reforms. International experience suggests that such support could be the most effective if it is aimed at providing a mix of federal incentives to states, including financial assistance (grants), political support, and technical assistance. To consolidate federal reform-related assistance to sub-national governments, several countries use a State Reform Assistance Fund mechanism.

International Perspective on Reforms in Federal Transfers

Intergovernmental finance systems worldwide show several stable common patterns, which could be easily explained on the basis of efficiency considerations. One of such patterns is significant asymmetry in expenditure and revenue-raising responsibilities. This results in a gap between relatively high centralization in revenue collection and much more decentralized pattern of public spending *(Vigneault, 2007)*. Such asymmetry explains a need to design an efficient system of federal transfers that would return a portion of centrally collected revenues back to lower levels of government to help them finance their expenditure mandates.

Another common pattern in intergovernmental finance is that expenditure responsibilities are pretty similar worldwide. States (subnational governments) are usually responsible for the provision of key public services, including basic health, education, social protection, roads, etc. And many of such state responsibilities, as assigned by national constitutions, are such that they are critical for achieving core national development objectives. This implies that the federal government has considerable interest in the manner in which the regions exercise their legislative responsibilities (*Broadway, 2007*). That is, the federal government is interested in the level of states' service delivery and quality of delivered services. It is expected to monitor sufficiency of resources allocated to services of national importance and try to influence state expenditure choices.

In addition to the need to ensure the achievement of national/common development objectives, the main reasons for such an "interventionist" position of the federal government include:

> *a) Equity argument:* the federal government has responsibility for equalizing the level of public service delivery across locations that have equal levels of taxation, and more generally equalize local opportunities for growth.
> *b) Efficiency argument:* that relates to a spillover effect of public services, and respectively to possible under-supply of services produced on the basis of decentralized decisions.

Within this framework, it is broadly acknowledged that development and implementation of national poverty alleviation programs should be a joint responsibility of different government levels. The federal government is supposed to provide most of the funding and set up general rules, while day-to-day implementation should be done by sub-national governments *(Rao, 2002b)*.

Respectively, federal grants to states are seen as a common instrument to improve efficiency of inter-governmental cooperation. They are used by federal governments to influence states' resource allocation and encourage them to improve financing of key services in line with national priorities. They do not mean a subordination of one government level to another, while instead aim at aligning interests and strengthening government cooperation. Sato (2007) calls intergovernmental transfers "glue for national unity". In particular, programmes of specific grants, linked to particular sectoral programmes/services, if properly set up, could provide for both budget autonomy of grant recipients and securing that additional funding is concentrated in key policy areas.

The main lessons from international experience on design of grant schemes could be summarized as following (Shah, 2007):

i) keep it simple
ii) aim at a single objective in each grant programme
iii) undertake periodic review of programme relevance
iv) build national consensus on objectives and design of grant programmes
v) combine (i) block grants to equalize fiscal capacity, using explicit standard of revenue potential with (ii) specific program-linked grants to equalize differences in needs
vi) avoid multi-factor formulae for fiscal equalization
vii) make grants output (not input) oriented at achieving minimum national standards in access to public services

In addition, to become sustainable, grant mechanisms need to be institutionalized and based on a clear legislative framework to ensure that it is implemented in a transparent and predictable way, and the federal government cannot manipulate the system in support of its own political agenda.

Recent Policy Developments in Nigeria

In Nigeria, there has been a gradual building of consensus that the federal government should start the withdrawal from the actual delivery of services and play a more active role in setting national policy, financing of priority services and monitoring. While there is no developed blue print to operationalize this strategy, the government has accumulated important practical experience under the Universal Basic Education (UBE) scheme. Further, as part of the 2007 budget cycle, the FGN has designed a new conditional transfer scheme.

In particular, as part of 2007 federal budget, the following new federal grant schemes were approved and should be seen as pilots, which if successful could be scaled up later:

a) *Conditional grants (N20 bn):* to support eligible state projects in primary health, rural electrification, and rural water supply and sanitation based on the approved federal guidelines
b) *Safety Net Schemes (N10 bn):* specific grants to be channeled to communities across the states for financing pre-selected poverty reduction interventions through National Poverty Eradication Programme (NAPEP) and SME Development Agency (SMEDAN)

In the area of federal monitoring, the federal government has accumulated important experience in 2005-06 through undertaking the first SEEDS benchmarking exercise. The FGN has also made efforts recently to improve its capacity to monitor state expenditure patterns, but these efforts are constrained by the lack of constitutional authority to request proper budget reporting and disclosure by states. It is expected that, when adopted, the Fiscal Responsibility Law would create a better framework for fiscal disclosure and accountability, as well as for federal monitoring of sub-national fiscal performance.

Another major promising recent development in the area of policy coordination relates to the preparation of Medium Term Sector Strategies (MTSS) during the last two budget cycles, i.e. in the course of preparation of 2006 and 2007 annual budgets. Several MTSS documents made a serious emphasis on strengthening inter-governmental policy coordination in respective sectors. For instance, in health, the federal ministry is committed *inter alia* to pursue its Goal 1—to improve governance in the sector, including policy formulation, regulation, coordination, monitoring, and evaluation. In particular, the FGN has been working to secure a passage of the National Health Bill, which is supposed to strengthen the regulation of the national health system by establishing the standards of service delivery, clarify responsibilities at each level of the government, and set up national health information systems.

Other federal initiatives for 2007-09 to promote inter-governmental coordination in the health sector, as reflected in the MTSS, include the following:

a. construction of national health accounts,

b. providing technical assistance to states and LGAs,
c. strengthening federal monitoring of health sector performance, including through a) the establishment of countrywide monitoring and evaluation of hospital services, and b) undertaking a regular survey of health workers at the LGA level,
d. supporting activities of the National Council on Health.

Relevant International Experience of Using Federal Fiscal Transfers to States

There is a great deal of international experience in the creative use of federal grant schemes to facilitate national development through better inter-governmental cooperation. This section is focused on examples from India and Russia, (two large federations) which still have major unresolved problems in their models of federalism, but which have made considerable gradual progress in this area. Box 1 presents relevant examples from a number of other, both developed and developing countries.

India has used 3 main complimentary channels to provide federal transfers to states *(Rao, 2002a; McCarten, 2003):*

a. *Finance Commission* (which distributes about 60% of all federal financial support to states) provides unconditional block grants, which are formula based, and mostly aimed at achieving equalization objectives. Distribution of these grants is linked to the size of state population and local incidence of poverty. Individual states' funding shares are linked to the local tax potential, but not to actual tax collection.
b. *Planning Commission* (22% of all transfers) is responsible for formula-based support to implement state development plans provided as a combination of grants and soft loans to states in proportion 30:70. There is a soft policy conditionality attached to this funding in the form of federal certification of state development plans.
c. *Sectoral schemes* administered by sectoral ministries (18% of all transfers): federal co-financing of state programs (in proportion of 50-80% of overall program budget) to improve provision of public services with significant spillover effect and facilitate achievement of national goals, including in the area of primary education expenses, child nutrition, family planning, self-employment support. India has more than 180 of such individual programmes, several of which show strong populist flavour .

Overall, about 50% of all federally collected taxes in India is shared back with states through federal transfer programmes. The total amount of resources involved exceeds 7% of GDP.

Box 1. International experience with the grant schemes: selected examples

Indonesia operated (before 2001) a highly successful programme of federal support to primary schools managed by local governments (LGs). The programme included two components: a) operating grant to LGs based on school age population, and b) capital grants for school construction to communities that do not meet national standard of access.

South Africa adopted a Municipal Finance Management Act that introduced a Treasury-managed grant system for municipalities to encourage an upgrade in municipal budget management practices. This represents an example of "money for reforms" type of scheme.

Tanzania operates a Local Government Capital Development Grant (LGCDG) system of allocating performance based grants for local development. Those municipalities that fail to meet performance requirements are eligible for smaller grants for local capacity building.

In 1976, the **USA** operated 412 different federal specific grant programmes with the overall budget of $170bn a year.

Since 1996, **Germany** has allocated 18% of federally collected oil product excises to states to finance local investment projects in public transportation.

Russia's example is interesting from the perspective of relatively rapid progress made by the country in reforming its fiscal federalism arrangements. It took Russia about a decade to introduce rather a modern system of federal transfers basically from scratch (Figure 3). Most federal funding currently distributed in Russia to sub-national governments is formula-based, quite transparent and predictable. Significant attention is paid to the equity dimension of federal funding, while local differences in revenue potential are explicitly taken into account. Since 2000, Russia has introduced specific grant schemes to compensate regional governments for administering and financing federal responsibilities in the area of social protection *(World Bank, 2004).*

In 1998 Russia piloted an innovative federal grant scheme called the "Fund for Regional Fiscal Reforms", a special grant window to encourage fiscal reforms in line with the federal priorities. To qualify, regions had to meet specific policy targets in the PFM area, such as reduction in debts and deficits, establishment of regional treasury, improvement in cost recovery in the utility sector, etc. One could see this policy conditionality as an IMF-type of reform program run by the Federal Ministry of Finance for regions that are interested in policy adjustment.

The programme is administered by the designated Department in the Federal Ministry of Finance, which also has responsibilities for federal monitoring of regional fiscal performance, technical support to sub-national governments, and dissemination of regional-best practice. It is worth noting that the overall size of the programme has been relatively small (participating regions have been awarded grants in the range of $10m per region). However, many reform-minded governments found participation in the programme beneficial because of its attractive combination of cash and non-cash benefits.

Figure 3. The structure of the federal transfer system

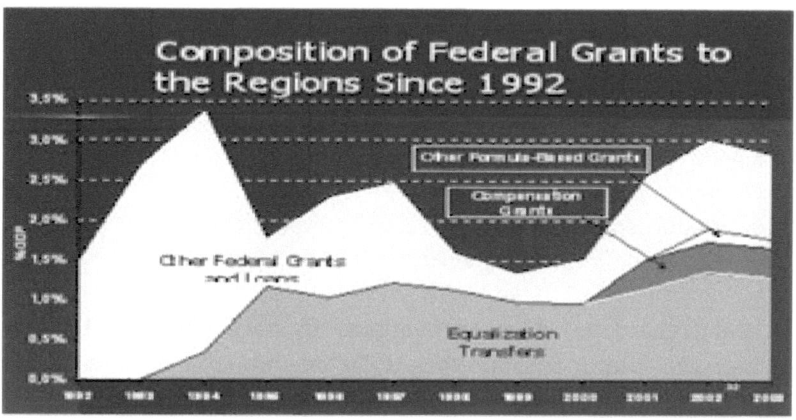

Source: *World Bank (2004)*

Lessons for Nigeria from recent Russian experience with fiscal federalism reforms could be summarized as following:

a) fiscal federalism reform is a long term process, which could not be completed in 1-2 years,
b) it is extremely politically sensitive, and may need a popular central government to facilitate a consensus building across different government levels,

c) the environment of strong economic recovery and broadly shared growth is very conducive to reduce states' opposition to reforms and facilitate consensus building,
d)improvements in social and fiscal statistics are important to illustrate deficiencies of the pre-reform situation (e.g. inequalities) and properly estimate potential reform impact (e.g. winners and losers of the proposed change),
e) clarification of expenditure/revenue mandates and improvements in equalization formula is not enough to improve efficiency in the intergovernmental finance system. To encourage adjustment in states' performances, these must be complimented by adequate fiscal rules and intergovernmental policy coordination mechanisms.

Nigeria: Is there a need for some more Radical Changes in the System of Intergovernmental Transfers?

Given the above analysis, this paper suggests the following priority directions for reforming inter-governmental financing arrangements in Nigeria:

a. more attention to the equity dimension of revenue sharing;
b. strengthening government accountability for utilization of public money in general, and for use of a common pool of funds such as the Federation Account in particular; and
c. introduction of specific grant schemes directly linked to expansion of sub-national government financing in key sectors.

With regard to these innovations, in particular specific grant schemes, the natural question then is: "what should be a source of their funding?" In this respect, it may be worth considering some relatively radical changes to the existing revenue sharing arrangements, such as the following:

a. conversion of allocations from the existing VAT account into a specific grant scheme, tied to spending on primary health: all sub-national governments would continue to receive the same shares of the common VAT pool, but they would agree to channel those proceeds to primary health within the agreed national framework.
b. use of off-shore oil revenues, which are not produced at the territory of any state, for a new fiscal equalization scheme, (i.e. distribute this money across states differently than on-shore oil revenues).

Should off-shore oil revenues be freed from the derivation principle to improve general equity of fiscal allocations to states?
c. agreement that future revenues from natural gas production be distributed across government levels differently from the existing arrangements with respect to oil revenues in order to focus these funds more directly on improvements in service delivery in key sectors, such as education and health.

If there is an appetite for these type of reforms, Nigeria could start with a pilot programme to test block grant arrangements tied to the implementation of a particular national programme of primary importance by sub-national governments, such as child immunization. The underlying rationale for this innovation could be (a) the need to encourage a nationwide increase in sub-national spending in the selected area, and (b) potential efficiency gains from better coordination across governments. This could be viewed as a federal policy aimed at accelerating the achievement of core MDGs and the implementation of SEEDS in key sectors.

Conclusions and Recommendations

The analysis in this paper suggests the following main directions for reforms to strengthen inter-governmental coordination:

a) shift from joint service delivery towards co-financing, state/local delivery, and joint monitoring,
b) more attention to equalization dimension of federalism,
c) expansion in specific grant schemes focused on key MDG areas,
d) strengthening accountability arrangements for how public money is spent, especially at state level,
e) strengthening capacity of institutions responsible for intergovernmental policy coordination with NPC becoming a central player, and
f) facilitating inter-state competition on the basis of quality of service delivery.

Development partners could support Nigeria's efforts in this area by:

i. helping the FGN to carry out unbiased evaluation/monitoring of state performance,
ii. supporting FGN efforts to accelerate capacity building in states,

iii. concentrating donors' support in reform-minded states, in particular states that are eager to cooperate with the federal government in service delivery, and
iv. providing advice on the best international practice in organization of inter-governmental fiscal relations.

REFERENCES

Broadway, Robin. "Grants in a Federal Economy: A Conceptual Perspective." In Broadway and Shah (2007, eds.), *Intergovernmental Fiscal Transfers. Principles and Practice.* (Washington D.C.: World Bank., 2007), pp. 55-74.

Broadway, Robin and Anwar Shah (Eds.) *Intergovernmental Fiscal Transfers. Principles and Practice.* (Washington DC: World Bank., 2007).

Collier, Paul. Africa: *Geography and Growth.* (Oxford: Oxford University, 2006)

Development of a Strategic Framework for the Financing of Local Governments in Tanzania. (Georgia State University. Andrew Young School of Policy Studies. June, 2005).

Improving Intergovernmental Collaboration and Coordination in National Service Delivery Process. (SLGP. Consultants' Report No. 184. Abuja. May, 2005).

McCarten, William J. "The Challenge of Fiscal Discipline in the Indian States". In Jonathan A. Rodden and Gunnar S. Eskeland (eds.) *Fiscal Decentralization and the Challenge of Hard Budget Constraints.* (MIT Press, 2003), pp. 249-286.

Rao, M. Govinda. "Fiscal Decentralization in Indian Federalism". In Ahmad, Ehtisham and Vito Tanzi (eds.). *Managing Fiscal Decentralization.* Routledge: (London and NY, 2002), pp 286-305.

Rao, M. Govinda. 2002b. "Poverty Alleviation under Fiscal Decentralization". In Rao, M. Govinda. (Ed). *Development, Poverty and Fiscal Policy. Decentralization of Institutions.* (Oxford University Press: New Delhi, 2002), Chapter 14, 278-298.

Sato, Motohiro. 2007. "The Political Economy of Interregional Grants". In Broadway and Shah (2007, eds.), pp. 173-202.

Shah, Anwar. "Comparative Reflections on Emerging Challenges in Fiscal Federalism". In Blindenbacher, Raoul and Abigail Ostien Karos (eds.) *Dialogue on the Practice of Fiscal Federalism: Comparative Perspectives.* Vol. 4. Forum of Federations: (Ottawa, 2006), pp. 40-45.

Shah, Anwar. "A Practitioner's Guide to Intergovernmental Fiscal Transfers". In Broadway and Shah (2007, (eds.), pp. 1-54.

UNDP. 2006. *Niger Delta Human Development Report. Abuja.*

Vigneault, Marianne. "Grants and Soft Budget Constraints". In Broadway and Shah (2007, eds.), pp. 133-173.

World Bank. 2003. *The Capacity of the Nigerian Government to Deliver Basic Education Services.*

World Bank. 2004. *Fiscal Federalism in Russia: Progress and Challenges. July.*

World Bank. 2006. *Nigeria: Realigning Health Sector Development. Draft Report,* September.

World Bank. 2007. *Nigeria: A Fiscal Agenda for Change. PEMFAR. (Draft).*

PART IV

FISCAL FEDERALISM: TOWARDS COPING WITH AND RESOLVING FUTURE CHALLENGES

CHAPTER 8

FISCAL FEDERALISM: TOWARDS COPING WITH AND RESOLVING FUTURE CHALLENGES

Attahiru Jega

Introduction

The challenges of fiscal federalism in Nigeria are enormous and a concerted effort and action are required to cope with, and resolve them. Even under normal circumstances in the so-called mature federations, these challenges require careful navigation and skilful management. Years of practice and the accompanying experience in inter-governmental relations have not totally resolved frictions, controversies and disagreements over federal fiscal arrangements, especially over the sources and sharing of revenues. However, the institutionalization of mechanisms for rational generation, allocation and sharing of resources in most mature federal democracies has ensured relative stability of fiscal federalism than in newer federations in post-colonial countries, such as Nigeria. In the Nigerian context the challenges are profound and very consequential, largely because of the colonial and military foundations of the development of fiscal federalism. Colonial rule was characterized by intriguing manipulations in, while military rule was characterized by reckless and poor handling of, the management of diversity. These have consequences for fiscal inter-state relations. One of the consequences has been the constant complaint and conflicts associated with vertical and horizontal revenue sharing. As an illustration, states quarrel with the federal government and the local governments quarrel endlessly with the states. Similarly states bicker and contest their allocations relative to others, and mobilize sentiments and perceptions of discrimination and/or marginalization. The oil producing states in particular have been embroiled in militant demands for a larger share of the revenues from oil and gas using the principle of derivation. In the circumstances, now perhaps more than ever before, creative political solutions are required for coping with and meeting the challenges of fiscal federalism in Nigeria.

In general, from the colonial period to date, controversies surrounding fiscal federalism in Nigeria have been associated with (i), which revenue sources are to be defined as federal for sharing and (ii) the utilization of, and the relative weight assigned to the principles of revenue sharing. Revenue sharing criteria have historically involved such principles as derivation; equity; even or balanced development; landmass; population; and others, each assigned different weight. Excessive politicization and use of governmental fiat, which characterized fiscal relations in the post-colonial period, ensured that these principles have not been neatly counter-balanced, with dire negative consequences on the stability of the federal system as a whole. The colonial origin of the Nigerian federal system combined with the centralizing, undemocratic and arbitrary impact of a long period of military rule to give rise to the prevailing conundrum of fiscal federalism and complicate the management of inter-state relations. There is no doubt that Nigeria has to go back to the basics and adapt and institutionalize tested fiscal principles and arrangements, which have worked well in other federal systems and which could enable it cope with and resolve the challenges in the future. For, only by doing so could Nigeria accelerate on the path to stable democratic development.

Overview of the Challenges

The Nigerian federal system has been a very precarious balancing act. Introduced and nurtured by British colonial rule to achieve colonial objectives and, subsequently, conditioned and influenced by military authoritarian rule to serve selfish and parochial objectives, the Nigerian federation became characterized by sharp ethno-regional and religious divides, which for decades have threatened to upset the balance required for attaining unity in diversity. The British colonial masters constructed the federal arrangement using divide and rule tactics and the manipulation of mutual fears and suspicions of ethnic, regional and religious domination. They somehow maintained unity in diversity by attempting to politically counter balance the northern with the southern region.[1]

Colonial intrigues were complex and not easily discernible when it came to management of diversity and using divide and rule technique to achieve their objectives. Thus, in order to assuage the fears of southern domination by the elite in the educationally backward, economically weaker and predominantly Muslim north, the British introduced a loose federal system with a multi-party electoral democracy. Through this it ensured the political control of the federal government by a northern-led coalition government at the time of independence in October 1960.[2] The educationally advanced and predominantly Christian southern elite controlled the economy and the federal bureaucracy. The northern elite were assuaged somewhat with the control of federal power, and saw it as a means of reducing the educational and economic gap separating the regions. However the southern elite could not fathom why they should concede political power to the northerners since economic power goes in tandem with the control of political power. They therefore, strove to capture power from the northerners. Threatened by the possibility of losing power in multi-party electoral competition based on a parliamentary system of government, the northern-led coalition government strove to guarantee political hegemony by controlling the military through massive recruitment of northerners and rapid promotions to command positions. Perceptions of favoritism, marginalization and discrimination, among other things, led some junior southern officers to organize the January 15 1966 coup. Though a failure, it resulted in the assassination of leading northern politicians and military officers. Thus heightening ethnic and religious tensions. It was therefore not surprising that a counter coup led by northern officers occurred in July 1966.[3]

Hence, a relatively politicized and ethnically factionalized military junta ruled Nigeria between 1966 until 1999, except for a brief period of four years (1979-83). During this period of about 29 years, the Nigerian federation was re-structured (from four regions to 36 states); it was centralized (with the federal government having more powers, responsibilities and resources than the states). At the same time while national resources were vandalized by authoritarian rulers, reckless strategies were deployed by them to manipulate Nigeria's diversity by mobilizing ethno-regional, religious and communal identities, thus reinforcing mutual suspicions and fears as well as acute perceptions of marginalization by some groups who felt excluded from the prebendal process of governance. In other words, military authoritarian rulers corruptly enriched themselves and their clients from public coffers.[4] The processes of governance and institutions were weakened and made exclusive rather than inclusive, intensifying perceptions of marginalization and exploitation of one group by another. Similarly, ethnic, regional and religious identities were mobilized and exploited by successive rulers, thereby heightening mutual fears and suspicions.[5] Under these circumstances, even where fiscal principles introduced for revenue sharing were not out-rightly discriminatory, they were nonetheless perceived to be so and were therefore contested.

Between 1999 and 2007, the Obasanjo civilian government tried, but did not succeed, in resolving the problems of marginalization and the mutual fears and suspicions of ethno-regional and religious domination. Indeed, while under military rule, the northern elite bore the brunt of accusations of marginalization, under the Obasanjo government, some members of the northern elite who felt excluded, mobilized sentiments and identities and reinforced suspicions and fears of marginalization. While the Obasanjo government tried to pump more revenues to the oil producing states in an effort to redress deep-seated perceptions and feelings of deprivation, the failed promises and politicization of the revenue sharing formula further alienated the restive youth in the Niger-Delta. The result was more violent conflicts, assassinations and abductions for ransom in the region, purportedly to back up demands for resource control broadly and vaguely defined as the control/ownership of revenues from petroleum resources by states from where these resources are produced.

In the circumstances, the Obasanjo government merely reinforced mutual suspicions and fears of marginalization without fundamentally addressing the structural defects of the Nigerian federal system. Thus, in many respects it magnified the crises of fiscal federalism. Reforming the federal arrangement through constitutional reforms, which would reduce the powers of the federal government, give more powers to the states and enshrine a more equitable and politically acceptable fiscal regime are among the formidable challenges facing the new government of President Umaru Musa Yar'Adua.

Towards Coping with and Resolving Future Challenges

At least, four problem areas demand urgent resolution by President Yar'Adua's government in handling of the prevailing crisis of fiscal federalism. First is the deep-seated perception of inequity in the sharing of federal revenues. At issue, is how to equitably share national resources with minimal perceptions of discrimination and marginalization, using (popularly) acceptable revenue sharing criteria formula.

Second, is the mono-cultural and rentier nature of the main source of revenues (i.e. export of crude petroleum and now gas). This problem is further complicated by the almost exclusive regional concentration of this revenue source. In this regard it is important to diversify the national revenue sources, and the national spatial spread of sources of revenue. Third, is the problem of environmental degradation and economic devastation of the petroleum producing areas in the Niger-Delta region. How does one marshal a realistic quantum of federal resources in a rescue package to be devoted to environmental regeneration, infrastructure development and poverty reduction in the Niger-Delta? This is a major area of concern. Fourth, is the problem of youth restiveness, militancy and criminality in the Niger-Delta region. How best does one speedily demilitarize the region, restore peace and stability, introduce effective youth employment programmes and provide adequate security to checkmate rising tides of restiveness, communal conflicts and, worse, criminality? These are real challenges for any government.

There is no doubt that one of the pre-conditions for assuring the future of Nigeria's democratic development is associated with coping and resolving the challenges of fiscal federalism and strengthening the institutional mechanisms for effective management of diversity in the Nigerian federal system. This must be given priority by the government under a new dispensation. Specifically, steps must be urgently taken to evolve an equitable and popularly acceptable revenue sharing formula. Indeed, no serious attempt to review the revenue sharing criteria/formula in a professional and rational manner has been done in Nigeria in the past two decades. It is, therefore, imperative to give priority to the setting up of a non-partisan fiscal commission, consisting of experts and key stakeholders, which is to be assigned the task of dispassionately reviewing existing revenue generation and sharing practices and recommending better and more equitable ones. The experience of the recent years, especially the 2005 National Political Reform Conference, suggests that no matter how well-intentioned, the task of reforming fiscal federalism is better conducted separately from that of wide-ranging political and constitutional reforms. Otherwise, extraneous and excessive political considerations and partisanship would come to becloud rationality, which is necessary in resolving matters associated with fiscal federalism.

Indeed, any constitutional reform process in the near future must focus appropriate attention on reforming the institutional mechanisms for monitoring, guiding and regulating fiscal federalism. Whereas one such institution, the Revenue Mobilization, Allocation and Fiscal Commission (RMAFC), has striven to discharge its constitutionally stipulated roles from 1999 to 2007, the disagreements and quarrels, which characterized the relationship between the Presidency and the Commission, including court cases over disclosures and sharing of excess petroleum related wind-falls, suggest that the Commission needs to be strengthened. In addition, constitutional ambiguity should be cleared, to minimize presidential or executive interference and facilitate transparency and accountability in the management of public funds in the Federation Account and the Distributable Pool Account. Also, as I argued elsewhere, there is the need to make the RMAFC not only non-partisan, but also, and especially, professionally and technically more competent and efficient. Such a reorganized Commission can help to design relatively scientific, equitable formula for revenue sharing that balances all the critical variables, such as derivation, need and equalization.[6]

Nigerian federal courts, especially the Court of Appeal and the Supreme Court, have acted courageously to protect and strengthen the institutions and processes of democratic development in the period of transition from merely civilian rule to democratic rule (i.e. 1999 to 2007). They have generally provided dispassionate and progressive adjudication and constitutional interpretations, significant among which relate to disputes on fiscal and revenue matters. Nonetheless, the courts need to also be strengthened and protected against executive interference and lawlessness so that they continue to play positive roles in Nigeria's democratic development.

The introduction of Value Added Tax (VAT) has gone some way to generate additional revenues for the federation and to beef up the revenue shares of many non-oil producing states, such as Lagos and Kano. VAT has highlighted the expanded scope of taxation in increasing, as well as diversifying, revenue base in a mono-cultural economy. There is therefore, no doubt that tax reforms and additional justifiable taxes can go a long way to increase the revenue of federal as well as individual states and local governments. The challenge here, however, is associated with avoidance of arbitrary and multiple taxation, and the mere hiking of taxes by percentage increases. States and local governments taxing powers need to be sanitized and enhanced. The methods of tax collection need to be made much more effective and efficient.

But even more significantly, diversifying the federal revenue base would require diversifying the Nigerian economy, and moving away from not just reliance on crude oil exports, but also moving away from primary commodity export generally. Pursuit of industrialization, for the production of goods and services not just for export, but also for the home market, is imperative.[7] Nigeria's manufacturing enterprises must be supported and encouraged, and their capacity strengthened by deliberate, focused and sustained government effort.

In its last year in power (i.e. in 2007) the Obasanjo government succeeded in articulating a framework / road map, for addressing the challenge posed by the problem of environmental degradation and economic devastation in the form of the Niger-Delta Master Plan. The Yar'Adua government has tried to build upon that by expressing commitment to the actualization of the proposed Master Plan, and continuing with relatively more inclusive stakeholder consultations to facilitate its execution. Under the proposed Plan, billions of dollars are earmarked to be spent, over a defined period, to clean up the environment, build infrastructure, improve social provisioning and provide jobs and economic empowerment targeted at poverty reduction. The much touted Master Plan has received favourable comments from a range of stakeholders both from within and outside the Niger-Delta region. However, there are growing concerns about the effective and efficient execution of the plan. The Niger-Delta Development Commission (NDDC) which is assigned a pivotal role in the execution of the Master Plan has credibility and legitimacy problems associated with allegations of lack of transparency, accountability and inclusiveness in the execution of their funded programmes. There are concerns that these problems if not decisively addressed would obstruct the attainment of the defined objectives of the Master Plan. There is no doubt that success in the execution of the Master Plan would depend to a large extent on reforming and strengthening the institutions and agencies, as well as the key stakeholders saddled with the responsibility of seeing it through to successful execution.

Conclusion

There is great need as well as the opportunity for improving upon and strengthening the management of diversity in the Nigerian federal system. The scope for improved inter-state relations, as well as more equitable and better fiscal arrangements is vast. While democratization and good democratic governance would go a long way to improve the general challenges associated with the management of diversity occasioned by colonialism and prolonged military rule (e.g. transparency, accountability and inclusiveness under good democratic governance would reduce mutual fears and suspicions and accompanying perceptions of domination and marginalization), great headway would be made only when (i) the constitutional and legal framework / requirements of a federal democracy are reformed and institutionalized and (ii) the fiscal foundations of the federal system are properly and adequately reformed to ensure diversified multiple sources of revenue, equitable sharing of revenues, as well as a diversified national economic base, in which each state or region has its own stable source of revenue and which does not rely on export earnings from one primary (mineral or agricultural) commodity. Hence, it is necessary to, as a matter of priority initiate a credible process of constitutional review to deal with the most glaring weaknesses/ deficiencies of the 1999 Constitution, such as concentration of powers and resources in the federal government at the expense of state governments. And it is equally necessary to have a separately constituted fiscal commission to review both the principles and the practice of fiscal federalism in Nigeria with a view to improving and enhancing these for stable and desirable democratic development. Doing these represent the major challenges, which have to be coped with and resolved in the near future.

NOTES AND REFERENCES

1. For details on Nigeria's political development, see: J. S. Coleman, *Nigeria: Background to Nationalism* (Berkeley: UCLA Press, 1958); R. Sklar, *Nigerian Political Parties* (Princeton: Princeton University Press, 1963); H. M. A. Kirk-Greene, *Crisis and Conflict in Nigeria* (Ibadan: Oxford University Press, 1971); J. P. Mackintosh, *Nigerian Government and Politics* (London: Allen and Unwin, 1966); B. J. Dudley, *Instability and Political Order: Politics and Crisis in Nigeria* (Ibadan: Ibadan University Press, 1973).

2. Attahiru Jega, Nigeria after the 2007 Elections: The Tasks Ahead; Keynote Address presented at the international conference on "Nigeria: Too Rich for Dignity and the Law?" (*Loccum*: The Evangelische Akademie, 15th - 17th June, 2007).

3. See O. Oyediran, *Nigerian Government and Politics Under Military Rule, 1966-79* (London: The Macmillan Press, 1979); A. Ademoyega, *Why We Struck* (Ibadan, Evans, 1981); Mainasara, *Why They Struck* (Zaria: Hudahuda Press, 1977); A. Said and A. Momoh, *The Political Economy of Nigeria Under Military Rule* (Harare: SAPES Books, 1995); B. Gbulie, *Nigeria Five Majors* (Africana Educational Publishers, 1982).

4. See A. Momoh and A. Said, *The Political Economy of Nigeria Under Military Rule*, op. cit.

5. See Attahiru M. Jega, ed. *Identity Transformation and Identity Politics under Structural Adjustment in Nigeria.* (Uppsala: Nordiska Afrikainstitutet, 2000).

6. Attahiru M. Jega, *Resource Control: Issues, Contradictions, Paradoxes and Implications for National Development* (Abuja: National Development Project, 2002).

7. Y. B. Usman, *Nigeria Against the IMF: The Home Market Strategy* (Kaduna: Vanguard Publishers Ltd., 1986.

Other Readings

Attahiru M. Jega, The Political Economy of Nigerian Federalism, in Elaigwu, J. I. And R. Akindele, (eds.), *Foundations of Nigerian Federalism*, 1960-1995. (Abuja: National Council on Intergovernmental relations 1996).

Attahiru M. Jega, *Democratization in Nigeria: Problems and Prospects*. The 8th Claude Ake Memorial Lecture (Port Harcourt: Centre for Advanced Social Sciences, 2006).

J. Isawa Elaigwu, *The Politics of Federalism in Nigeria* (Jos: Aha Publishing House Ltd., 2005).

A. B. Akinyemi, P. D. Cole and W. Ofonagoro, *Readings on Federalism* (Lagos: NIIA, 1979).

CHAPTER 9

FISCAL FEDERALISM: TOWARDS COPING WITH AND RESOLVING FUTURE CHALLENGES

Milton Iyoha

Introduction

Nigeria has operated a federal form of government since 1954. However, the nature and structure of fiscal federalism in Nigeria has undergone a steady evolution and has been subjected to several social, political and economic upheavals. Thus, the current system of political and fiscal federalism is the outcome of several influences – historical, cultural, legal, political, and economic. In addition, the character of the Nigerian polity as a heterogeneous, pluralistic, multi-ethnic, and multi-religious one has had implications for the evolution and current state of its system of fiscal federalism. Furthermore, the military intrusion into Nigerian politics and its domination of the political landscape for approximately 30 years (out of the 47 years of the country's existence between Independence from colonial rule in 1960 and 2007) has had lasting effects on the nature, structure, and problems of the system of fiscal federalism in Nigeria.

Since the adoption of the federal structure of governance in 1954, Nigeria has had 3 tiers of government. Originally, the designation was federal, regional, and provincial. Today, in addition to the federal government, we have state governments and local governments. The number of sub-national governments has expanded over time. From 3 regions in 1954, the number increased to 4 in 1963. The nomenclature then changed to "state" and the number steadily increased from 12 in 1967 to 19 in 1976, 21 in 1987, 30 in 1991, and finally it rose to 36 states and the Federal Capital Territory (FCT) in 1997. From 299 in 1970, the number of local governments rose to 301 in 1979 (when they were officially recognized in the Constitution as a separate tier of government for the first time), and to 774 in 1997.

There was a natural tendency towards over-centralization of powers and responsibilities during the period of military rule. In many important respects, the army ruled the country as if there was a unitary system of government. Military Governors in charge of each state were named by the Head of the federal government and served at his pleasure. Apart from the use of military decrees to centralize powers at the federal level, many ad-hoc measures and policies, including the setting up of dedicated accounts and special funds, were used to increase the proportion of total revenues accruing to the federal government. The proliferation of off-budget funds made it possible for the federal government to undertake and finance huge amounts of extra-budgetary spending. These contributed to making Nigerian public finance opaque and non-transparent, further emphasizing the lack of accountability of military governance. In the area of inter-governmental fiscal relations, the multiplicity of special funds and management of the Federation Account by the federal government aggravated the problem of vertical imbalance. The state and local governments were reduced to waiting for transfers from the federal government in order to undertake even basic responsibilities such as payment of salaries. Meanwhile, the over-abundance of revenues in the hands of the federal government led to fiscal indiscipline, profligacy and an excessively high level of official corruption.

Nigeria's overall economic performance during the past 3 or 4 decades has been less than impressive. Despite the availability of huge oil resources, its growth rate has been quite feeble. Available data show that between 1964 and 1997, per capita GNP rose from US$120 to US$280, (i.e., it barely doubled in 33 years). Between 1960 and 2000, the average annual growth rate of GDP was only 3.7%. Taking the most recent decade, 1988-2000, (i.e., the period since the adoption of the Structural Adjustment Programme (SAP)), the average annual growth rate of GDP improved, but could only equal 3.9%. Many Nigerian scholars attribute the weak performance of the economy during this period—most of which was under military rule—partly to the over-centralization of government finances. According to Okunrounmu (1999:453), "The imposition of a centralized unitary system on a federal structure under the military administration partly explains our experience of poor fiscal management and low economic performance which, over the years, had adversely affected national development".

In addition, the excessive budget deficits, made possible by unwarranted fiscal over-centralization, have been widely blamed for the rapid inflation of the first half of the 1990s, when the rate of price increase reached an annual rate of 72% in 1995. Thus, there have been calls for some significant fiscal decentralization, particularly as decentralization is expected to contribute to a more rapid rate of economic growth. However, while there are grounds for believing that a system of *true federalism* with a significant degree of fiscal decentralization has the potential for encouraging more responsible fiscal management and promoting rapid economic growth, there are also theoretical arguments for believing that decentralization may damage economic growth. Tanzi (1996) and Prud'homme (1995), using different arguments, suggest that decentralization may be inimical to economic growth.

Basically, Prud'homme argues that corruption may be more pervasive at the local level, especially in developing countries. Given the expected negative effect of corruption on economic growth, he draws the conclusion that increasing the amount of revenues available at the local level will lead to less growth. But then, empirical evidence adduced by Huther and Shah (1996) and Kim (1995) support the hypothesis that decentralization improves economic performance. In particular, using econometric techniques to estimate a Barro-type growth model with international panel data, Kim obtains the result that a measure of fiscal decentralization is significantly and positively associated with the rate of economic growth.

The return to democratic governance in May 1999 was expected to lead to the practice of a more balanced system of fiscal federalism, more transparency and fiscal accountability and more devolution of powers to lower tiers of government, and hence more fiscal decentralization. While a greater degree of decentralization could contribute to greater grass-roots participation, generate more local development, increase efficiency and equity, create employment opportunities, and promote poverty alleviation, care must be taken to ensure that it does not unduly complicate the pursuit of the national objective of macroeconomic stabilization. Accordingly, in this paper, an attempt will be made to provide a comprehensive analysis of the current state of fiscal federalism in Nigeria, analyze its problems, and proffer suggestions towards coping with and resolving future challenges.

Fiscal Federalism in Nigeria

Fiscal federalism is the area of economics that deals with the principles, canons, arrangements, practices, and modalities of intergovernmental fiscal relations in a multi-tier government structure. According to Oates (1999:1120):

> As a subfield of public finance, fiscal federalism addresses the vertical structure of the public sector. It explores, both in normative and positive terms, the roles of the different levels of government and the ways in which they relate to one another through such instruments as inter-governmental grants.

Depending on the initial conditions, size, history, evolution, and legal framework, the nature and outcome of fiscal federalism varies from country to country. The current state, structure, and nature of Nigeria's system of fiscal federalism are the outcome of the interplay of various forces including:

a) the application of the precepts of public finance as enunciated by Oates (1972, 1994, and 1999), Musgrave and Musgrave (1989), and Musgrave (1959);
b) the interplay of political and legal influences as reflected in various constitutional provisions;
c) the reality of a pluralistic, multi-religious and multi-ethnic society;
d) the dominance of petroleum as a source of government revenue; and
e) the intrusion of the military into Nigerian politics and its sustained stay in power for almost 30 years.

Thus, while there are several commonalities, Nigeria's system of fiscal federalism is different in many important respects from what obtains in other countries that operate a federal constitution like the U.S.A., Canada, Australia, Germany, Switzerland, India and Brazil.

Assignment of Functions

By and large, Nigeria, like other federal countries, has been guided in the assignment of functions to different levels of government (and the appropriate fiscal instruments for accomplishing the tasks) by the classical theory of fiscal federalism and the normative framework, which it presents. According to Oates (1999:1121):

> ... this theory contends that the central government should have the basic responsibility for the macroeconomic stabilization function and for income redistribution... In addition to these functions, the central government must provide certain 'national' public goods (like national defence) that provide services to the entire population of the country.

In most countries, the national public goods over which the central government have authority have included foreign affairs, citizenship, international trade, banking, national currency, and the environment.

Sub-national governments are expected to provide goods and services whose consumption is limited to their geographical areas of competence ("local" public goods) in the interest of efficiency and welfare maximization. With regard to this assignment, a Decentralization Theorem has been established which states that

> ...in the absence of cost-saving from the centralized provision of a [local public] good, and of inter-jurisdictional externalities, the level of welfare will always be at least as high (and typically higher) if Pareto-efficient levels of consumption are provided in each jurisdiction than if any single, uniform level of consumption is maintained across all jurisdictions. (Oates 1972:54)

In Nigeria, assignment of responsibilities has been done by including them in the various Constitutions and military decrees and in various *ad hoc* provisions introduced by military governments. In particular, the bulk of what currently obtains is contained in Section 4 (second schedule) of the 1979 Constitution. The practice has been to list functions exclusive to each tier of government and those that are concurrent. As an illustration, national defence is the exclusive responsibility of the central (federal) government while education and agriculture are on the concurrent list (which comes under the purview of both federal and state governments). Indeed, education (in this case, primary) also comes under the auspices of the local government. Table 1 gives the main functions currently assigned to the different tiers of government.

Table 1: Nigeria: Federal, State, and Local Expenditure Assignments

Assignment	Jurisdiction
Defense	Federal
Foreign affairs	Federal
International trade	Federal
Interstate trade	Federal
Environment	Federal
Air and rail transport	Federal
Agriculture	Federal & state
Education	Federal & state
Health	Federal, state, & local
Police	Federal
Natural resources	Federal, state, & local
Highways	Federal, state, & local

Source: *Presidential Commission on Revenue Allocation. 1980,* vol. 1, *Main Report*

Note that the assignments of some functions have changed over time. A case in point is "Police" which used to be under state and local but was later switched to federal. With the return to democratic governance and the demands of political decentralization and increased autonomy, there are now increasing and strident demands for allowing state governments to have their own police force.

Assignment of Fiscal Instruments

The other side of the coin of assignment of functions is the assignment of fiscal instruments, mainly tax bases. In other words, a workable system of fiscal federalism requires the assignment of specific fiscal instruments to the various tiers of government for financing their expenditures. The primary source of finance is usually taxation. This is supplemented when needed by borrowing (debt instruments) and in the case of vertical fiscal imbalances, revenue sharing and intergovernmental grants. In addition to the assignment problem, there is the issue of which tier of government should collect specific taxes. This is because one tier of government (such as the central) may collect a tax but the revenue may accrue to another tier of government (such as the state). Who should collect taxes is often determined *inter alia* on efficiency grounds. Assignment of tax bases to various levels of government is very important because of differences in the buoyancy of tax bases. One way out is centralization of collection and then sharing of revenue among the different tiers of government.

Economists and practitioners often make a case for the central collection of taxes, particularly those like income taxes where taxpayers are mobile and may avoid taxes levied by geographically localized units of government. Central collection of many taxes is often canvassed on the following grounds:

a) it is consistent with the redistribution and stabilization functions of the federal/central government and the adequate provision of national public goods;
b) it is likely to generate economies of scale in tax administration and avoid loss of revenue due to the mobility of taxpayers; and
c) it is desirable if there is a preference for uniformity of taxes across states and local government areas.

However, centralization of tax collection implies that tax revenue would be allocated back to state and local governments, thereby encouraging transfer-dependence and undermining fiscal autonomy. In general, central collection of all or most taxes leads to non-correspondence of functions and revenue, accentuating the problem of vertical fiscal imbalance among the various tiers of government. Note, however, that even allowing state and local governments to collect taxes could still result in vertical fiscal imbalance since all tax bases are not equally buoyant or income elastic. Besides, decentralized tax collection could aggravate the problem of horizontal fiscal imbalance among states or local governments since tax handles, like income, are not uniformly distributed across states.

In Nigeria, assignment of fiscal instruments has also been based mainly on constitutional provisions. In particular, the 1979 Constitution bestowed the power to levy and collect key taxes like customs and excise, company tax, petroleum profit tax, mining rents and royalties on the federal government. Thereafter, military decrees gave the federal government the power to levy and collect the personal income tax and the Value Added Tax (VAT). States and local governments have been left with the power to collect other taxes and fees. However, note that while state and local governments retain revenues collected by them, those collected by the federal government (except the so-called independent revenue) are expected to be paid into the Federation Account, which is shared among the three tiers of government. Table 2 provides information on the assignment, jurisdiction, and retention of key taxes.

Table 2: Nigeria: Federal, State, and Local Tax Jurisdictions and Assignment

Tax	Legal Jurisdiction	Collection	Retention
Import duties	Federal	Federal	Federation Account
Excise duties	Federal	Federal	Federation Account
Export duties	Federal	Federal	Federation Account
Mining rents & royalties	Federal	Federal	Federation Account
Petroleum profits tax	Federal	Federal	Federation Account
Capital gains tax	Federal	State	State
Personal income tax[1]	Federal	State	State
Sales tax[2]	Federal	State	State
Company tax	Federal	Federal	Federation Account
Stamp duties	Federal	State	State
Gift tax	Federal	State	State
Property tax	State	State	State

Tax	Legal Jurisdiction	Collection	Retention
Licenses and fees	Local	Local	Local
Motor park dues	Local	Local	Local
Motor vehicle tax	State	Local	Local

Source: *Presidential Commission on Revenue Allocation,. 1980, vol. 1, Main Report.*

Note: Personal income taxes of the armed forces, external affairs, and the Federal Capital Territory are federally legislated, collected, and retained.

[1] Now collected by the federal government.

[2] Now abolished and replaced by a national Value Added Tax collected by the federal government but shared by the three tiers of government.

Revenue Allocation, Inter-Governmental Grants and Borrowing

Since the exact correspondence between functions and revenues is rare, imbalances between required expenditure and available revenue to some federating units are a common occurrence in federal systems. Revenue gaps are often filled through the instrumentality of intergovernmental grants. According to Oates (1999:1126),

> Intergovernmental grants constitute a distinctive and important policy instrument in fiscal federalism that can serve a number of functions. [These include] ... the internalization of spillover benefits to other jurisdictions, fiscal equalizations across jurisdictions, and an improved overall tax system.

Grants may be "conditional" or "unconditional". In the case of conditional grants, the tier of government giving the grant places one or more restrictions on its use by the recipient tier. Unconditional grants are basically lump-sum transfers to be used as desired by the recipient tier of government. By their very nature, unconditional grants are the perfect vehicles for undertaking fiscal equalization. The purpose of such a transfer is to channel funds from relatively buoyant localities to less wealthy ones, based on some measure of "fiscal need" or "fiscal capacity".

Revenue sharing or revenue allocation is one of the most important examples of intergovernmental grants. In this case, the grant is unconditional and the primary purpose is to sustain a more efficient overall tax system. It can also be used to ameliorate the problems of vertical fiscal imbalance among tiers of government and horizontal fiscal imbalance across jurisdictions. In developing countries like Nigeria where the central government collects key taxes for various reasons including low capacity for effective tax administration by state and local governments, the case for revenue sharing is strong. The case is even stronger in Nigeria because a high proportion of total government revenue comes from petroleum, which is highly localized in the Niger-Delta. Revenue sharing then becomes a systematic way of transferring funds to other states and localities. Indeed, revenue sharing has been a consistent though contentious issue in Nigerian public finance since it became a federation in 1954. The issue has become even more controversial since the rise of petroleum to a dominant position as foreign exchange earner in the early 1970s. Several commissions have been set up to propose revenue allocation formulae but an acceptable formula has remained elusive.

In Nigeria, there are three main inter-governmental revenue accounts, viz., the federation account, the autonomous foreign exchange market (AFEM) profits account, and the value-added tax (VAT) account. The VAT revenues come from a 5% national value-added tax. The revenue-sharing formula for the funds in this account is determined on a yearly basis. Currently the formula is 30% to the federal government, 50% to the state governments, and 20% to the local government councils. Revenues are generated in the AFEM profits account when government oil foreign exchange receipts are sold in the AFEM. Currently the federal government receives its pro-rata share of the profits while it holds the balance in trust on behalf of the state and local government councils. The Federation Account is a depository for the following nationally generated revenue: receipts from crude oil exports, domestic petroleum product revenue, revenues generated from the company income tax and from customs, excise and fees. However, prior to distribution, certain "first charges" are deducted and put aside. These include funds for external debt service payments, national priority projects, oil-related cash-calls, the Nigerian National Petroleum Corporation (NNPC) priority projects, the special reserve, and the excess proceeds reserves. Net federation proceeds, which in recent years have approximated 35% of total federation revenue, are then distributed, using the statutory revenue-sharing formula to the three tiers of government and the special funds. Currently the federal government gets 48.5%, the state governments get 24%, and local government councils obtain 20%, while 7.5% goes to the Special Funds. The special funds consist of the Federal Capital Territory Fund, the Ecology Fund, the Statutory Stabilization Fund, the Mineral Derivation Fund, and the Mineral-Producing Areas Fund. The special funds are controlled and managed by the federal government.

Borrowing is an option for any tier of government whose expected expenditure exceeds its expected revenue. The federal government can borrow domestically and from abroad. State governments can borrow domestically; they can also borrow externally but only with the prior approval of the federal government. The local government councils can only borrow domestically. Generally, state and local governments are expected to borrow to finance capital projects only.

Table 3: Nigeria: Shares of Revenue by Tiers of Government in Total Government Revenue, 1993-1997 (%)

Year	Federal	State	Local
1993	71.12	18.92	9.96
1994	67.89	23.13	8.98
1995	80.72	14.19	5.09
1996	79.01	16.57	4.42
1997	79.30	15.63	5.07
Average	**75.61**	**17.69**	**6.71**

Source: Anyanwu, J.C. 1999, p. 133.

Table 3 provides data on the shares of revenue by tiers of government in total government revenue. It is seen that for the 1993-1997 period, the share going to the federal government averaged 75.6%, the share accruing to all the state governments averaged 17.7% while the share going to the local government councils averaged only 6.7%. In effect, more than three-quarters of all government revenue went to the federal government. Many believe that this over-abundance of funds at the federal level encouraged fiscal irresponsibility, profligacy, and rampant corruption. On the other hand, the inadequacy of funds for the sub-national governments slowed down economic development at the grassroots level. Table 4 provides data on federal transfers as a proportion of sub-national governments' total revenue during the 1993-1997 period.

Table 4: Nigeria: Federal Transfers as Proportion of Sub-national Governments' Total Revenue, 1993-1997

Year	State	Local
1993	84.83	94.79
1994	77.92	93.73
1995	74.58	91.35
1996	78.17	91.53
1997	71.95	91.89
Average	**77.49**	**92.66**

Source: Anyanwu, J.C. 1999, p. 135.

For the five years in the sample, it is seen that on the average, federal transfers accounted for 77.5% of total state government revenues while they accounted for 92.7% of the revenues of the local government councils. This is a demonstration that there was little or no fiscal autonomy at the sub-national level. Indeed, for many of the sub-national governments, the situation was so bad that they waited to receive federal transfers before they could pay salaries of teachers and civil servants.

Problems of Nigeria's System of Fiscal Federalism

The main problems of Nigeria's system of fiscal federalism include:

(i) the existence of significant vertical fiscal imbalance between central and sub-national governmental units;
(ii) the lack of fiscal autonomy regarding state and local governments;
(iii) the existence of horizontal fiscal imbalance across jurisdictions;
(iv) the lack of a widely accepted revenue allocation formula;
(v) the debt overhang problem at the center; and
(vi) the threat to macroeconomic stabilization and management caused by (i)-(v).

Towards Coping With and Resolving Current and Future Challenges

In May 1999, a civilian government came to power after many years of military misrule. The emergence of civilian governance offers the country a golden opportunity to discard some old habits like massive extra-budgetary spending and over-centralization of funds at the federal level. It also offers an opportunity to introduce other changes in the system of fiscal federalism in order to make it a better instrument for rapid and sustained economic growth and development. It is believed that implementation of some or all the recommendations below will go a long way to solve identified problems in the current system. and position the economy for rapid economic growth in the new millennium.

Recommendations

Since the basis of Nigeria's system of fiscal federalism is legal as well as political, some of the proposed changes that are structural, fundamental, and/or of a long-term nature would necessarily require amendment of constitutional provisions. Others, which are technical or procedural, could perhaps be implemented rather quickly.

Modification of Assignment of Fiscal Instruments

This study finds that the assignment of functions in Nigeria's system of fiscal federalism conforms by and large with that proposed by the classical theory of fiscal federalism and to what obtains in many other countries. However, there seems to be some deficiency in the assignment of fiscal instruments. In particular, there is over-centralization of revenue at the centre leading to high transfer-dependence and a severe lack of fiscal autonomy with regard to the sub-national governmental units. The remedy may be to transfer some tax bases or tax handles to the sub-national governmental units without seriously undermining the efficiency of tax collection.

Establishment of a Permanent Commission on Revenue Allocation

There is a need for a more equitable and functional revenue allocation procedure and revenue sharing formula. A desirable way to bring about these changes is the establishment of a permanent Finance Commission on Revenue Allocation, like those that exist in countries like India and Mexico. The Commission, whose tenure could be for a period of 7 to 10 years and whose membership would include experts in public finance, would be empowered to manage inter-governmental revenue accounts, including taking decisions on items to include in the distributable pool and determination of a revised revenue sharing formula. It would also be given the task of designing a more scientific set of principles to use in allocating funds to the different tiers of government. Presumably, principles like tax effort and need would be accorded significant weight. Under this new proposed dispensation, unilateral *ad hoc* adjustments to the formula by the federal government would cease, dedicated accounts would remain abolished, special funds would be eliminated – all of which would do away with the ready means formerly available for financing federal government extra-budgetary expenditures. This definitely would contribute to a more transparent, effective, and responsible, non-inflationary system of budgeting and also promote rapid growth.

Establishment of a Macroeconomic Stabilization Fund

Given the extreme dependence of Nigeria's public revenues on volatile oil prices, there is a need for the establishment of a macroeconomic stabilization fund as a vehicle for effecting a credible counter-cyclical macroeconomic stabilization policy. Currently, there are three special funds – the special reserve account and the two excess proceeds reserves accounts–which could theoretically serve this purpose. However, they are not being used for this task. Rather, the federal government uses the proceeds of these funds as it pleases, often for undisclosed purposes. A true stabilization fund would be used solely for counter-cyclical output stabilization and the funds optimally should be in the custody of the permanent Finance Commission. Oil receipts above a certain agreed level would be automatically paid into the stabilization fund. When the price of oil falls and receipts fall below a certain level, required funds would be released by the Finance Commission, at the request of the federal government, to all tiers of government – using the ruling revenue allocation formula.

Since the onset of the current economic reform program, government has attempted to achieve fiscal prudence by setting up an excess crude oil account to be used as a counter-cyclical macroeconomic stabilization devise. A Fiscal Responsibility Bill, containing aspects of this principle, has recently been passed by the National Assembly.

Federal Government Regulation of Borrowing by Sub-national Governments

The idea is steadily gaining ground in the literature on fiscal federalism that while increased fiscal decentralization may promote efficiency, increase welfare and enhance economic development, it is likely to reduce the ability of the central government to carry out its traditional macroeconomic management functioning. In a recent study, Teresa Ter-Minassian (1997b:3) concludes that fiscal decentralization "can entail significant costs in terms of the effectiveness of the central government in stabilizing the economy". The potential for spending by sub-national governments (SNGs) to conflict with national stabilization policy is larger when state and local governments are free to borrow at will to finance budget deficits. According to Ter-Minassian:

> Substantial deficits of SNGs – especially the larger states and cities – if financed from abroad or by domestic bank credit can undermine the conduct of monetary policy, and, even if not financed monetarily, can 'crowd out' the private sector (1997b:7).

One way to mitigate the potential disrupting effect of SNGs is to require them to have balanced budgets. If this is not possible, strict controls should be placed on their borrowing activities. Above all, foreign borrowing by SNGs should be discouraged – both for the sake of macroeconomic stabilization and to prevent exacerbating the debt overhang problem.

Currently, in Nigeria, state governments are allowed to borrow abroad with the express permission of the federal government. They are also allowed to borrow domestically from financial institutions. Local government councils are also allowed to borrow domestically from financial institutions. In order to improve the central government's ability to stabilize the economy, it would be desirable to ban

SNGs from borrowing abroad and to restrict their domestic borrowing to the non-bank public.

Need to Improve Fiscal Administrative Capacity of SNGs

It has been argued above that more tax responsibilities should be given to SNGs in order to increase their levels of fiscal autonomy. However, for the proposed recommendation to work, it would be necessary to take concrete measures to increase the fiscal, administrative and budgetary capacity, especially of local government councils. Weak tax administration would only result in loss of tax revenues and would do nothing to improve the much cherished fiscal autonomy.

Summary and Conclusion

In this chapter, an attempt has been made to analyze and assess the present system of fiscal federalism in Nigeria with particular reference to its expected impact on macroeconomic management. Given its history and evolution, and in particular, the influence of military governance on its development, it was found that the current system of fiscal federalism is over-centralized especially with respect to revenue collection. Although inter-governmental grants are used to moderate the concentration of financial resources at the centre, it is nevertheless still true that the lower tiers of government are under-funded and hence relatively ineffective as agents of development. On the other hand, the overabundance of resources at the centre has contributed to fiscal indiscipline, unnecessary use of extra-budgetary expenditure, and pervasive corruption.

The chapter has attempted to analyze the critical problems buffeting the current system of fiscal federalism in Nigeria. They were found to include:

a) the existence of large vertical inter-government fiscal imbalances;
b) the lack of fiscal autonomy for state and local governments;
c) the wide horizontal fiscal imbalances across jurisdictions;
d) an inequitable and flawed revenue allocation system; and
e) an inadequate and ineffective macroeconomic management framework.

Next, solutions to the identified problems were proposed with the aim of making fiscal federalism a tool of rapid and self-sustained economic growth in the years ahead.

REFERENCES

Agiobenebo, T.J. "Assignment Criteria and the Fiscal Constitution: An Excursion into a Theory of Rational Fiscal Federalism."in Aigbokhan, B.E. (ed.) *Fiscal federalism and Nigeria's Economic Development.* Selected papers presented at the 1999 Annual Conference of the Nigerian Economic Society. (Ibadan: NES, 1999).

Aigbokhan, B.E. "Fiscal Federalism and Economic Growth in Nigeria." In Aigbokhan, B.E. (ed.) *Fiscal Federalism and Nigeria's Economic Development.* Selected papers presented at the 1999 Annual Conference of the Nigerian Economic Society. (Ibadan: NES, 1999).

Anyanwu, J.C. "Fiscal Relations among the Various Tiers of Government in Nigeria." In Aigbokhan, B.E. (ed.) *Fiscal Federalism and Nigeria's Economic Development.* Selected papers presented at the 1999 Annual Conference of the Nigerian Economic Society. (Ibadan: NES, 1999).

Anyanwu, J.C. "Revenue Allocation and Stable Fiscal Federalism." *Journal of Economic Management*, Vol. 1, No. 2, October, 1995 pp 1-27.

Davoodi, H. and Heng-fu Zou. "Fiscal Decentralization and Economic Growth." *Journal of Urban Economics*, 43, 1998, pp 244-257.

Ekpo, A.H. "Fiscal Federalism: Nigeria's Post-Independence Experience, 1960-90." *World Development*, Vol. 22, No. 8, 1994, pp.1129-1146.

Emenuga, C. "The Search for an Acceptable Revenue Allocation Formula." *The National Question and Economic Development in Nigeria.* (Ibadan: Nigerian Economic Society, 1983).

Gandhi, V.P. "Intergovernmental Fiscal Relations and Economic Performance." In Roy, J. (ed.) *Macroeconomic Management and Fiscal Decentralization.* (Washington, D.C.: World Bank, 1995).

Iyoha, M.A. "Nigeria's Growth Performance, 1960-2000: Lessons for Policy". *AERC: Explaining African Economic Growth Project*, 2006.

Iyoha, M.A. "Fiscal Federalism, Decentralization and Macroeconomic Management in Nigeria". *NCEMA Policy Analysis Series*, Vol. 6, No. 2, 2000.

Iyoha, M.A. "Introduction and Overview of Leading Issues in Macroeconomic Policy Design and Management." In Obadan, M.I. and M.A. Iyoha (eds.) *Macroeconomic Policy Analysis: Tools and Techniques with Applications to Nigeria.* (Ibadan: NCEMA,1997).

Kim, S.L. Fiscal Decentralization, Fiscal Structure, and Economic Performance: Three empirical studies. Unpublished Ph.D. Dissertation. (United States. Maryland, 1995).

Mbanefo, G.F. "Unsettled Issues in Nigerian Fiscal Federalism and the National Question." Proceedings of the 1993 Annual Conference of the Nigerian Economic Society, 1993, pp. 61-77.

Mered, M."Nigeria." In Ter-Minassian, T. (Ed.) *Fiscal Federalism in Theory and Practice*, (Washington, D.C.: International Monetary Fund, 1997).

Moser, G., S. Rogers, and R.. van Til. *Nigeria: Experience with Structural Adjustment*. Occasional Paper No. 148. (Washington, D.C.: IMF, 1997).

Musgrave, R.M. *The Theory of Public Finance*. (New York: McGraw Hill1959).

Musgrave, R.M. and P.B. Musgrave. *Public Finance in Theory and Practice*. (Singapore: McGraw Hill, 1989).

Oates, W.E. "An Essay on Fiscal Federalism." *Journal of Economic Literature*, vol. xxxviii, No. 3, Sept., 1999,. pp 1120-1149.

Oates, W.E. "Federalism and Government Finance." In Quigley, J. and E. Smolensky (eds.) *Modern Public Finance*. (Cambridge, MA: Harvard University Press, 1994), pp 126-151.

Oates, W. *Fiscal Federalism*. (New York: Harcourt, Brace, and Jovanovich, 1972).

Okunrounmu, T.O. "Policy Issues in Fiscal Federalism and National Development"in Aigbokhan, B.E. (ed.) *Fiscal Federalism and Nigeria's Economic Development*. Selected papers presented at the 1999 Annual Conference of the Nigerian Economic Society. (Ibadan: NES, 1999), pp. 453-475.

Okunrounmu, T.O. "Fiscal Federalism: Revenue Allocation for Economic Development in Nigeria." *Bullion*, vol. 20, No. 2, April/June, 1996.

Olomola, A.S. "Restructuring Nigeria's Fiscal Systems: Rationale, Strategies and Policies In Aigbokhan, B.E. (Ed.) *Fiscal Federalism and Nigeria's Economic Development*. Selected papers presented at the 1999 Annual Conference of the Nigerian Economic Society. (Ibadan: NES, 1999).

Olowononi, G.D. "Federalism and Vertical Intergovernmental Financial Imbalance in Nigeria" in Aigbokhan, B.E. (ed.) *Fiscal Federalism and Nigeria's Economic Development*. Selected papers presented at the 1999 Annual Conference of the Nigerian Economic Society. (Ibadan: NES, 1999).

Osakwe, J.O. "Fiscal Relations among the Three Tiers of Government in Nigeria: Some Policy Issues" in Aigbokhan, B.E. (ed.) *Fiscal Federalism and Nigeria's Economic Development*. Selected papers presented at the 1999 Annual Conference of the Nigerian Economic Society. (Ibadan: NES, 1999).

Phillips, A.O. *Nigeria's Fiscal Policy, 1998-2010*. NISER Monograph Series, No. 17. (Ibadan: Nigerian Institute of Social and Economic Research, 1997).

Prud'homme, R. "The Dangers of Decentralization." *The World Bank Research Observer*, Vol. 10, No. 2, 1995, pp. 201-220.

Roy, J. (ed.) *Macroeconomic Management and Fiscal Decentralization*. (Washington, D.C.: World Bank, 1995).

Shah, A. "The Reform of Intergovernmental Fiscal Relations in Developing and Emerging Market Economies." *Policy and Research Series* No. 23. (Washington, D.C.: World Bank, 1994).

Suberu, R. T. *Federalism and Ethnic Conflict in Nigeria.* (Washington, D.C.: United States Institute of Peace Press, 2001).

Taiwo, I.O. "Fiscal Federalism: A Theoretical Framework" in Aigbokhan, B.E. (ed.) *Fiscal Federalism and Nigeria's Economic Development.* Selected papers presented at the 1999 Annual Conference of the Nigerian Economic Society. (Ibadan: NES, 1999).

Tanzi, V. "Fiscal Federalism and Decentralization: A review of some efficiency and macroeconomic aspects" in Bruno, M. and B. Pleskovic (eds.) *Annual World Bank Conference on Development Economics, 1995.* (Washington, D.C.: World Bank, 317-322, 1996).

Ter-Minassian, T. (ed.) *Fiscal Federalism in Theory and Practice.* (Washington, D.C.: International Monetary Fund, 1997).

Ter-Minassian, T. "Inter-governmental Fiscal Relations in a Macroeconomic Perspective: An Overview" in Ter-Minassian, T. (Ed.) *Fiscal Federalism in Theory and Practice.* (Washington, D.C.: International Monetary Fund, 1997), pp. 3-24.

World Bank. 1997. *Study on the Evaluation of the Revenue Powers and Responsibilities of the Three Tiers of Government in Nigeria.* Report submitted to the National Revenue Mobilization Allocation and Fiscal Commission, the Presidency, Abuja.

World Bank. 1996. *Nigeria: Federal Public Expenditure Review.* Report No. 14447-UNI. (Washington, D.C.: World Bank).

World Bank. 1999. World Development Indicators CD-ROM. (Washington, D.C.: World Bank).

CHAPTER 10

REFORMS AND FISCAL FEDERALISM IN NIGERIA

Eghosa Osaghae

Bringing Politics and Federalism Back Into Reforms

Programmes of economic reforms have emerged as key drivers of the reconstruction of local and global formations according to neo-liberal (market) precepts. Inspired, authored and led by the Bretton Woods Institutions – the World Bank and the International Monetary Fund (IMF) – the reforms trajectory suffered initial credibility problems in the Third World owing partly to the externalities and conditionalities that heralded its introduction (some would say imposition) and partly to the unproven success of the reforms therapy.

Since then, attempts have been made to contextualize reforms and build local support constituencies. These have seen the movement from reforms without a human face to poverty alleviation and reduction; from state recession to good governance and regime change, as well as the rise of reforms elite amongst others, all of which have ameliorated the massive opposition that initially greeted its entry. Thus, although doubts continue to be raised about the actual objectives of reforms (some suspect they are meant to legitimize the post-cold war hegemonic global order) and their overall benefits to reforming countries (as opposed to global capital for instance), there is obviously a more tolerant attitude towards them. Nevertheless, the reforms discourse has remained somewhat fixated on appraising the efficacy of reforms in terms of the avowed goals of recovery, growth and development. The result is that some crucial aspects of the reforms regime suffer neglect or do not get the attention they deserve.

One such aspect is the political framework and consequences of reforms. Admittedly, issues of governance are integral to reforms, as the concern with curbing corruption, better management of resources (including, most importantly, foreign aid) as well as institution building and effectiveness clearly show. For countries that have suffered from endemic problems of legitimacy and rent-seeking, these would appear to be laudable objectives, but the political correlates of reforms are deeper and more fundamental and may in fact jeopardize reforms if not well understood and addressed. The suggestion by a recent commentary that the promotion of more open political systems in Africa is more important than financial assistance by donors and development partners (Calderisi, 2007) provides a lead here. What exactly is the problem?

It is that by the logic of design and implementation – as embodied in such instruments as poverty reduction strategy papers (PRSPs), public sector reforms, privatization, debt management and anti-corruption strategies – reforms are essentially centrist projects and have demonstrably promoted fiscal and political (over) centralization of the state as well as its derivative of increased authoritarianism. As such, reforms pose a serious challenge to thorough-going federal systems whose structuration into multiple centres of government is guaranteed by the principle of fiscal and political autonomy. Coming at a time when federal systems are struggling to salvage *true* federalism from the forces of centralization and the diminution of the powers of constituent units and redeem its utility as a model of efficient service delivery based on the principle of subsidiarity amongst others, the challenge requires full interrogation to properly situate reforms within the federal framework.

It is against this background that we examine the interface between the ongoing reforms in Nigeria and the country's federal system, which has been in crisis for several decades. At the heart of the crisis is the erosion of the fiscal, jurisdictional and administrative competences of the state (and local) governments and their subjugation to an imperial and omnipotent central government. This has constrained the efficacy of the federal solution in all of its ramifications and provoked the clamour for *true federalism* beginning from the mid-1990s. In particular, the emasculation of the fiscal competencies of the state governments and the ensuing loss of capacity to serve as centres of service delivery and development has been a major factor in the intractable crisis in the Niger-Delta region. The long period of military rule whose directive principles of unity of command and hierarchical authority as well as "lawless autocracy" created a peculiar blend of highly centralized federalism characterized long ago by Elaigwu (1976) as *military federalism* which has been identified as a major source of the crisis. However, though the effects of reforms dating back to the Structural Adjustment

Programme (SAP), which was introduced in the mid-1980s has so far been discounted.

Be this as it may, the return to civilian democracy in 1999, complete with multiparty politics, constitutionalism, rule of law and political liberalization, was expected to create the necessary impetus for salvaging the federal system. This was based on the experience of the Second Republic (1979-83) in which the civilian operators of the states fought hard to redeem the federal system especially in the area of reclaiming state powers taken over by the centre under military rule. But after eight years, the civilian democracy federalism has not been put back on track; instead, the central government has waxed stronger than ever before, especially in fiscal terms.

The boom that followed the high prices of crude oil, the country's main revenue earner which is controlled exclusively by the federal government, and has strengthened the imperialist tendencies of the centre, the hangover of military federalism especially given the dominance of retired military officers and their cohorts in the ruling coalitions and government, as well as the centralist inclinations of the political parties, are some of the factors that can readily be cited as being responsible for the continued travail of federalism. But by far the most important factor, which has served to position the federal government as the master government in all spheres is the regime of reforms. The rest of the paper will interrogate how this has been done.

Reforms as a Centralist Project

Reforms are designed to engage the central state, to be implemented by it and, in the final analysis, to strengthen it. Evidently, no exception is made for federal systems as a reading of reform packages in Zambia, Nigeria and Ghana will show. The central authorities are expected to install the macroeconomic fundamentals with regard to deregulation, privatization, trade liberalization, public sector reforms, debt and exchange management, anti-corruption measures, poverty reduction, disease control (HIV/AIDS, Avian Flu), etc, and ensure their effectuation throughout the country. Although decentralization, civil society, consultation and participation are integral to the reform packages, it is the central government that has responsibility for reforms. In Nigeria, since the mid-1980s when SAP was adopted as the mainstay of reforms, the federal government has been fully in control and very few attempts have been made, even by way of consultation, to involve the other tiers of government.

The formulation of NEEDS and SEEDS as blueprints for reforms at the federal and state levels respectively might suggest an improvement in the necessary federalization of reform packaging, but in reality, SEEDS (and LEEDS) were centrally directed and were designed to (uniformly) fit into centralist schemes. The same can be said of the Poverty Reduction Strategy Paper (PRSP) which gives the central state responsibility for poverty alleviation, whereas poverty is actually located in the states and localities and therefore ought to be their responsibility. In fact, in virtually every area that has been subjected to reforms, the states have lost grounds to the federal government. The reforms in the education sector illustrate the point very well.

The introduction of the Universal Basic Education (UBE), fundamental changes in tertiary education such as the affiliation of polytechnics and colleges of education to universities, elevation of some polytechnics to city universities, monetization of allowances, changes in pensions, restrictions on programmes offered in higher institutions, and so on, have all been done without reference to the states and private sector operatives, even though education is a concurrent matter and its deregulation has engendered private sector participation. The reforms have evidently put state and private institutions at grave risk as they lack the financial muscle of the federal government to cope with the very expensive transformations. But even more fundamentally, rather than take federal authorities away from primary and secondary education in accordance with the rules of subsidiarity, reforms have extended federal participation and control.

Reforms and Fiscal Federalism

If reforms were cognizant of Nigeria's federal structure, then they would have addressed the structure of fiscal relations with a view to strengthening the overall capacity of the country to deliver on social services, infrastructure and overall development. They would, for example, have created incentives for state (and local) governments to demand and build structures of fiscal autonomy (what in Nigeria is known as internally generated revenue), enjoy a greater share of federally collected revenues necessary to enable them discharge their constitutionally allotted responsibilities, and given states and localities responsibility in non-centrist spheres of education and healthcare. But this has not been the case, as fiscal relations have been further centralized with the very rich federal government in control.

All that has happened therefore is that state nationalists – and not so much state governments – have merely struggled to get more from the federal government's oil windfall – the clamour for higher allocation weight to be assigned to the principle of derivation is a case in point. Even the fiscal responsibility bill, which seeks to tie fiscal allocations to the state and local governments to service delivery and therefore has the potential to address some of the anomalies we have highlighted, is a federal formulation designed to make the states accountable to the federal government. It goes without saying therefore that 'fiscal responsibility' promotes a notion of federal 'ownership' of resources and is a device for ensuring greater federal control over states when what are needed are state-level structures of responsibility and accountability. As these operated under the regions and in the period before 1976 (that is even under the military), regional and state governments were held responsible for developmental failures and poor service delivery and overall performance by their citizens. Today, it is the federal government that is held responsible for failures and poor performance on matters that should ordinarily belong to state and local governments, which clearly shows the anomalous structure of fiscal relations. What states need is not more allocation from a benevolent centre, but the institution of viable structures of fiscal autonomy that are not controlled by the federal government. The clamour for resource control, which was popularized by the Niger-Delta minorities desirous of wresting control over the material benefits of crude oil production from the federal government is a pointer to what needs to be done. If reforms do not have a way of addressing this critical issue, then they are in need of reforms themselves.

The Way Forward

If reforms have had any major failing in Nigeria, it is that the macro political framework and correlates necessary to make them effective–in this case, federalism variables and imperatives – have so far been neglected. The stipulation of good governance variables (transparency, responsiveness, accountability, rule of law, zero-tolerance for corruption) as political conditionalities of reforms is necessary but not sufficient for reforms to have the desired impact. For a federal system transiting from low-federalism to high federalism, reforms have to be reconfigured to strengthen federal capacity, and the aspect to focus upon is restructuration of fiscal relations. It is another matter if reforms as designed by the Bretton-Woods institutions to perpetuate the hegemonic world order of the post cold war era – for which only the central state and its power holders are needed – can be reformed this way, but that is the challenge that Nigeria faces and has to address from within (this may yet be the country's contribution to the political economy of reforms). The political parties, state governments, civil society, ethno-regional and state nationalists have to champion the political reforms because the federal government which has been the main beneficiary is not capable of leading a process that challenges its awesome power and omnipotence.

REFERENCES

Calderisi, R. *The Trouble with Africa: Why Foreign Aid isn't Working* (New Haven & London: Yale University Press, 2007).

Elaigwu, J.I. "The Military and State-Building: Federal-State Relations in Nigeria's 'Military Federalism'" in A.B. Akinyemi et al, (eds.) *Readings on Federalism* (Lagos: NIIA,1979).

Nwabueze, B.O. *Nigeria '93: The Political Crisis and Solutions* (Ibadan: Spectrum, 1994).

CONCLUSION

SUMMARIES, CONCLUSIONS AND RECOMMENDATIONS OF THE NATIONAL WORKSHOP ON "FISCAL FEDERALISM IN NIGERIA: FACING THE CHALLENGES OF THE FUTURE", MARCH 18-21, 2007

Nelson Ochekpe, Habu Galadima and Filikus Adakai

Introduction

The Institute of Governance and Social Research (IGSR), Jos, in collaboration with Canadian International Development Agency (CIDA) and the Department for International Development (DFID), co-sponsored a National workshop on "Fiscal Federalism in Nigeria: Facing the Challenges of the Future". The workshop, which was organised by IGSR, began on Sunday, March 18, 2007 at Chida International Hotel, Jabi, Abuja, and ended on Tuesday, March 21, 2007.

The workshop was well attended by seasoned academics; distinguished public servants (retired and/or serving); Permanent Secretaries of some states; civil society groups, including the Nigeria Labour Congress, the media; member of donor agencies, and many others. About 67 people registered and participated at the workshop.

The objectives of Workshop included:

i) identifying the major issues and challenges to fiscal federalism in Nigeria;
ii) proffering practical solutions to these challenges; and
iii) recommending a road map for more functional intergovernmental fiscal relations for a stable federation.

In order to achieve these objectives, the participants attempted to provide answers to the following questions: What is the nature of fiscal federalism in Nigeria? To what extent is the distribution of tax powers a reflection of the distribution of powers and responsibilities among component units of the federalism? What are the current powers and responsibilities of each tier of government? Why is revenue-sharing such a sensitive issue in Nigeria? What kinds of fiscal equalization measures do we have - vertically and horizontally? What are the issues of the Niger-Delta; and the politics of fiscal federalism – towards dealing with current and future challenges?

The methodology adopted for the workshop was two-fold. First, was the plenary session where papers were presented by seasoned academics, administrators, public servants (retired and/or serving) using the PowerPoint projector for ease of presentation. Each segment of the presentation was followed by question and answer sessions. This enabled participants to have a more in-depth discussion on the issues raised by the paper presenters. A total of Nine (9) papers were presented at the National Workshop. These were:

i. The Challenges of Federalism in Nigeria: An Overview – Prof. J. Isawa Elaigwu, (President IGSR);
ii. Division of Powers and Responsibilities (including Tax Powers) – Dr. Habu S. Galadima (Department of Political Science, and Deputy Director, Academic Planning Division, University of Jos);
iii. Fiscal Federalism in Nigeria: The Challenges of the next Decade – Professor Akpan Ekpo (Former Vice-Chancellor, University of Uyo);
iv. Resource or Revenue Sharing - Dr. Phillip Usman, (Special Assistant to Governor of Bauchi State);
v. Revenue Sharing (Vertical and Horizontal)– Professor Eghosa Osagie (Former Vice- Chancellor, Idahosa University, Benin);
vi. Intergovernmental Fiscal Relations and Fiscal Equalization – Professor Mike Obadan (University of Benin);
vii. Fiscal Federalism: Towards Coping with & Resolving Future Challenges - Prof. Milton Iyoha, Chief Economist (National Economic Summit Group);
viii. Intergovernmental Policy Coordination in Nigeria: Improving Service Delivery in Core Sectors – Dr. Lev Freinkman, Senior Economist, World Bank, Abuja.
ix. Reforms and Fiscal Federalism – Professor Eghosa Osaghae (Vice-Chancellor, Igbinedion University).

In addition, Roundtable sessions were also organized around major National challenges within the thematic area. Three Roundtable sessions were held, i) The Niger-Delta Conundrum-Towards Resolution and Development; ii) and iii) have the same title: Fiscal Federalism: Towards Coping with and Resolving Future Challenges. Each session was chaired by seasoned academics and administrators, and had a lead discussant.

Participants made a number of observations and recommendations; and arrived at some conclusions.

Opening Ceremony/Reception

The opening ceremony was preceded by a welcome cocktail/reception party organized for the participants from 6.00pm, March 18, 2007. This enabled the participants to familiarize themselves with the programme as well as set the stage for opening ceremony. The opening ceremony commenced around 8.00pm with a National Anthem. Professor Okon Uya, former Chairman of the defunct National Electoral Commission (NEC), chaired the opening ceremony. Professor Uya welcomed all the participants and drew their attention to the challenges of fiscal federalism. He commended the organizers and asserted that the survival of democracy would be largely determined by fiscal federalism in Nigeria and the resolution of the Niger-Delta crisis, and not necessarily by throwing more money at the problem. He pointed that there should be a systematic approach to understanding the underlying causes of the crises in the Niger-Delta rather than throwing money at the problems in order to suppress them.

In his introductory remark, the President of the Institute of Governance and Social Research, Professor Jonah Isawa Elaigwu commended the Canadian International Development Agency (CIDA) and the Department for International Development (DFID) for agreeing to co-sponsor the National Workshop. He expressed the appreciation of many Nigerians for the interest which Canada has always shown and the support it has always given to the democratic process in Nigeria. He emphasized the importance of fiscal federalism and noted that it is the oil that lubricates the wheels of the federal system. It is possible to argue therefore, he continued, that without fiscal federalism there can be no federation. He introduced the objectives of the workshop and identified the central areas of focus during the National Workshop. He thanked all the participants for honouring the invitation to participate at the workshop, even at short notice.

The Canadian High Commissioner to Nigeria, Mr. David Angell noted that the sponsorship of this workshop by the Canadian International Development Agency (CIDA) shows his country's commitment to strengthening fiscal federalism and comparative studies on federalism in Nigeria and Canada. Canada, when it was founded 140 years ago, had 80% of her population as rural, while the reverse is the case today, as a result of a strong federal system. He opined that an alignment between fiscal capacities and responsibilities should be established.

Observations

The following observations were made at the National Workshop: That:

1) the trend world over is increasing interdependence and centralization as the complexity of modern governance, the need for homogeneity within the state, as well as the nature of foreign trade (among other reasons) have contributed to the increase in the power of central government in most federal states.
2) the logic of the distribution of powers in Nigeria, has been to strengthen the central government politically and economically to enable it intervene in essential areas and to keep the country together.
3) the Nigerian federation is characterized by strong unitary streaks, as a response to almost three decades of military rule, and is under intense pressure for a review of the legislative lists to devolve many powers concentrated at the centre to sub-national units. This was due largely to: i) long military rule; ii) response to the civil war; iii) the creation of states; iv) the increase role of in petro-naira; v) demands for federally desirable harmonization; and vi) International trade and globalization.
4) states have complained that the federal government has too much powers and that the legislative lists should be revised in their favour.
5) the issues of resource distribution and management have become important issues of debate as Nigerian groups reassess the federation in the context of the new democratic polity.
6) three major dimensions of federal politics can be observed in the political arena since May 1999. These are:

i) issues of centralization and decentralization in the relations among the three tiers of government.

ii) issues of resource distribution and/or management::

a) the clamour for resource control.
b) the politics and intrigues of revenue sharing formula.
c) vertical tax powers and proportional allocation.

iii) the politics of federalism and aggressive sub-nationalism:

d) horizontal equalization versus derivation.
e) aggressively defensive and defensively aggressive ethno-regionalism.
f) emergence of militias and increase in communal violence.
g) the minority question
h) the Shari'a controversies
i) the Confederal demand
j) the resource control controversy

7) the Nigerian fiscal federalism is distinguished by the overwhelming concentration of tax jurisdiction and collection at the level of the federal government, while the state and local governments have jurisdiction only over minor and low-yielding revenue sources, with the exception of personal income tax at the state-level and property tax at the local level.
8) since 1954, Nigeria's system of fiscal federalism has steadily evolved as a result of social, political and economic influences and upheavals.
9) the problems of fiscal federalism in Nigeria include:

i) the existence of large vertical inter-government fiscal imbalances;
ii) the lack of fiscal autonomy for state and local governments;
iii) the wide horizontal fiscal imbalances across jurisdictions;
iv) an inequitable and flawed revenue allocation system; and
v) an inadequate and ineffective macroeconomic management framework.

10) most of the discussions and controversies over the structure of fiscal federalism and the accompanying dynamics centered more on revenue-sharing than on sharing the responsibility and authority for raising the revenues that go into the Federation Account.
11) the fiscal capacity of state and local governments are very weak and are reflected in their internally generated revenue.

12) the federal government in Nigeria still behaves as both the custodian and owner of the Federation Account inspite of the Supreme Court ruling of April 2002.

Recommendations

1) The quality of leadership is important in effecting necessary compromises in Nigeria's reconciliation system. Thus, there is the need for the following:

a) the transformation of political contractors and touts into genuine politicians.
b) a new search for political leaders and statesmen.
c) the sanitization of electoral process to restore electoral legitimacy.

2) In order to respond to the challenges of distribution of resources, there is need for the following:

a. revision of legislative lists;
b. revisiting the on-shore/offshore dichotomy;
c. empowering the RMFAC to monitor and work out formal mechanism for vertical and horizontal fiscal equalization;
d.increasing intergovernmental interaction.

3) Functions which can be more efficiently performed by the federal government than lower levels of government should be assigned in the exclusive legislative list. These include national defence, external relations (including borrowing and external trade), banking, currency, nuclear energy, etc.
4) Adoption of fiscal rules must be accompanied by setting up an Independent Inter-Governmental Committee to promote a framework of fiscal discipline and fiscal policy coordination.
5) There is the need to decentralize tax administration; this will enhance the fiscal capacity of the federating units.
6) Review or amend the 1999 Constitution to examine the issue of the devolution of more powers to lower levels of government.
7) The following recommendations were made for the vertical allocation of revenue among the three tiers of government:

i) 30 per cent of mining rents and royalties (without making any distinction between on-shore and off-shore petroleum production) should go to producing areas; and 70 per cent allocated to the Federation Account. In addition, mining rents and royalties should be split on a ratio of 50:50 between the state and local governments where the minerals are produced, and earmarked for appropriate capital projects.
ii) Proceeds derived from sale of gas should be accounted for separately, and treated in the same way as revenue from crude oil sales.
iii) Surpluses from the operations of the Central Bank, NNPC, and other public sector commercialized enterprises should be paid into the Federation Account.
iv) When the federal government uses crude oil to pay for capital projects executed by foreign contractors, the value of such oil swaps should be calculated at current spot prices and the federal government should pay an amount into the Federation Account equivalent to the spot market value.
v) The share of the Federal Government in the Federation Account should decrease from 48.5 per cent to 40 per cent.
vi) The share of the States in the Federation Account should rise from 24 per cent to 30 per cent in agreement with recommendations of the National Revenue Mobilization, Allocation and Fiscal Commission in 1989.
vii) The share of the local governments in the Federation Account should remain at 20 per cent.
viii) 10 per cent of the Federation Account should be allocated to Special Funds as follows:

a) Research, Science & Technology: 7.0%
b) Ecology: 1.0%
c) National Emergency & Contingency: 2.0%

8) Also, on vertical revenue allocation, the following were recommended:

ix) the recognition of the derivation principle as an autonomous criterion for vertical revenue allocation.
x) the drastic reduction in the share of the federal government in the Federation Account from 48.5 per cent to 40 per cent to curb the *Santa Claus* and *Ali Baba* propensities of the centre.
xi) Thirty percent of mining rents and royalties to be returned to producing States.

9)Meaningful dialogue and compromises will reduce tensions emanating from the practice of fiscal federalism.

10) To cope with the challenges to fiscal federalism in Nigeria, there is need for the modification of assignment of fiscal instruments; reduction of over-centralization of revenue at the centre; as well as transfer some tax bases and/or tax handles to the SNGs without undermining efficiency of tax collection.
11) Establish a *Macroeconomic Stabilization Fund* to provide a vehicle for effecting a credible counter-cyclical macroeconomic stabilization policy to held solely by the permanent Fiscal Commission (RMAFC);
12) Increase the fiscal, administrative and budgetary capacity of SNGs, especially LGAs.
13) Federal Government of Nigeria should start the withdrawal from the actual delivery of services and play a more active role in setting national policy, financing and monitoring.
14) Shift from joint service delivery towards co-financing, state/local delivery, and joint monitoring.
15) More attention to equalization dimension of federalism.
16) Expansion in matching grant schemes focused on key MDG functional areas.
17) Strengthening arrangements for accountability; how public money are spent, especially by states (but at all levels of government).
18)Strengthen capacity of institutions responsible for intergovernmental policy coordination, with National Planning Commission (NPC) becoming a central player.
19) Facilitate inter-state competition on the basis of quality of service delivery.

Conclusions

The participants concluded that there were needs for a complete overhaul of the nature of fiscal federalism in Nigeria. To this end, it was agreed that a follow-up workshop should be organized to examine specific issues raised at the National Workshop.

BIODATA OF AUTHORS

BELLO-IMAM, I. B.

Professor I. B. Bello-Imam is a Professor of Political Science with emphasis on Public Administration. His Research Interest spans Nigerian Government and Politics, Governance issues, Comparative Politics and Public Administration including Local Government Administration. He has taught in many universities including Obafemi Awolowo University (OAU), Ile-Ife, Ambrose Alli University (AAU), Ekpoma, University of Birmingham, United Kingdom and University of Northern Iowa, United States. Professor Bello-Imam was the pioneer Head of Department of Political Development of NISER, Ibadan and he was once the Deputy-Vice-Chancellor (Administration), AAU, Ekpoma. He has several publications to his credit in his areas of research interest. He is currently the Dean of Post-graduate School, Lead City University, Ibadan and a member of many national and international professional organizations.

ELAIGWU, J. Isawa

Jonah Isawa Elaigwu is professor emeritus of political science at the University of Jos. He obtained his first degree from the Ahmadu Bello University, Zaria. He holds a masters and a doctorate from Stanford University, California USA. He served as Director-General and Chief Executive of the National Council on Intergovernmental Relations, Abuja from 1992 to 1996. He also served as chairperson of the Board of Trustees for the United Nations Institute of Training and Research. He has many publications to his name, both internationally and within Nigeria. He is currently the President of the Institute of Governance and Social Research, Jos, Plateau State, Nigeria.

EKPO, Akpan H.

Akpan H. Ekpo obtained his Ph.D in Economics from the University of Pittsburgh, PA. USA in 1983. He is Professor of Economics, former Vice-chancellor, Federal University of Uyo (2000-2005) and presently Pioneer Vice-chancellor, Akwa Ibom State University of Technology. Professor Ekpo has advised all levels of Government (Municipal, State and Federal) in Nigeria on economic matters. He has published extensively in his areas of specialization (economic theory, public finance and development) in national and international journals. He was one-time Chairman, Ministerial Advisory Committee, Federal Ministry of Finance, Abuja (1993-1997) and Editor of the prestigious *Nigerian Journal of Economic and Social Studies* (1996-2003). He consults for several national and international organisations and is a Non-Executive Director, Central Bank of Nigeria, Abuja.

FREINKMAN, Lev

Lev Freinkman is a senior economist with the World Bank office in Abuja. He joined the World Bank in 1992 and until 2005 was working mostly on economies in transition. His main areas of professional interest include public fiscal management, fiscal federalism, and intergovernmental relations. In 1998-2002 he held a position of the Bank country economist for Armenia and led various Bank teams that were involved in development of several credits to the Armenian government. In 2002-2004 he was a main author of several Bank reports, including Russia Public Expenditure Review, Ukraine Trade Study, and Belarus Country Economic Memorandum. In Nigeria he has been working mostly on fiscal management and governance issues. He led the Bank team that recently produced Nigeria Public Expenditure Management and Financial Accountability Review PEMFAR). Lev Freinkman has Ph.D in economics from the Moscow State University, Russia.

GALADIMA, Habu

Dr. Habu Galadima is Senior Lecturer with the Department of Political Science and Deputy Director, Academic Planning Division, University of Jos, Nigeria. He was Assistant Director, Defence and Security Studies, Institute for Peace and Conflict Resolution, the Presidency, Abuja. He was Research fellow with the National Council on Intergovernmental Relations, Abuja. He holds Ph.D in International Relations and Strategic Studies (Jos, Nigeria). He has a number of articles in peer-reviewed Journals. His publications include "Peacebuilding and Sustainable Human Security: The Nigerian Experience" in *African Renaissance* (Volume3. No.5, September/October 2006) Adonis-Abbey, London. Pp. 141-153; "The Human Security Deficits: Challenges of Peacebuilding and Sustainable Development in Nigeria" in *State – Society Relations in Nigeria: Democratic Consolidation, Conflicts and Reforms* (London: Adonis & Abbey Publishers Ltd, 2007) and co-authored an article with Professor J. Isawa Elaigwu, "The Shadow of Shari'a over Nigerian

Federalism" in *Publius, The Journal of Federalism, USA.* Summer 2003. Pp 123 -144.

IYOHA, Milton A.

Milton A. Iyoha, Ph D (Yale), is Professor of Economics in the Department of Economics and Statistics, University of Benin, Benin City, Nigeria. A former Research Fellow at the Brookings Institution in Washington, D.C., Dr. Iyoha has taught at the State University of New York at Buffalo, USA and has been a Visiting Professor of Economics at the University of Lagos and the University of Botswana. A former Chief Economist of the Nigerian Economic Summit Group, he has also served as a Consultant to the IMF, ILO, ACBF, AERC, AfDB, IBRD, UNECA and UNDP. Professor Iyoha's research focuses on macroeconomic policy, trade and growth, and international finance.

JEGA, Attahiru

Attahiru Jega is a professor of Political Science at Bayero University, Kano. He obtained his B.Sc from Ahmadu Bello University, Zaria and M.A. and Ph.D from Northwestern University. He has published widely on Nigerian politics. He was one time Director, Centre for Democratic Research and Training, Kano and is currently the Vice-Chancellor of Bayero University, Kano.

OBADAN, Mike I.

Mike I. Obadan has had an exciting professional career as an economist, educationist and administrator in the University system and the wider public sector. He has engaged in active teaching and research in Universities and related institutions in Nigeria and abroad and, at different times, he served as Head of Economics Department, University of Ilorin and Dean, Faculty of Social Sciences, University of Benin. Professor Obadan has also served as the Director General of the Nigerian Centre for Economic Management and Administration in Ibadan, Nigeria and also as President of the Nigerian Economic Society. He is deeply committed to research, publications and knowledge sharing and has published extensively in the areas of macroeconomics, international trade and finance and development issues, in the form of books, monographs, journal articles and chapters in books. Currently, Professor Obadan is a professor of economics at the University of Benin, Nigeria.

OSAGIE, Eghosa
Professor Eghosa Osagie was a Professor of Economics, University of Jos, a former Director of Research, National Institute of Policy and Strategic Studies (NIPSS) Kuru, Plateau State, Nigeria and former Vice-Chancellor Benson Idahosa, University, Benin City, Nigeria. He has published many books and articles.

OSAGHAE, Eghosa
Professor Eghosa Osaghae is a Professor of Political Science, University of Ibadan; currently Vice-Chancellor, Igbinedion, University, Okada, Edo State, Nigeria. He is widely published.

USMAN, Philip Sulaiman
Dr. Phillip Usman is a trained economist and a seasoned administrator. He had his first degree (B. Sc. Economics) at Ahmadu Bello University, Zaria; a Masters degree in Financial Economics at the University College of North Wales, Bangor, U.K; and a doctorate degree in Economics at University of Connecticut, U.S.A. Dr. Usman worked in both the private and public sector. He had a stint in the academia at the School of Basic Studies, ABU, Zaria. He started his career in the public service as a Planning Officer with the North Eastern State. He was one-time Commissioner of Finance and later Special Assistant to the Bauchi State Governor on NEPAD. He also served as the Managing Director of ECWA Productions Limited. He is currently managing his businesses and serves as a Chairman and Board Member of many organizations.

Appendix A

INSTITUTE OF GOVERNANCE AND SOCIAL RESEARCH (IGSR)

NATIONAL WORKSHOP ON "FISCAL FEDERALISM IN NIGERIA: FACING THE CHALLENGES OF THE FUTURE", MARCH 18 – 21, 2007 AT CHIDA INTERNATIONAL HOTEL, JABI-ABUJA, NIGERIA.

REGISTRATION FORM FOR PARTICIPANTS

S/ No	NAME	ADDRESS	E-MAIL	TELEPHONE/FAX OFFICE/HOME
1	Dr. Habu S-. Galadima	University of Jos	galadimaha@yahoo.com	0803 703 1006
2	Dr. Nelson Ochekpe	University of Jos	ochekpen@yahoo.com	0803 700 6372
3	Prof. Eghosa Osagie	Benin City	eghosaosagie@yahoo.com	0803 336 3504
4	Prof. J. Isawa Elaigwu	IGSR Jos	elaigwu2033@yahoo.com	0803 315 5301
5	S. A. Asemota	Benin City	adunasemota@yahoo.com	0805 522 1669
6	Michael Orobator	Benin City	mikinator@yahoo.com	0805 603 816
7	Y.A. Ochefu	Lagos	yakubu.ochefy@gmail	
8	Mary Mom	Makurdi	maryomom2007@yahoo.com	0802 607 1318
9	S.A. Ibrahim	NSUK	sianibrahim@yahoo.com	0803 320 3387
10	Prof. Milton Iyoha	NESG, V_I. Lagos	iyohama@yahoo.com	0802 337 4166

11	A.O. Odumu	Makurdi		0805 367 0900 08022005817
12	Dr. Ambita'a, SS	MOH-Jalingo	ambisisi@yahoo.com	0803 438 5325
13	Dr. Usman, PS	NEPAD Secretariat Bauchi		0805 264 4099
14	Stephen Okhonmwa	Igbinedion Uni. Okada	swiks@hotmail.com	
15	Dele Sobowale	Vanguard	biolesobowale@yahoo.com	0805 506 9026
16	Anyalewa A. Ajonye	Gotit, Otukpo	aajonye@yahoo.com	0803 592 0370
17	C. J. Nnamani	MOH Enugu		0803 475 0990 08051264397 042-311380
18	Maureen Egbuna	Intercellular Nig. Plc Lagos	maureenegbura@yahoo.com	0805 307 8553 01-4708399
19	Chief Efiong Essien	Calabar		0803 335 1160
20	Dr. Fatima Danladi, mni	MOH.Lafia N/State	phatidan@yahoo.com	0803 589 4871
21	Mairo Danladi	AGIS. Wuse II Abuja	mairodanladi@yahoo.com	0803 393 2548
22	Dr. Ibrahim Y. Lame	No. 12 1st Avenue, Gwaringo Housing Estate, Abuja		0803 315 5770
23	Amb. Prof.	University	oronewya@yahoo	0803 710

	O.E. Uya	of Calabar	.co.uk	6070
24	David Angell	Canadian High Commissioner		09-413-9910
25	Anthony Okoye	Enugu	Okoyetu@yahoo.com	0802 364 5283
26	Akpan H. Ekpo	Akutech Uyo	ahekpo@skannet.com ahekpo@yahoo.com	0802 777 5555
27	Sarah Andrew	Abuja	Omale_sarah@yahoo.com	0803 632 5135
28	Sunday Ameh	NIPRD	sjitodo@yahoo.com	0805 369 1277
29	Dan Agbese	Lagos	achiwa44@yahoo.co.uk	0803 321 8058
30	John Odah	Abuja	johnodah@nccng.org	0802 290 4113
31	E. Agodo	Abuja		0803 332 0672
32	Ijoma A.A.	Per. Sec. Min. of Fin. Abia State	abaraije@yahoo.com	0803 312 4909
33	Ginigeme Mbanefoh	Dept. of Eco. Uni. Of Ibadan	ginimbanefoh@yahoo.com	0803 311 8464
34	Dan Rogger	OSSAP.MDGS	danrogger@hotmail.com	0806 582 8233
35	Lev Frienkman	World Bank	lfreinkman@worldbank.com	0803 909 6856
36	Ilaria Chessa	DFID	i-chessa@dfid.gov.uk	09-4137710+19
37	Dr. Haroun	Adam	Haroun44@yahoo	0803 704

	Adamu	Consultant	.com	3144
38	Barr. S. Obande	"	"	
39	Maimuna L.Ibrahim	DMO	Mamarus200@yahoo.com	0803 311 0767
40	Nurudeen Ogbara	Citizens centre/NBA 4, Owolowo st, Ikorobu	Ogbaraco3000@yahoo.com	0802 307 2749
41	Rev. F. Cyril Nwafor	OLQN, Garki Abuja	cyrileberka@yahoo.com	0803 721 2339
42	R.N. Egbuniwe (Mrs)	Local. Govt Dept Pol. Affairs Office (SGF) Abuja	Franciscamillenium@yahoo.com	0803 314 6275
43	Chief A.K Horsfall	5 Moor house Rd, Ikoyi	hosfallco@yahoo.com	0803 721 6030
44	Onaiyekan John	Bishop's House, Abuja	Onaiyekan7@yahoo.com	09 2340 661
45	Godwin Aidenagbo	Yakubu Gowon Centre, Asokoro, Abuja	goddieaide@yahoo.com	09 3140 613
46	Mairo Ahmed	Adekunle Fajayi close, Asokoro, Abuja	Mairo_4real@yahoo.com	0803 4889 338

47	Mike I. Obadan	University of Benin, Benin City	mikeo-badan@yahoo.co m	0802 3250 853
48	T. Zibiri	Min. of Finance, Benin City, Edo State		0803 4084 171
49	Agnes Baba	Min. of Health, Kaduna	babaag-nes@yahoo.com	0802 3462 584
50	Alh. A. Musa	Min. of Finance		0802 7818 291
51	Adejoh Jo-seph	Min. of Agric.	adejohjo-seph@yahoo.com	0803 4372 297
52	Chinedu O. F	Min. of Education		0805 5834 712
53	Alh. A. Wasin	Min. of Agricul-ture	wasin@yahoo.co m	0803 3412 628
54	Labara A	NSOC		0802 3475 132
55	Nelson O	CLO		0804 2423 030
56	Oke-chukwu I	IMO	Ike_okey@yahoo. com	0803 6252 627
57	Chuang J. E	Lagos		0802 2334 405
58	B Usman	FIRS		0805 5282 340
59	Gidado Mohd	TVLA	Gi-dado_m@yahoo.c om	0803 3782 645
60	Danlami M S	Min. of Education	Danlami2004@ya hoo.com	0803 3155 32
61	Nneka Naji	CLWS		0802 8186 391
62	Philip Osafo	Fed Min. of Finance	phili-posafo@gmail.co	0806 972 6508

			m	
63	Dr. Sir Clement Oriaichi	The Economics Institute, Abuja	ieeconomicsinstitute@yahoo.com	0803 700 8385
64	Celestine Ukatu	IGSR	Igsr2003@yahoo.com	
65	Ali Garba	"	"	
66	Mrs. Azuka Chime	"	"	
67	Abigail Gyang	"	"	

Index

E

F

G

H

I

J

L

M

N

O

P

R

S

www.ingramcontent.com/pod-product-compliance
Ingram Content Group UK Ltd.
Pitfield, Milton Keynes, MK11 3LW, UK
UKHW041638031026
15587UKWH00001B/366

9 781906 704032